SOIL

CONSERVATION

SOIL
CONSERVATION

SELLERS G. ARCHER

NORMAN

UNIVERSITY OF OKLAHOMA PRESS

BY SELLERS G. ARCHER

(with Clarence E. Bunch) *The American Grass Book*
(Norman, 1953)

Soil Conservation (Norman, 1956)
Rain, Rivers and Reservoirs (New York, 1963)

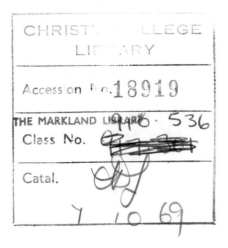
Library of Congress Catalog Card Number: 56–6002
Copyright 1956 by the University of Oklahoma Press,
Publishing Division of the University.
First edition, May, 1956.
Second printing, November, 1960.
Third printing, February, 1965.
Manufactured in the U.S.A.

*In writing this book
I have had four inspirations:*

My wife, Lorena

My daughter, Constance

*Farm leaders who have served faithfully
without remuneration on soil conservation
district boards and other committees to
promote conservation*

*Professional workers who have served
Conservation as a "cause" rather than
as a career*

To them this book is dedicated

Preface

JOHN IS PROBABLY one of the best conservation farmers that I know.

It is not simply that John follows the standard conservation practices recommended for his farm, or that he maintains all of these practices—from terracing to conservation crop rotations—in the best tradition year after year. He is a good conservationist because he studies the cause and effect of every bit of soil movement on his land, and when he learns the cause, he remedies it immediately.

A case in point is the location of a garden plot for the family. First it was near the house on sloping land. Clean tillage in the garden permitted considerable erosion, so the next year it was about two hundred yards from the house on nearly level bottom land. There was still some soil movement caused by erosion, and the next year the garden was on even flatter land, with the rows directed across the slight slope. Then when fall came, the land was planted to wheat for a winter cover.

After the second year he told his wife that she would have to confine her gardening to sown crops because he couldn't afford to let his soil wash away. Of course, she vetoed this idea, and that was why he moved the garden plot to the most nearly level land on the farm and adopted the contour and cover crop program to protect the soil.

He is a good conservationist because he knows that the soil is not expendable, and he will not permit himself either to use it up or to waste it.

No one taught him these things— at least, not intentionally. He looked about and saw what was going on. He formed his own conclusions about what was going to happen to his county, his state, and his nation if soil wastage continues—this makes him a good citizen. He has learned that since World War II we are helping to feed the world and that, in the future, we will have to help feed more and more hungry people in many nations. This helps him to identify himself with all mankind and adds meaning to his Christianity.

What has he done? In his humble way, he has lived and taught soil conservation. He has no position in public life. He does not write, and he does not speak before the public. But he is a good farmer and a good neighbor.

Once he rigged two one-row drills together so he could pull them behind his tractor and plant vetch and rye in his cotton middles to protect the soil during the winter. He parked the rig where passing neighbors could see it, and when anyone asked about it, he explained why he used it and offered to lend it to him. If the neighbor hesitated, he offered to bring it over behind his tractor to show him how it worked. If the neighbor had no seed, John would lend him some. Sometimes he planted the neighbor's field, and sometimes he did not get the seed back. But he never felt that he was imposed upon.

"If my neighbor's field blows, it is apt to start mine to blowing. But if we all tie down our sandy soils with a good winter cover crop, I will be protected. And if my neighbor finds that this practice pays off, he will repay me in many ways." John is always generous and optimistic, and he can always see profit in conservation for himself.

Throughout the years both of his farms have been unobtrusive conservation lessons. The sandy-land farm where the soil is never left bare during the windy or rainy seasons, and the tight-land farm where good alfalfa bottom land is edged by steep and eroded slopes which are always sown to permanent grass or small grains and clover—these are classrooms without conscious teaching, sanctuaries without conscious preaching.

John comes to me with many questions and problems, like these:

"I've got a gully that I can't stop. Can you help me?"

"I want to take a crop of alfalfa seed. Someone said I should have bees in the field. What about it?"

"The dirt keeps moving in that field behind the house. Have you got a grass that will tie it down for good, and that I can use for calf pasture following wheat?"

When I said that John is one of the best conservationists I know, I did not mean to imply that he has all of the answers. But he has eyes that detect even the slightest erosion on any of the land that he farms; he has the initiative to find the solution to his erosion problems, and he has the heart to search for the right answers.

Today's answers are different from yesterday's, and there will be better answers tomorrow—because of the combined efforts of research, field workers, and farmers like John who have the hand and heart to apply themselves to the great task of soil conservation.

Many people have helped me gather the material in this book and have helped to edit and revise the manuscript. And to all of them, I am grateful. We have searched for good answers for all of the questions that John might ask and have set them down for him, and for all of the other Johns who are serious about this business of conservation farming—good farming.

Sellers G. Archer

Cordell, Oklahoma
March 1, 1956

One of the best rewards of conservation thinking is the increasing force it is exerting upon Americans in all walks of life. I am all the more pleased to acknowledge it because, since my book was first published, the general demand for the principles it contains has made two large printings necessary, now followed by a third. Reviewing the progress that has been made in conservation in the few years since the book first appeared, I find nothing of substantive character to change. But I do recognize the splendid progress that has been made in many sections of our country, on the basis of which still further improvement may be expected in the next decade.

SELLERS G. ARCHER

Fort Worth, Texas
January 15, 1965

Acknowledgments

I WISH TO EXPRESS appreciation to the many individuals who gave me ideas, facts, and encouragement. Among those who offered constructive criticism, specific ideas for improvement, or encouragement are Messrs. Jack W. Adair, Clarence E. Bunch, Harry M. Chambers, Alvin M. Clements, Alfred M. Hedge, Earl K. Lowe, James B. McBride, Leon J. McDonald, Herbert A. Prevett, Edd Roberts, N. E. Rowley, Ray Walker, Lawrence J. Ward, H. R. Wells, and Clay E. Wilson. All of these people, and others, helped in the making of this book, but they are not responsible for any of the ideas, interpretations, or conclusions presented by the author.

Also, my thanks to the Soil Conservation Service for supplying the illustrations for this book.

Sellers G. Archer

Contents

Results of soil loss; conservation benefits; the goal; government in conservation provides research, information, technical, and financial assistance; other favorable aspects.

1. A Definition and History. Conservation in its beginning; its development. Prevention of erosion; land use; soil improvement related practices. A new meaning. The importance of good planning based on sound analysis. Assistance in planning through soil conservation districts. The conservation agreement. The principle of planning. Aids provided by the district.

2. Land Capability. The Basis for Soil-Conservation Planning. Development of soils: parent material, age, slope, climate, and vegetation. Classifying the soil by units and groups to indicate texture, permeability, and depth. Definitions. Land capability, the key to proper use and treatment. Eight land classes. Definitions of the land classes. Erosion reduces the potential of land and lowers its capability class. Interpretations. Conservation activities of U.S.D.A. based on this system. Farmers can get land-capability inventory of their lands.

3. How to Develop and Use the Conservation Plan. Principles, more than details, are needed. Needs of the land versus needs of the farmer. Examples. Combinations of treatment vary with the conservation program. The conservation plan is a delicately balanced but flexible system of practices based on certain land uses and cropping programs. Minor treatments not overlooked; reason from cause to correction. A conservation plan is a growing thing. For the farmer not ready to make

basic decisions, the plan must be incomplete and tentative. Using the plan; beginning its application; examples; first things come first. Checking effectiveness of treatments; mechanical measures; check plots for fertilization and rotation studies; comparing results with neighbors.

Contents

field arrangement, fields within fields, acreage determinations, preparation of map or sketch. Land preparation: methods, equipment; planting; problems in plowing and planting terraced fields; harvesting crops; use of guide lines.

5. Waterways. Definition. Conservation uses. Location. Construction: shaping the waterway, equipment, replacing the topsoil. Protection and maintenance: waterway protection, structure and vegetation. Protecting the end of the waterway: diversion terrace, sod flume, overfall structure, drop-inlet and erosion-control dams. Maintenance of the waterway.

Introduction: Depletion of native grasslands; better management practices needed; rebuilding and re-establishment.

1. Planning Grassland Development. Planning based on land capability; grassland rotations for cropland; permanent cover for some lands. Yearlong grazing; outline of program for permanent and supplemental grazing needs. Preparing the land: smoothness, tilth, fertility, seedbeds, land clearing, drainage, denuded areas. Planting: seed, equipment, planting methods. Development of the planting: time required, protection during early stages, avoiding competitive growth, cultivation, fertility. Planting and Care of Bermudagrass. Cost of permanent grassland plantings.

2. Management of Grasslands. Basis of management: stocking rates, protection of green growth, use of mulch, fertility. Managing native pastures and ranges: variation in plant growth, classifying the range: excellent, good, fair, poor; using the range classification; small pastures; seasonal grazing; rotation grazing. Other range management practices: control of competing plants, fertilization. Managing tame pastures and meadows: grazing control, maintaining the desired plants, discouraging undesirable plants, hay making.

Contents

3. Farm Drainage. Importance of proper drainage. Types of drains: surface drains, subdrains, vertical drains. Drainage costs. Surface drainage. Tile drainage: advantages, planning, materials, outlet protection, surface inlets, silt wells, relief wells. Maintenance.

VIII : *Public Assistance in Conservation* . . . 249

Agencies and groups serve the farmer in many fields; technical assistance in soil conservation through soil conservation districts; behind-the-scenes aids to farmers; supervised aid on the local level by trained specialists; special aid.

1. Farmer-Controlled Groups. Soil conservation districts: local, independent organizations under state laws; liaison office between farmers and agencies offering conservation services; their responsibilities. Agricultural Stabilization and Conservation Service committees: supervise cost sharing in conservation by federal government; community, county, and state levels; election rules; duties; Agricultural Conservation Program; co-operation between district governing bodies and Agricultural Stabilization and Conservation Service committees. Special district organizations, for special purposes. Associations to promote special interests.

2. Technical Field Assistance Agencies. Soil Conservation Service: history, responsibilities, organization. Soil and Moisture Conservation Operations Office: responsibilities on Indian-owned land. Forest Service: responsibilities on publicly-owned grasslands and woodlands and on privately-owned woodlands; protection of resources and control of watersheds.

3. Financial Assistance in Conservation. Agricultural Stabilization and Conservation Service offers federal assistance in sharing costs of conservation work; administration of funds; relationship to S.C.S.; lines of authority. Farmers' Home Administration, lending agency of federal government; eligibility, terms.

4. Agencies Which Assist in Education or Research. Agricultural Research Administration: co-ordination of research activities; basic research; field trials; dissemination of information. Educational agencies: county agents, vocational agriculture teachers, land grant colleges, Extension Service, vocational agriculture departments, 4-H clubs, F.F.A. groups; other assistance in soil conservation education.

5. Co-ordination of Public Assistance in Conservation. Confusion and conflicts in programs; responsibility of Extension Service in co-ordinating information programs; stronger local groups of farmers can best resolve problems and promote programs.

Figures

Tables

xix

Illustrations

SOIL
CONSERVATION

I: The Field of Conservation

"THE CHIEF HARVEST of the land is man himself. From the soil comes the quality of his bone and muscle. What he is, what he does, and how he does it are determined by the acres he tills. His courage, his ambition, his very way of thinking grow out of the furrows at his feet as truly as the wheat, the cotton, and the clover he tends." So speaks Wellington Brink, editor of *Soil Conservation Magazine*. Few will dispute his statement, yet not many persons really stop to consider that abuse or conservation of the land reaches into the homes and lives of all the people, whether they live on the land or in towns and cities.

This fact was emphasized when the National Farm and Home Hour recently reported over a national radio network the results of a fifty-year study of two rural communities—one where the land was conserved and one where it was abused. The report included the following data:

	Conserved	*Abused*
Number of families in each community	10	10
Number of children in each community	26	33
Number of father-son partnerships	9	0
Number married and in business locally	11	8
Number at home going to school	3	2
Number who had left the community	3	23

3

Nearly 90 per cent of the children in the community where conservation was practiced remained there to make their homes. Only 30 per cent remained in the vicinity of the eroding farms.

In another graphic example, a public service company reported the results of a decline in the rural population in a thirty-county area in southwestern Oklahoma during the fourteen-year period from 1934 to 1948. When the number of farms in the area was decreased by thirteen, one retail business in town closed its doors, and three families who lived in town lost their source of livelihood. Truly the chief harvest of the land is man himself, with his churches, his schools, his businesses, and all the other facets of his complex civilized society.

Soil conservation is no less important to the town and city dwellers than it is to the farmer who will be forced off of his land when the soil erodes from under his feet. Sterling North, former editor of the *Chicago Daily News*, pointed this out when he stated: "It takes a productive land to support a democracy. Every time you see a dust cloud or a muddy stream, a field scarred by erosion or a channel choked with silt, you are witnessing the passing of American democracy, for the crop called MAN can wither like any other."

Recognizing the stake that the people as a whole have in the land, the federal government appropriates millions of dollars each year for many activities ranging from conservation to reclamation and flood control. State governments make appropriations to assist in conservation, particularly in supporting research and educational work and bolstering local soil conservation districts, which are local units of self-government whose sole purpose is to promote conservation. County and city governments also support such activities. The trend has been toward greater support from governmental units of all classes, although the federal government still bears the major share of the burden.

But it is the farmers, representing 15 per cent of the nation's population, who bear 75 per cent of the costs of the total soil-conservation activities, which are designed to insure present and future food and fiber needs for the 85 per cent of the people not living on farms as well as for the farmers themselves. Their motives are at once altruistic and practical.

On the practical side, farmers increase the capital worth of their own holdings and at the same time produce more from their land for cash sales. For example, there is Delmar Hammond, a co-operator with the Tompkins County Soil Conservation District, Jacksonville, New York, who reclaimed a 125-acre dairy and cash-crop farm. Corn production increased to 100 bushels per acre from a pre-conservation production of 40 to 50 bushels. Hay production jumped from three-fourths of a ton to 3 tons per acre, bean production from 15 to 26 bushels, and his pastures now feed 3 animals per acre where they could formerly support less than half that number.

Lloyd McKinnon of the Southern Aroostook Soil Conservation District, Bridgewater, Maine, raised potato production from 127 barrels in 1948, before conservation, to 165 barrels in 1949, and 195 barrels in 1950, and is saving his land to produce again and again.

One hundred bushels of corn per acre has become the goal of good conservation programs in the corn belt. H. George Thompson of St. Mary's Soil Conservation District, Leonardtown, Maryland, beat that figure on land that formerly grew only 35 to 40 bushels. Even in Kansas, where there is less rainfall, Perry W. McPheeters of Baldwin increased corn production from 30 to 80 bushels per acre with a good conservation program. And Vernon Pfister of Hiawatha, Kansas, increased corn yields from 25 to 30 bushels to 75 to 90 bushels and reduced erosion 90 per cent.

Thirty-eight co-operators of the Bryan County, Oklahoma, Soil Conservation District reported that conservation farming

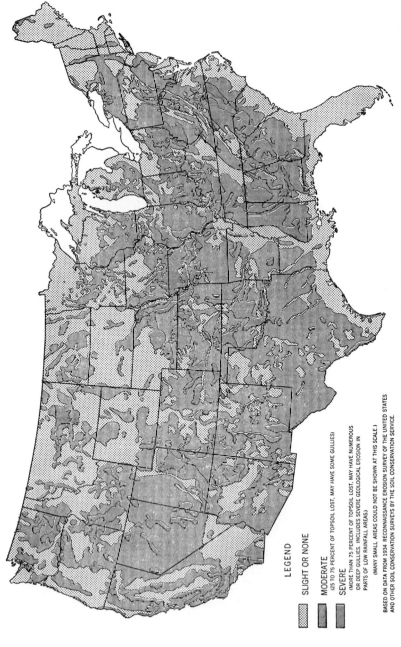

LEGEND

[ ] SLIGHT OR NONE

[ ] MODERATE
(25 TO 75 PERCENT OF TOPSOIL LOST, MAY HAVE SOME GULLIES)

[ ] SEVERE
(MORE THAN 75 PERCENT OF TOPSOIL LOST, MAY HAVE NUMEROUS
OR DEEP GULLIES. INCLUDES SEVERE GEOLOGICAL EROSION IN
PARTS OF LOW RAINFALL AREAS)

(MANY SMALL AREAS COULD NOT BE SHOWN AT THIS SCALE.)

BASED ON DATA FROM 1934 RECONNAISSANCE EROSION SURVEY OF THE UNITED STATES
AND OTHER SOIL CONSERVATION SURVEYS BY THE SOIL CONSERVATION SERVICE.

FIGURE 1.   *Generalized Soil Erosion.*

had increased their total production by 93 per cent. In Oklahoma, moisture conservation is vital to crop production. A federal-state experiment station at Cherokee, Oklahoma, reported that contour cultivation reduced the runoff of rainfall by 22 per cent over a five-year period, and contour cultivation plus terraces reduced the runoff by 42 per cent. A similar station at Guthrie, Oklahoma, found that a rotation of cotton, wheat, and sweet clover reduced runoff 33 per cent and soil losses 76 per cent.

Complete conservation on all of the nation's agricultural land by 1975 is the goal set by conservation leaders. Perhaps this date has been selected because statisticians have estimated that by that time the nation's supply-demand factors will be in balance. The rising demands of an increasing population (nearly 170,-000,000 in 1955, approximately 3,000,000 more than in 1954) and the falling production of eroding fields and deteriorating pastures will bring an end to agricultural surpluses. Then either the standard of living must be lowered or new sources of supply must be found. In that event the United States could not continue to be the "bread basket of the world," but would join the ranks of the "have-not" nations.

Meantime, one cubic mile of good soil is washed annually from the fields of the Mississippi Basin into its streams. Less than one-twentieth of the conservation measures needed was applied last year. Moreover, there is evidence of persisting indifference on the part of many of the nation's leaders and a large percentage of the landholders to the extent of the continuing damage to agricultural lands.

The government entered the picture belatedly, but for reasons that are basic to the welfare of the nation. Early conservationists, Washington and Jefferson among them, regarded soil wastage as an unholy thing, but to them it was a matter of personal principle rather than a subject for national policy. To most farmers it did not seem important to their own welfare, for when one farm was washed away, there were new lands to settle, new forests to be cleared, and new sod to be broken.

But this situation no longer existed after World War I. Too much timber had been cleared and too much sod broken, and too much of the exposed soil had been washed into creeks and rivers and into the sea. Too much land was mutilated by gullies, robbed of its productivity, and abandoned.

Then prophets were heard. H. H. Bennett, regarded as the father of soil conservation in this nation, J. N. "Ding" Darling, Paul B. Sears, and others engaged in a great crusade to awaken the nation's consciousness, to organize public assistance, and to mobilize private agencies and the landholders.

Although the real beginnings of the great conservation effort were clouded by close association with "made-work" relief programs of the depression years, public assistance was brought to the farmer to help him solve his conservation problems. Government entered the picture in the four general fields of research, information and education, technical assistance, and financial assistance, for in spite of the great benefits accruing to the individual farmer from the application of a soil conservation program to his own land, there are many things that he cannot do for himself. In addition, there are many farmers who are not yet willing to accept new methods.

Soil conservation is new in the United States. The establishment of erosion control experiment stations in 1930 was the first public effort to find the cause of erosion and to develop methods of dealing with it. There is still much to be learned and much to be developed in this field.

Research will point the way. When new facts are learned and new procedures are developed, they must be not only offered to millions of farmers but also presented in a manner that will motivate farmers to accept them. This is the task of the informational and educational programs of the schools, extension services, and action agencies.

Expert direction is needed in the application of permanent practices, in starting new farming methods, and in the maintenance and improvement of new scientific programs. This is the field of the technical agencies, or so-called action agencies. Many farm conservation practices are too expensive for the farmer to adopt. He is given financial assistance through cost-sharing plans, loans, and tax relief. Government agencies, by means of cash grants and technical assistance, aid groups of farmers in installing irrigation, drainage, flood-prevention, and watershed-protection projects.

Public assistance for these activities is justified and necessary. It is insurance against the days of want which will almost surely come to future generations without them, and which could come during the lives of many now operating farms and ranches or directing the affairs of the nation. Unless new sources of food are found or the potential productivity of our agricultural lands is increased beyond present expectations, the day of reckoning will surely come and there will be a shortage of bread, meat, and milk. Some people in the United States will not have enough to eat—not because they can't afford it, but because there will not be enough food to go around. And each year, barring bumper crops, there will be less and less.

But the picture is not all dark. Even as erosion is accelerated as it progresses, its dangers become more frightening to the tillers of the soil and to farsighted leaders. The sense of urgency grows. More farmers start their own conservation programs. More city dwellers realize their dependency on agriculture. More people, when they see a stream running muddy, know that it contains soil from fields that must produce food and fiber for them and their children. More people realize that this is not a fight for the farmer alone, and they find ways to give him aid and encouragement.

Perhaps the goal of complete conservation by 1975 is not too optimistic. By that date every man in the nation should be able to see that erosion and soil depletion must be stopped. Before that time, national, state, and community leaders should develop sound national policies, co-ordinate all agricultural activities with them, and provide really adequate assistance to the farmer.

In that day, federal appropriations for soil conservation will exceed the cost of a battleship, and more attention will be given to conservation than to a Congressional investigation. State appropriations for soil and water conservation will be greater than those for a single highway, and more thought will be given to conservation than to the organization of the legislature. Conservation will be the most important goal of every local civic and commercial club in agricultural areas.

II: Planning for Soil Conservation

1. DEFINITION AND HISTORY

THERE IS NOW a whole field of technology in soil conservation, and assistance in its many phases is available to farmers who need and want it. This was not always true.

Once conservation meant the digging of hillside ditches to intercept runoff from fields or pasture land and protect crop-land below. Rock, brush, or wire dams across natural watercourses were added to trap silt from the slopes or reduce gullying. Sometimes gully banks were sloped and covered with brush mats in an effort to stabilize them. Then earth fills across gullies replaced the loose rock or brush dams.

At this time gullies were regarded as evidence of erosion. The insidious sheet erosion occurring on the upper slopes, where there was no great concentration of water, went unnoticed. As these slopes lost their dark color and the yellow, white, or red subsoil began to show up, the problem of sheet erosion was recognized, and the idea of terracing was conceived.

At first, ditches or dykes were used to collect water from points of concentration and lead it out onto a pasture or wood-land area. Gradually there evolved a system of ridges across slopes. These ridges had varying grades, shapes, and sizes. To get a suitable gradient in the ridge line was a problem, but the ingenious American farmer contrived several devices to aid in establishing a line across the slope on the approximate contour.

One early method used a water-filled hose, with ends held up to prevent spilling. When the water in the elevated ends of the hose stood at the same height, say at three feet above the ground, the two points or "stations" under the ends of the hose were at the same elevation. The stations were marked, and the man carrying the rear end of the hose advanced to the last station while his partner sought another point of the same elevation. A succession of such points or stations determined a level line across the slope.

Another innovation was based on the use of a carpenter's level. A large A-frame was made of three twenty-foot lengths of 1 x 4-inch lumber. The frame was set up on two points previously leveled, and a carpenter's level was attached to the cross-member, with the bubble centered. In operation, two men carried the frame, the rear man holding the point while the forward man moved his end uphill or downhill until a third man, who was watching the bubble, signaled that the bubble was centered. On plowed land, the ends of the frame were set on boards. If a grade was wanted in the line, one board would be thicker than the other. But in either event, the bubble was centered between stations. Progression across the slope was made in the same manner as with the hose.

Farm levels, based on the principle of surveyors' levels, were later made available through county and community organizations. Now most conservation surveying is done by trained survey crews under the direction of competent engineers, and such service is available through soil conservation districts and cooperating technical-assistance agencies, without cost to the farmer.

Research and experience led to the development of the modern system of terraces, with size, shape, spacing, and gradient standardized. Thus soil conservation progressed from hillside ditching to gully control and then to terracing.

When the professional worker began to run terrace lines and help provide adequately protected outlets for the terraces, he observed that terraces did not stop all of the erosion. Therefore he recommended contour farming, cover crops, and stubble mulching, or the maintenance of crop residues in or on the surface to help control erosion between the terraces. Perhaps the greatest stride made in soil conservation came with the understanding that it usually takes more than one kind of device or practice to control soil erosion.

Nevertheless, the conservation worker continued to survey terraces on all types of land and to recommend a system of conservation farming between the terraces. By this time there were ten or twelve "recognized" soil conservation practices, and later there were others as the conservation field expanded. But it became increasingly clear that conservation could not be attained on all cropland by terraces and the other practices then employed.

At this stage emphasis was on the prevention of erosion. Since this goal could not be achieved on all lands by the conservation practices available, the logical conclusion was that some land could not be kept in cultivation indefinitely, even with the best of the known conservation and farming practices. This led to the next step in soil conservation: land use.

Obviously, if some types of land could be ruined by continued cultivation, they should be used in such a way that erosion would be halted and their productivity maintained. The crops chosen for these lands should occupy the land permanently, or nearly so, and not require regular tillage. The use of trees and grasses for this purpose led to advances in securing planting materials, in the selection of site and variety, and in methods of management and harvesting for maximum returns.

Silviculture, the care and management of forests, was a well-developed science when the planting and care of farm forests became a recognized need in soil conservation, and the principles of this science were embodied in the general field of conservation. On the other hand, the development and use of tame grasses had not progressed rapidly until this type of cover was also needed for soil conservation. Then grassland agriculture came into the conservation picture. Native rangelands were becoming depleted and eroded. Abandoned cropland in the rangeland areas required a protective cover, and the native grasses were the only types of plants which could meet the needs of land protection and give returns to the farmer. So variety selection, the development of seed sources, planting equipment and methods, and related activities entered the field of soil conservation.

Then new questions arose. If there were lands which must be retired from cultivation, what distinguished them? How were they to be classified? The present system of land classification was evolved from efforts to answer these questions. It was refined to indicate the intensity of treatment needed for all land in any use, and another activity was added to the field of conservation. The following section details the basic facts concerning land classification and explains how this subject concerns the farmer and his conservation program.

The technology of soil conservation was advancing at a rapid rate, but had not as yet attained maturity. It became evident that the condition of a soil cannot remain static. The soil is being improved, or it is deteriorating. Mere protection is not enough. To attain full conservation, there must also be improvement. The acceptance of this fact marked another advance for soil conservation.

Improvement of the soil brings greater yields and more profits. Conservationists very practically took advantage of this "selling point" and consciously directed their efforts toward a soil improvement program which would do a better job and at the same time appeal to every farmer. Improved yields meant, too, that the farmer could concentrate his efforts on the better croplands and free the poorer acres for a grass or tree cover. Improved production from pastures and woodland helped the farmer to diversify his operations, increase his income, and make the adjustments necessitated by changes in land use.

Improvement also came to mean drainage, irrigation, and water conservation projects, wildlife habitat improvement, watershed treatment, and flood prevention. Thus conservation workers found themselves engaged in fields not always directly connected with the prevention of soil erosion in its original sense.

The new meaning of soil conservation is based on a realization that soils are different—that they have different capabilities. On some sites almost anything suited to the climate can be grown with little soil protection, as long as fertility is maintained. Other soils can produce well over long periods with varying intensity of treatment. But no feasible treatment can keep other soils safely in cultivation over many years. These differences are determined by land capabilities, and a sound conservation program is based on a thorough knowledge of land capability. This is the basic principle of soil conservation.

Once soil conservation practices were experimental, halting, incomplete, and ridden with many failures. Now a conservation program can be as complete, safe, and rewarding as the farmer wants it to be.

Medicine has a similar history. Diagnoses were once not too accurate, and science had not developed enough medicines and treatments to combat the majority of the ills that were prevalent. Now most illnesses can be identified, the cause determined, and treatment prescribed to cure the patient or at least make him more comfortable. This is attested by the fact that man's life span was around forty years in grandfather's day, but is up to sixty-seven now. The patient has developed confidence in his doctor. He seldom says, "I will try the white pills to see if they will make me well, but I will omit the red capsules, the shots, and the operation you advise." He has learned that the doctor is usually right, and that if he does not follow the prescribed medical regimen, he will suffer.

A great number of farmers are developing similar confidence in their conservationists. He is their land doctor. Generally he can diagnose the ills of the land, determine their causes, and recommend a system of treatment which will halt deterioration and begin rebuilding the land. Often he can suggest a number of alternative treatments, and from these the farmer may choose the system that he wishes to follow.

Great emphasis is placed on planning an adequate program of soil conservation for each farm or ranch. Conservation is a major enterprise for the landholder, for it is of prime and basic importance to all other farm activities. The soil and water, and sometimes the permanent types of vegetation on the farm, are the only basic resources, aside from man himself. Their use, preservation, and improvement afford the only hope for the continued success of any type of farming, ranching, or woodland enterprise.

The symptoms of land ills should be carefully diagnosed, and the causes should be found. Plans should be carefully laid for a complete treatment of the farm, field by field and acre by acre. These resources are of such importance that no less than full soil protection and improvement, beneficial water conservation and management, and careful development of the vegetative resources to their fullest capacity would be wise farm management. To attain this goal, every acre must be used in accordance with its capabilities and treated in accordance with its needs for protection and improvement. This is the conservation goal of the U. S. Department of Agriculture. It should be subscribed to by every good farmer.

Planning for Soil Conservation

A complete conservation plan can seldom be made in a day—or a week. Often most of the steps involved can be foreseen, noted, and applied to the land in their proper order. Usually most of the needs of the land can be spotted and a general plan developed, with details to be completed as the work progresses. But often the farmer is not ready to make the required decisions at the time planning is begun. He may lack the cash or find it necessary to solve some personal problem. Or he may want to put part of the plan in operation now and wait until his income increases before attempting to work out the entire project.

None of these factors should deter him from accepting a plan and starting work. He can get help for as much or as little as he is able to do. The important thing is that he not lose sight of the goal—a complete conservation project for the treatment of every acre of his land.

Most conservation planning and action is handled by local soil conservation districts (which are local subdivisions of government organized and operated by the farmers themselves) and a co-operating agency, the Soil Conservation Service of the U. S. D. A. The latter makes detailed conservation surveys of private farm lands, as described below, which form the basis of farm planning and other conservation activities of the department.

The farmer secures assistance for conservation work by making application to his soil conservation district office. Each applicant receives assistance in accordance with the policies set up by the board of supervisors, the governing body of the district. Unless the board has established a system of priority or other policy which will delay action, the local conservationist will place the applicant in line for assistance in the order in which the application is received. He will go over the farm with the owner or operator as soon as his schedule permits, perhaps within a day or two.

If the soils on the farm have not been mapped for land capability, he schedules this task for a soil scientist who has been specially trained for this work in the local area. If the farmer is in no hurry for assistance, the conservationist may delay his visit to the farm until this map is prepared. If there is need for immediate assistance, the visit will take place as quickly as possible, and the necessary decisions will be made on the basis of the conservationist's recognition of the needs and capabilities of the land. More complete plans will be made later when the soils survey is available. Actually the first steps in planning are merely being speeded up to clear the way for starting the actual work.

The farmer is asked to sign a conservation agreement when assistance is given. This is necessary since the Soil Conservation Service works with farmers only through their soil conservation districts and, to a limited extent, through the county Agricultural Stabilization and Conservation Service committee. The farmer-district agreement forms vary somewhat, since each district chooses its own, but their general principles are as follows:

1. That the farmer understand that his soil conservation district is an independent subdivision of state government, organized and operated by local farmers to promote soil and water conservation in the area, and for no other purpose.

2. That the farmer is entering into the agreement with his district and not with the Soil Conservation Service or any other agency.

3. That the district will supply the farmer with an inventory of his soil and vegetative resources, with written explanations of each variation in soil, range, or woodland capability, with discussions of general conservation problems and alternatives in land use as they might apply to his land.

4. That other assistance in planning and application, such as the time of S. C. S. personnel assigned to the district, will be made available to the farmer as he needs them and as they

may be scheduled, in helping the farmer to plan and apply conservation measures.

5. That the agreement is voluntary and may be canceled by either party when due notice is given to this effect.

6. And that, in return for this assistance, the farmer will use his land within its capabilities, treat it in accordance with its needs for protection and improvement, develop as rapidly as feasible a conservation plan for his farm, start applying one or more conservation practices, and maintain the effective practices which have been applied.

In areas where soil conservation districts have been in operation, farmers know that this agreement is just what it implies— a joint effort of farmers within the district to conserve natural agricultural resources, with no strings held by any outside agency.

When the farmer signs the formal agreement, he becomes a district co-operator. He may have worked with the conservationist and made a complete (or basic) plan, a partial plan, or no plan at all. But the formal agreement signifies that he desires to do conservation work and is entitled to the assistance and guidance enumerated above. He gets assistance when he asks for it and when it can be scheduled. He can get it for one field only or for the entire farm—as long as he does not leave out some link which can cause the project to fail. There are technical standards which the S. C. S., or any other agency, must follow in planning these projects. However, if there is disagreement on any practice, the farmer may continue to receive assistance in other practices which meet the district standards.

The important principle of planning assistance is this: A scientific inventory of the soil and vegetative resources of the farm is made available to the farmer. The survey, when properly interpreted, indicates the various treatments which will control erosion and improve the farm. The suggested conservation measures are based on the facts about his resources, and experience has shown that the suggested conservation measures are sound. What the farmer does about these facts is up to him, but he can have the assistance of trained personnel to interpret the survey and plan and to help apply needed conservation measures. How the conservationist will work with the farmer is discussed more fully in Section 4 below.

The agreement docket will include the following items:

1. An aerial photograph of the farm, showing existing and planned permanent features, such as field boundaries, roads, farmstead, etc. Planned fields will be numbered with approximate acreages shown. On the face of this map or photograph will be shown land-capability boundaries with their designations. Around the borders of this map, notes will briefly describe the conservation measures which were planned at the time the map was prepared.

2. Land-capability guide sheets for each type of soil found on the farm, as shown on the aerial photograph.

3. Supporting information, such as job sheets for each type of work planned.

4. A copy of the agreement form, signed by the farmer and a representative of the soil conservation district.

In the district's copy of the agreement will be kept engineering notes, soil-test information, and other information concerning the progress of conservation work on the farm.

If the farmer originally made a basic plan, he should have in the docket a brief outline of all the conservation work he intends to do. If he made only a partial plan, he should have the basic information which will enable him to complete the planning. Of course, he may need further assistance in completing the plan, in applying practices, and in making revisions or improving the original plan.

If the farmer makes at least tentative plans for all of the conservation work needed on his land, he will be able to arrive at a close approximation of the cost, in money and labor, and the benefits to be derived. He can estimate the productive capacity of his fields, pastures, and woodlands under the new program and discover whether they will be sufficient for his needs. He will have a good picture of his present and future prospects.

If this picture meets with his approval, he can lay plans to do the first things first; and, although establishment of the complete plan may take a long time, he will find that there is less lost motion and that the completed job will be cheaper and better than if he planned the work piecemeal.

The result of the co-operation of farmer and conservationist will be a co-ordinated conservation plan for the entire farm. The farmer should not find himself with too many cattle and too little feed, or too much hay and not enough pasture. When he starts with a complete plan, he can go about the work job by job, rather than field by field. The parts of the conservation plan will fall into order. He is likely to arrive at a farm arrangement in which each part fits with every other part, and every farm enterprise is founded on good soil, pasture, and woodland, well managed and producing to its maximum.

This is a background picture of soil conservation and the usual methods of planning and applying the needed conservation measures. In the next section the principles of land classification will be discussed, and later the planning process will be more carefully examined.

2. LAND CAPABILITY: THE BASIS FOR SOIL CONSERVATION PLANNING

The success of any agricultural enterprise is limited by the ability of the land to produce. Any farm or ranch plan should be based on land capability, just as an adequate plan for soil conservation should be based on the capability of each acre and its need for protection and improvement.

Soils vary for many reasons. They were built from, or on, many types of parent material: muck, peat, sandstone, shale, limestone, granite, sand, chalk, gravel, lava, and others. They have been moved by water, wind, or glaciers. Some have been developing for a long period of time, and others are young, geologically speaking. The type of vegetation that grew on the soils has had a marked effect on them.

The slope on which certain soils developed affected their quality. Steep slopes lose much of the soil as it develops. Some bottom-land soils are largely accumulations from these slopes. Some lands, now uplands, were once lake beds. Some soils were developed on nearly flat uplands where little was lost to erosion; here the vegetation grew rank and produced deep, fertile soils. Temperature variations caused the parent material to break down faster in some places than in others. Rainfall variations affected the vegetation and the rate of erosion. Other soils were affected by mineral, salt, and rock deposits.

All of these factors, and many others, resulted in a wide variation of soil types. There are many hundreds of soils that are recognized as distinct units in conservation mapping. Once soil scientists mapped these soils by name. Now broader groupings are made of soil units having the same capabilities and treatment needs and the same qualities of slope, texture, and depth.

The new soil units were given numbers. Soil unit 1 is defined as a deep, fine-textured, very slowly permeable, upland soil. Unit 2 is similar, varying only in the degree of permeability. It is slowly permeable, instead of very slowly permeable. This may seem a small matter in definition, but it makes considerable difference to the crops that grow on the two soils.

To amplify the definitions a little: Soil unit 1 is a heavy clay soil with a subsoil so dense that there is almost no possibility for the feeder roots of field crops to penetrate below the surface soil, and there is almost no movement of air or water into or out of the subsoil. Soil unit 2 has almost the same surface texture, but the subsoil has some granulation, allowing some penetration by roots and some movement of air and water. The subsoil of unit 1, when exposed, has the appearance of layers of tinfoil, while the subsoil of unit 2 tends to break in vertical columns.

The classification process continues through the deep soils according to texture and permeability, including soils less dense than 1 and 2, through mixed soils, sands, and the bottom-land soils. Then the classification includes the shallow soils with different degrees of texture and permeability, then the very shallow soils, and finally rough, broken land, escarpments, and river wash.

These classifications are based on texture, permeability, and depth. Texture and permeability, as the terms are used by soil scientists, both relate to the density of the soils or the fineness of the individual soil particles, but the former relates to the surface soil while the latter concerns subsoil. In soil mapping, there is no description of the parent material below the soil, but the conservationist's definition of a soil unit may indicate that the soil lies on a deep sand or other material that will affect its use. Generally, however, all soils of a given texture in the surface and permeability of subsoil are mapped as the same unit if they have the same topographical location; that is, if they are either upland or bottom land. As has been pointed out, however, there are different classifications for the bottom-land and the upland soils.

The individual particles of sands are much larger than those of clays. There are more air spaces, and water enters and leaves the soil much more readily. These facts are important in all aspects of soil use, and must be indicated in mapping.

Fine-textured soils, then, have a surface that is composed of clays. Coarse-textured soils are sands. Usually the subsoil is similar to the surface soil, but as this is not always true, the conservationist must also indicate the kind of subsoil. Since the primary functions of the subsoil, in relation to crop production, are to receive and store moisture and to permit roots to penetrate in search of this moisture and minerals, its qualities can best be described in terms of permeability. Therefore the clay subsoils are shown as "slowly" or "very slowly" permeable to indicate that water, air, or roots cannot enter them readily. Coarse, sandy subsoils are indicated as "freely" or "very freely" permeable. Between these extremes are those soils which have a good balance between clay and sand. When the surface has this balance, it is called "medium textured." A similar subsoil would be "permeable."

Depth is the other basic consideration in the classification of soils. It refers to the thickness of topsoil and subsoil down to the unaltered parent material, or the layer on which the soil was built. It is the normal zone of root activity and is measured without consideration of soil losses from erosion or its virgin state.

A layer of rock may limit root activity and clearly mark the lower boundary of the soil. In a sand, this boundary may not be so well defined. There will be a zone below the topsoil where the sand has definitely been altered by the presence of roots. Below this there will be another zone where there is no evidence that roots have ever penetrated. The first zone is the subsoil, and the latter or deeper zone is the parent material. But between these two zones there may be an intermediate area where there is an indication that roots are beginning to alter the sand by leaving deposits of organic matter through decay. For soil classification purposes, this zone, or "horizon," is usually regarded as parent material and is not considered in measuring the depth of the soil.

Soils may vary in depth from an inch or two to many feet, but only three categories are considered necessary in mapping.

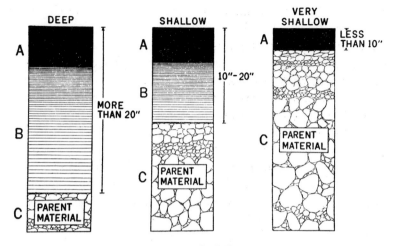

FIGURE 2. *Soil Depth.*

(1) A soil is called "deep" if it is more than twenty inches through topsoil and subsoil to the parent material. (2) It is "shallow" if the range is from ten to twenty inches. (3) It is "very shallow" if it is less than ten inches deep. Other factors also enter into soil classification.

The capacity of a soil to produce over a long period of time without being destroyed determines its *capability* and gives a key to its proper use. Capability is often confused with productivity. The latter refers to the balance of plant food elements and water in the soil at any certain time and the qualities of the soil which permit plants to use these materials and produce a desired yield.

In classifying soils as to capability, the soil scientist considers present productivity, but goes further. He wants to know whether they will continue to be productive for many years to come. He may say that a soil can be productive for coming generations, if it is properly used and given the proper treatment and care. *The use and treatment required to keep it pro-*

ductive is determined by its capability. That is the basis of modern conservation planning.

In all parts of the nation, soils have been put in cultivation that were productive for a time, but were later abandoned because they had lost their productivity. This loss of productivity has usually been attributed to the failure of the land operators to establish proper conservation measures. Just as often, however, the fault lies in land use. Although the proper combination of conservation practices and farming methods would in some instances have maintained the productivity of the land, often the land could not have been maintained in cultivated crops regardless of any reasonable type of conservation program. In such cases the land did not have the capability for the production of cultivated crops, and therefore would best have been used for tree or grass production or as a home for some form of wild life.

Seldom, however, do people realize that "this land should never have been plowed" until after irreparable damage has been done to the soil. That phrase is heard in all communities where productivity has been destroyed, and usually there is an implication of blame against those who originally "broke out" the land. Yet, in most of these same communities, there is land still under cultivation which "never should have been plowed," and sometimes the man who now owns or farms the land will admit it, in spite of the fact that he will not quite agree to put a permanent cover of grass or trees back on such areas. The man who realizes that his land is not suited to permanent cultivation is apt to retire it from such use sooner than the man who cannot see that it will not long remain productive.

Then there are types of soil which are not quite as unstable as the examples given above, but which can be kept in cultivation if treated and used properly. The treatment may include terraces, contour farming, and the use of a fertility-improving crop of grasses or legumes from one-third to two-thirds of the

Does conservation pay?
ABOVE: *Poor land makes poor people.*
BELOW: *Conservation planning and practices
mean progress and prosperity.*

CLASSIFYING THE LAND

Suitable for cultivation

    I Requires good soil-management practices only
    II Moderate conservation practices only
    III Intensive conservation practices necessary
    IV Perennial vegetation—infrequent cultivation

No Cultivation
Pasture, Hay, Woodland, and Wildlife

    V No restriction in use
    VI Moderate restrictions in use
    VII Severe restrictions in use
    VIII Best suited for wildlife and recreation

time. If properly used, the land may be restricted to sown crops at all times, with stubble maintained between crops. Other lands may require varying treatments, with few restrictions on use, to assure a long life under cultivation.

How, then, are the farmer and the conservationist to determine land capabilities from the soils mapping so that they may plan a realistic program for the conservation and improvement of the soils on the farm? Generally, more information is needed than was outlined above. Of course, some types of soil are not suited to cropping under any conditions, and others are unstable and require infinite care to be kept in cultivation. But in the case of most soils there are other factors that enter into land-capability determinations.

Chief among the other factors are erosion conditions and the slope on which the soil lies. To be considered also are such conditions as wetness, rock outcroppings, detrimental deposits of salt or other inorganic substances, and susceptibility to overflow. Some of these conditions may be recognized by the trained and the untrained alike as making the land unsuitable for cultivation. But usually an expert is required to make an accurate survey of all of these conditions and weigh them against texture, permeability, and depth classifications to determine land capability.

This is exactly what is required to determine a safe basis for the planning of an adequate program of soil protection and improvement, farm by farm, field by field, and acre by acre, all over the nation. It is the task assigned by the federal government to the United States Soil Conservation Service—the mapping of every acre of agricultural land in such detail that capability determinations can be made for use by farmers and all other agencies dealing with agricultural land use.

Eight *classes* of land capability are now recognized. In most classes there are literally thousands of combinations of soil units in various classifications of texture, permeability, and depth, as modified by slope, erosion conditions, and the inhibitory factors of wetness, stoniness, salinity, and overflow. And these conditions are interpreted for any locality in terms of climate, prevailing farming practices, conservation methods, and the types of crops which might be grown. A list and explanation of all the possible combinations of soils and conditions found in the United States would fill a book larger than this, and it would be impractical for field use by even the most expertly trained technician.

In each soil conservation district, a group of soils technicians make a general survey to discover all the types of individual soils to be found in the area and to determine in which of the texture and permeability groups they belong. Then, in consultation with practical conservationists familiar with the area, a prolonged study is made to determine how each of these soils, in any of its conditions, fits into tables of capability.

For example, the conservationists may have under consideration a fine sandy loam soil determined to be in the deep, medium-textured, permeable category. It is an upland soil without any of the inhibitory factors such as wetness or salinity. When it lies on a slope of three to five feet fall per hundred feet, with only moderate erosion, the group agrees that it is suited to long-time cropping with intensive treatment, including terraces for which proper outlets are provided, contour farming, strip cropping when in row crops such as cotton or peanuts, the frequent use of soil-improving crops such as vetch and rye every four or five years to maintain the structure of the soil and its fertility, and the management of crop residue to protect the soil between crops. In this instance there is no disagreement among the conservationists and the soils man. But when the soil lies on a steeper slope, or when erosion has become severe, there may be disagreement whether the land may be maintained in cultivation under any combination of conservation practices. Here field trips are required. Land in similar condition is found, and the opinion of the farmers who handle the land is sought. Consultations are continued until an agreement is reached.

This type of study results in a *land capability table* for the district. In it are listed all of the groups of soil, in all possible combinations of depth, slope, erosion conditions, and the other factors which affect either its productivity or its durability.

By using these tables, any field worker can quickly determine land capability for any soil on any farm which has been mapped by the soil scientist. By a further study of the recommendations which go with each table, a conservationist can help the farmer determine the best treatment and use for any acre on the farm, or he can help determine the best alternate treatments and uses in accordance with the farmer's needs.

It is clear, therefore, that the development of a basis for the planning of conservation treatment on the land is a highly scientific achievement in any soil conservation district, and is worthy of careful study by any farmer who has this information made available to him. He will need to know just what the eight land classes are, at least in general terms. Whether he lives in the United States or its possessions or in any other place in the world where this system of land classification is used, the farmer will find that he can fit his land into one or more of the eight land-capability classifications as described below.

CLASS I. Class I land is level, or nearly so. It may fall into one of many texture or permeability classes, but it is deep, does not deteriorate readily, and is subject to little if any erosion. It has none of the inhibitory factors. Its use is restricted only by climate. Conservation measures needed are only those required to maintain fertility. This class of land includes all of our best soils.

CLASS II. This soil is less level, or is composed of soils more erosible or otherwise less stable. There is no restriction on use, as any crop suitable to a similar Class I soil can be grown if

Soil Conservation

moisture and fertility conditions are adequate. However, simple conservation measures are usually required. These may include contour farming, strip cropping, stubble mulching, and the occasional use of a soil-improving crop to maintain the structure of the soil and its fertility. Occasionally terraces are used for more complete erosion control and for slowing down runoff rainfall so that more water may be absorbed by the soil. Water-spreading or detention type terraces greatly increase water absorption, and any type of terrace can be used to break up large concentrations of water on long slopes.

CLASS III. Soils in this category may be of many texture and permeability classifications, may be deep or shallow, and may vary in slope from nearly level to fairly steep. They may have some of the inhibitory factors, as long as these do not completely prevent cropping. The amount of erosion that has taken place may vary from slight to moderately severe. These soils are usually rather subject to wind or water erosion, or both.

Generally their use is not restricted as far as conservation is concerned, although site and fertility conditions may not permit the profitable growing of crops suited to better soils. Under continued cropping, maximum conservation treatments are needed to protect the soil from erosion and maintain or improve its fertility. Practices usually needed are those employed on Class I or Class II land, but applied more intensively and usually with some additions. Also, the maintenance of the soil generally will require a more intensive use of soil-improving crops.

CLASS IV. This class of land is suited to limited cropping if maintained in a sown crop and no row crops are used, and if soil-improving crops of grasses or legumes occupy the land a large part of the time and are handled in such a manner that large amounts of residue are incorporated into the soil to maintain its structure and fertility. However, such lands are better used if maintained permanently in grass or trees.

If cropped, the land requires all of the intensive erosion control measures used on Class III land, with the additional protection of near-permanent cover as outlined above. If the land is planted to grass or trees, erosion control measures are seldom necessary, except that adequate cover must be maintained.

CLASS v. These lands are wet and often saline. They may be poorly drained or overflow so frequently that cropping is impractical. If the soil can be economically drained or protected from overflow and put to cultivation, that treatment would, in effect, raise the land to a higher class.

Otherwise, this land should be used for grasses, trees, or wildlife habitats. The plant cover should be that which is found there or that which may be introduced and will survive under the given conditions.

CLASS vi. This group of lands is suited only for permanent cover and should never be plowed. If the cover has been destroyed, grasses or trees should be restored. Under a suitable cover of the proper type of permanent vegetation, this type of land should produce well and will need no auxiliary erosion control measures.

CLASS vii. This class of land is even less stable than Class VI land and may need auxiliary conservation treatment. If the land has been cropped, land leveling, an occasional diversion terrace, mulching of critical spots, or similar measures may be needed to protect the soil while a suitable cover is being restored. Sometimes erosion has damaged the land even though the native vegetation has not been removed. This may have been caused by overuse or misuse of that vegetative cover. In this event, the erosion control measures are based on a more moderate use of, or complete rest for, the woodland or range, sometimes accompanied by gully control practices, interplanting or overseeding, or mulching of bare spots.

CLASS viii. This class includes deserts, rock and shale outcroppings, soilless stretches of rock or lava beds, crags or bluffs, peaks, river-wash, etc. Such lands sometimes have value as homing or hiding places for wildlife, and occasionally they have nonagricultural values because of deposits or minerals or building materials in them.

Some of these lands may support a sparse plant population useful to wild animals or birds for food, shelter, and nesting places. The land cannot be used for grazing of domestic animals to any profitable degree, however, because erosion would be accelerated and even the sparse plant population would be in danger of destruction. If this were not true, the land would not be Class VIII, but would belong in a higher category.

Classes I, II, and III are all of the land classes suited to almost unlimited cultivation, even with the best of care, while the first four classes represent all of the land suitable for cropping. Except for Class V land, each of the other classes is successively less suited to profitable use or requires more protection. The first seven classes of land represent all land which is considered profitable in normal farming or ranching operations. But other portions of the earth's surface must also be classified, and they are all lumped into the last capability class.

Land can, and does, fall from a higher to a lower category. This is the result of erosion, which reduces the land's potential. Great areas of the United States which were once suitable for cultivation are now suitable only for a permanent cover of grass or trees, and even in this use the land's potential has been reduced—all because of the erosion which has been allowed to take place. Every year thousands of acres of the nation's farm lands are falling from Class II to Class III, from Class III to Class IV, and from Classes III or IV to Class VII, all because of improper farming methods, which include failure to employ the proper methods of erosion control.

Land cannot be upgraded, even by the best soil-building practices known—that is, not in our lifetime. Land classification presupposes that completely adequate land use and protective measures must be used to maintain the land in its class. The fact that proper use and treatment has stabilized the soil and built up its fertility to a high degree does not raise its classification, for within that class of land those measures were needed to achieve the desired results.

For example, Class IV land cannot be rebuilt to grow row crops by the use of measures needed for the maintenance of Class IV land. If it can, then the land was improperly classified in the first place. Of course, rock retaining walls may be built and the interval judiciously leveled with proper placement of topsoil. In such an event, one or more of the factors which originally entered into the land classification formula—slope and perhaps depth—have been changed, and the land may properly be given a higher classification.

This type of work may regularly be done in some of the older countries and would thus influence land classification and treatment considerations. In other words, a certain field would be capable of producing adequately over a long period of time if masonry retaining walls were built, the land properly leveled, and other measures applied; then it would be Class III land. But if the rock walls and leveling were not practices prevalent in the farming community, they would not be considered, and the land would remain as Class IV. And if the soil technician's judgment is not in error—and it usually isn't—then the commonly used intensive conservation treatments are necessary to protect the soil and maintain production over a long period of time. And, if the technician is right, a failure to limit the use to sown crops and to apply other conservation measures will result in further damage to the soil, so that it eventually will be suited only for a permanent cover of grass or trees—that it will be downgraded to Class VII.

Likewise, it is not uncommon for land that was suited for grass or trees to be abused to the extent that all soil has been washed from an underlying bedrock and the land downgraded to Class VIII.

33

On this base of land classification rest all of the conservation activities of the United States Department of Agriculture and the Indian Service of the Department of the Interior. Indeed, on this base rest all conservation activities the world over, whether applied consciously in this form or in another.

Soil erosion and deterioration always result from failure to realize the capability of land and to use it and treat it in accordance with its capabilities. This is the reason why millions of acres of the nation's agricultural lands have been depleted, sometimes to the point of total destruction. This is why our agricultural potentialities have been decreasing. And this is why it is highly important and urgent that an adequate land-capability survey be made for every acre of agricultural land in the nation, that such survey maps be placed in the hands of every owner and operator, who should accept the evidence and install the needed land use and treatment measures.

There are bright sides to the picture. Every year there are fewer acres being depleted because adequate land use and treatment measures have been established on them. Every year the rate of erosion and depletion is being reduced on many other acres because remedial measures are being started, and every year additional land owners and operators are realizing the toll that is being taken by erosion and are planning to do something about it. Farmers who want and need a complete land inventory for their land and assistance in its interpretation and in making plans for the proper use and treatment of their soil can get this aid through their soil conservation district.

3. HOW TO DEVELOP AND USE THE CONSERVATION PLAN

The conservation plan should embody the principles of conservation farming rather than details concerning the application of structural, cropping, or other conservation measures.

The farmer's general program may indicate the crops he plans to grow for cash income and their relationship to the crops he plans to use for conservation. This would be his conservation crop rotation in relation to the types of crops presently planned for the land. Often it may be difficult to distinguish the conservation crop from the regular cash crop, but the distinction can be made when it is determined which crops serve the needs of the land and which serve the needs or desires of the farmer. A few examples will be helpful.

(1) On a field of Class III land the farmer plans to use certain mechanical practices and also to use corn and soybeans in rotation with alfalfa-bromegrass meadow. A few years later corn prices are low, and the farmer wants to plant wheat, oats, or some other crop in place of corn in his rotation. Since corn is not a conservation crop and therefore not an essential part of his conservation crop rotation, substitutions may be made freely. However, if, because the price of corn is high and that of alfalfa-bromegrass hay promises to be poor, he decides that he would make more profit by delaying the planting of the meadow in favor of another year of corn, he is advised to proceed cautiously. Grass is a conservation crop intended to build up the structure of the soil.

Erratic and irregular use of his conservation crop is apt to result in a total decline in production and a net loss to the farmer. However, a more profitable crop which will meet the needs of the land may be substituted. For instance, alfalfa may be planted alone and harvested for seed. In making such a decision, the farmer would be well advised to seek the advice of his county agent or conservationist. No one can force him to discontinue planting corn, but if his conservation program has been properly gauged to the needs of the land, production will suffer in later years and likely he will lose in the long run.

(2) The farmer has planned to plant an area of Class VII land to a mixture of permanent grasses (or trees). He decides

later that it might be profitable to plant the area to wheat or cotton for a few more years before retiring it from cultivation. This decision would violate the principle of his conservation plan since the land needs the permanent cover now. Continued cropping would cause the loss of additional productive capacity so that lower yields of grazing or woodland products would result when the land is finally put to its proper use. The farmer might actually gain in immediate income, but the total production from the land would be lowered.

(3) The farmer has made a similar plan for Class IV land, but later decides that he wants to return it to cultivation. He may do so without violating the principles of conservation, but he must make additional plans for the protection and improvement of the soil. He should consult the guide sheet to determine which cropping systems are suitable for Class IV land in his area and, also, what other supporting conservation practices are needed. He may consult his conservationist again. When the costs of the added protection are balanced against the difference in yields, he may decide that it would be more profitable to leave the land in permanent cover. However, he may return it to cultivation with the proper safeguards. Again, he has made no contract concerning the use or treatment of the land, and the decisions are solely his, as they were in the first place. He may do as he likes, but the conscientious farmer will make his decisions according to the needs of the land and his own long-term profits.

(4) The farmer or rancher may have an area of original sod which was not mapped for land capability, and his conservation map will show only the range site and condition class of the grass cover. He may want to plow this land and put it into cultivation. First, however, he should ask his conservation office for a mapping of the soil and its capability class. Then, on the basis of its capability and with the advice of his conservationist, he can decide whether the land is suitable for cropping, and

whether the expected yields would make it profitable for him to plow up the sod.

(5) Often a farmer decides to retire more land to grass or trees before he establishes cropland conservation practices on the area. Obviously such practices are no longer needed for the protection of the land, but other practices or assistance may be needed; therefore, he should consult his conservationist again. This of course, would be land suitable for cultivation, and the planned practices might include a waterway, a complete terrace system, contour farming, stubble mulching, and a conservation crop rotation. If he decides to retire this land to pasture before these practices are installed, he will neither need nor want a complete terrace system and a sodded waterway for spill or any other cropland treatment. He may want a diversion terrace with a suitable spill. He may need to use fertility-building crops for a year or two and follow them with sudangrass or a similar crop to provide stubble as protection for the soil and young pasture plants until the planting is well established.

Combinations of treatment vary with changes in land use. Certain types of crops, which at first glance may seem to be used primarily for cash income, still have conservation benefits and may be relied upon heavily in conservation crop rotation. Such crops are sown small grains or grazing crops, as contrasted with row crops, which leave a large percentage of the land bare and without protection from rain or wind. They may be winter crops, which give the land protection during seasons of hard rain or strong wind, in comparison with summer crops planted on land that must be kept clean during these critical periods. They may be high residue-producing crops which leave large amounts of stubble or straw on the land during the fallow season, as compared with crops where most of the plant is removed for hay or other uses. In this category are small grains or feed grains combined for the grain alone, as contrasted with sorghum crops cut for bundle feed, ensilage, or hay, or grazed off. Another group of contrasting crops includes those which bear their fruit above ground, leaving the soil firm and with some cover, as opposed to those bearing fruit underground, such as potatoes or peanuts.

In all of these cases, if the cropping system is changed from the first listed crops to crops affording less ground protection, additional conservation practices may be required for adequate protection. Such practices might consist of cover crops to give the surface more protection during critical times or to add organic matter to the soil. They might include a strip crop pattern to provide a barrier against winds or running water or an additional crop in the rotation system. Other practices might even include mechanical treatment not originally considered necessary; this is required, for instance, when meadow crops, which may give almost perfect ground protection, are changed to row crops, which may require terracing to prevent soil movement. Therefore, combinations of treatment also vary with the cropping program.

The conservation plan, then, is a delicately balanced system of practices based on certain land uses and the employment of crops which afford varying amounts of soil protection and enrichment. The plan must be based on the uses and cropping system which the farmer desires at the time it is completed. When changes in the basic uses of the land are desired, or when the cropping system is materially changed, the balance must be maintained if the best returns are to be obtained from the land throughout the years and at the lowest cost.

If there is a change in land use from regular crops to trees or permanent grass, some of the planned practices should be discontinued. If changes are made from planned pasture or woodland to cropland, additional practices should be added to give approximately the same protection that the permanent cover would have afforded—and if the land is of such quality that additional practices will not give it adequate protection, the change to cropland should not be made.

If crops which are less desirable from a conservation standpoint are substituted for the crops originally planned, something must be added in the way of cover crops, tillage practices, or mechanical treatment to offset the loss in protection that the original crops would have afforded. The conservation plan must balance every operation that would cause erosion or render the soil subject to erosion with measures that counter the effects of erosion or soil depletion. If treatment is not available to offset such harmful operations, then these operations must be stopped or altered, to reduce or eliminate damage being done to the land. On the basis of these principles, the conservation plan can be, and should be, a changing thing.

It is evident that only the major, basic principles of land use and treatment can be listed on the margin of the conservation-plan map or aerial photograph of the farm—and those only for the principal areas of the farm. Treatments should be related to the principles, according to types of crops, land use, and general problems. In this way, the principles do not become obsolete as long as the general type of farming visualized by the farmer and conservationist is followed, and they will need revision only when a new system of farming is desired.

Many minor conservation problems and their treatments are not set down in any written plan because they would increase the complexity of the plan and might tend to make it confusing. But many minor erosion hazards may be noted by the farmer and conservationist in going over the farm and simple solutions worked out on the spot. In this category are such problems as that caused by cattle following the same path down a narrow lane or through a pasture area until gullying begins to occur. The solution may be as simple as widening the lane, throwing temporary blocks across the paths, changing salting or feeding locations, making a new entry to the pasture, or other simple measures.

39

The cause of small gullies at the edge of the field or in the pasture may be removed when terraces or other conservation measures are installed on cropland above, although minor sloping and sodding may be required to eliminate the scar. Soil tests to determine fertilizer additions needed by cover and pasture crops are important, and the proper procedure for taking samples of the soil may be outlined to the farmer by the conservationist. Various methods of planting trees, sod, or seed may be discussed, as well as pasture management and weed and shrub control. The principles underlying all of the conservation practices recommended may be discussed in detail. If all of these details were made a part of the written plan, it could become so voluminous and complicated that it would not be easily usable, and the true purpose of the plan thus be obscured.

Most conservationists realize that they cannot provide ready answers for all of the existing or potential conservation problems on all of the farms they are called on to service. And if they could outline perfect solutions for the problems seen, the farmer would likely not be inclined to follow such complete instructions unless he, too, could understand the reasoning behind the recommendations. If he understands the fundamentals of the problems, their causes, and their cures, he will not need detailed instructions. This does not mean that the farmer should not take as many notes as he desires concerning his conservation problem. In fact, if he wants such notes for study or to make certain that he does not overlook details, he should make them or ask the conservationist to make them as they study the farm. This systematic approach appeals to some farmers, but for others it has little value.

Therefore, the conservationist will try to analyze, with the farmer, the cause of the erosion or soil-depletion conditions noted, and then work out the procedures necessary to reverse the trends. As the basic principles of the plan begin to take shape, they are listed as part of the plan. The many other details discussed are by-products of the plan—meant as helpful, concrete suggestions for action, or as means to increase the farmer's fund of basic information so that he may be better able to solve his own problems as they arise.

Most farmers are ingenious enough to take this information and work out treatments better suited to their own needs. Indeed, the success of the conservation program on any farm is more dependent on the understanding and response of the farmer than on the expertness of the assistance given by the conservation workers. Thus, the conservation plan can be considered only the skeleton of basic principles on which the farmer, through constant study and intelligent work, can build a conservation program for his land. The project should be considered only a beginning, a flexible plan to be improved—principally by the land operator—as new needs are seen and as new procedures are devised. The farmer should understand that the conservationist often leaves out recommendations concerning things that are of a "polishing" nature, to avoid confusing the basic issues for the farmer who is just beginning to farm the conservation way. As the farmer progresses with his plan, he will add new practices to his conservation program. Through his own initiative and through information obtained from neighbors and conservation workers, he will learn new and more effective ways to conserve his soil.

The conservation plan is not only a changing thing, but it is a growing thing. A complete and perfect plan cannot be visualized in its entirety at the beginning. The conservationist and the farmer can discuss their combined visions of the project, if the farmer knows just what type of farming he desires and if he is ready to accept the basic principles of conservation farming. And this discussion may result in an adequate basic plan. But it should be improved as the farmer improves his ability to see and solve his erosion and soil-depletion problems and as he takes measures to offset new problems or to "dress up" his

41

conservation plan. The farmer grows with his conservation plan.

Of course, for the farmer who is not ready to make basic decisions, the first plan will be incomplete and tentative. The conservationist will have suggestions for alternative land uses and treatments, but the farmer must make important decisions before he can have even a beginning plan for all of his land.

Once his conservation plan is completed, it is up to the farmer to use it as a program for constructive work. This is the only way it will ever be worth anything to him, and he will find it a great challenge and satisfying experience. Not only will it provide immediate and long-term benefits for him and his family, but he will have the satisfaction of knowing that he is protecting the land for future generations.

Of course, he really means to use the plan or he would not have gone to the trouble to get his conservationist to help him make it in the first place. So let's look into the work still required to get the plan in operation on his land.

Even though the farmer has a general conservation plan, details for the application of it must be worked out. Suppose the plan calls for the establishment of approximately four miles of field terraces, one-half mile of diversion terrace, two waterways, and a farm pond. Since the government will share the cost of these practices through the Agricultural Conservation Program of the Agricultural Stabilization and Conservation Service, the farmer must make application to the A. S. C. S. office for this assistance. He has learned that he must have the waterways before the terraces can be approved and that, since the field to be terraced will furnish the water for the pond, it is not advisable to build the pond until after the terraces are established. Perhaps, therefore, he should make application only for the waterways. But if the pond has pasture drainage and part of the terraces will spill onto pasture land, he may be able to apply for the terraces and pond, also. Such applications should be made to A. S. C. S. before the practice is started, so

ABOVE: *The vigor and density of this ladino–Kentucky 31 fescue pasture means abundant production.* BELOW: *The Slump Test. Soils were saturated, excess water allowed to drain off, then the soils dumped on white cardboard. The soil in good condition (left) remained in a crumb structure while the soil in poor condition (right) ran together and slumped like soft cement.*

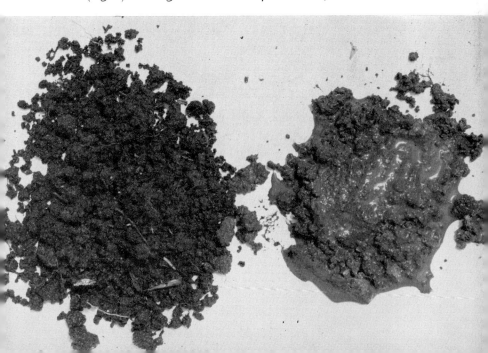

CONSERVATION PLAN MAP

Prepared By U.S. Department of Agriculture, Soil Conservation Service
Cooperating With
Garvin County
Soil Conservation District

Farm Owner ....Blow,Joe..
Farm Operator ...Blow,Joe... APPROX.
County ....Garvin........... State Oklahoma.... Photo No. CQV-3E-131
Acres 130.........Date Prepared ...7-55.... Approx. Scale 1"-660.'

(1) and (3)
Sod to Ber-
mudagrass,
overseed
annually to
hairy vetch.
Control graz-
ing. Dig
well on line
between fields
No. 1 and 3.

① 23 Ac. Pasture
② 65 Ac. Cropland
③ 25 Ac. Pasture
④ 35 Ac. Cropland
⑤ 10 Ac. Pasture
⑥ 3Ac.H

(2) Repair
terrace out-
let channel
by fertiliz:
with barnya:
manure and :
to Bermudag:
Maintain ol:
terraces.
tour farm.
tate crops
include a c:
crop of hai:
vetch at le:
once every
third year.

(4) Maintain old terraces. Contour farm. Rotate crops to include hairy vetch at
least once every three years or every year if row crops are grown.

(5) Annually overseed African weeping lovegrass with hairy vetch if needed.

(6) Farmstead. Sod east side of borrow ditch to Bermudagrass.

GENERAL TREATMENT:

Protect pasture and crop residue from fire. Inoculate all legume seeds. Apply
phosphate fertilizer as required.

The soil conservation district supplies the farmer with a Conservation Plan Map. The practices necessary for a successful conservation program are determined and indicated on map.

that approvals may be issued and government cost-sharing assured.

The farmer will plan to build the waterways as soon as possible. He will plan a method of sodding, adding the necessary manures or fertilizers to get them established as quickly as possible. Then he will build the terraces, and last of all he will build the farm pond. He may plan to install a pipe through the dam so that livestock can drink from a tank below, to fence the dam and pond basin to keep livestock out of the water, and to stock the pond with fish.

On the field, the farmer will consider the practices which may be started immediately. They may include the planting of a portion of the land to meadow or pasture crops or to legumes for seed production, as recommended in his land-capability guide sheets and discussed with his conservationist as part of his conservation crop-rotation program. He may be able to begin the practice of leaving larger amounts of crop residue in or on the surface for soil protection, and he may plan to exchange some of his tillage implements for tools that will be more satisfactory for this practice. But he may see that he cannot begin contour farming until the terraces are built to serve as guide lines. Although he cannot start some of these conservation practices immediately, he will lay plans to begin them as soon as possible.

Deciding upon the order of establishment is an integral part of conservation planning. Some things must precede others. If terraces are built before waterways are shaped and well enough sodded to be capable of handling the discharge of water from the terraces, an uncontrollable gully may result that will prevent the successful establishment of the entire program. If the pond is built before erosion is stopped in the field which supplies the water for the pond, it may be filled with mud and the site ruined. Certainly fish would not prosper in the mud to furnish sport and food for family and friends.

Where the land use is to be changed for part of the farm, with a resulting change in the farming enterprise, some careful planning is required. The farmer may wish to increase the amount of cattle on the farm and plans to plant one area to permanent pasture and devote another to hay and supplemental pasture crops. He definitely will not buy the livestock until he has planted the permanent pasture, or before it has developed sufficiently to carry the increased herd. And, of course, he must also plan to adjust his cropping so that the additional acreage is free to grow the hay and furnish the supplemental pasture. These things seem elemental and hardly worth mentioning, but farmers do buy livestock before they have established pasture and feed for them. The result is that the permanent pastures are grazed before they are ready, and are either destroyed or their productivity so damaged that profits are greatly reduced. Sometimes the farmer discovers that he has to dispose of livestock bought too soon and begin again the establishment of the permanent pastures.

As he establishes his conservation plan, the farmer must check its effectiveness continually. During the first good rain after his terraces are built, he will don a raincoat and boots, take a long-handled shovel, and go to the field to see how the terraces are functioning. He may see that one needs a little wider opening into the waterway or onto the pasture. If the terrace is in danger of breaking, he can open it up with the shovel. Another terrace may have a low place in the ridge or a high place in the channel that needs correcting. He may find that water is rushing out of the end of one terrace too fast and scouring the channel. This indicates to him that there is excessive grade in the terrace channel at that point. He may be able to determine what the grade should be, or he may have to ask a conservation worker to survey the field after it is dry and tell him where to move the end of the terrace uphill to reduce the grade.

If the farmer is using fertilizer, he may want to compare yields by leaving a check plot without fertilizer, harvesting the two areas separately. If he is using fertility-building crops for the first time, he should check yields by planting a portion of the succeeding crops on land that did not have the improvement. He should follow the same course every time he adopts a new practice for improving fertility: harvest the crops separately, so that he can determine just how much the yields have increased. This information will be valuable to his neighbors and to conservation workers, and it will be of even more value to him. If he knows that the method is paying off, he will certainly not neglect his conservation practices. He should keep a record of yields on the treated plots and the check plots for future reference.

In a pasture program, he can weigh beef cattle or calves when they go into a pasture and when they come off, to determine pounds of gain per day or per acre. He may experiment by dividing the pasture, stocking one portion heavier but for a shorter period. If he has better gains for the shorter period on the same pasture, he may learn that gains decline as the grass becomes shorter or less palatable, and he can therefore plan to modify his system of grazing management to secure the better gains. If he co-operates with his neighbors in similar experiments, together they can determine the best grazing management practices for their community. If the experiment concerns dairy cattle, day-to-day measurements may be more easily determined from milk production. In any event, adequate records are the only reliable evidence of the success of any management program, and only by a study of them can the farmer or dairyman or rancher make adjustments for greater profits.

III: Cropland Treatment

1. THE CONSERVATION CROPPING SYSTEM

CLINTON HARBERS of West Point, Texas, produces 780 pounds of lint cotton per acre on land that formerly produced 125 pounds. He does it by following a method of conservation cropping as precise as a mathematical equation. His method meets all of the needs of his soil for health, protection, and productivity.

He went in debt $34,000 in 1946 for less than one hundred acres and the necessary tools, equipment, and planting materials. Seven years later he had bought and paid for other land. In 1955, the United States Junior Chamber of Commerce named him one of four "outstanding young farmers of America" for "converting swampland into a $100,000 farm."

In 1946, his land was poorly drained and in poor physical condition. It would neither receive nor release moisture to plants efficiently. After he had constructed the necessary drainage ditches, he turned his attention to improvement of the soil itself. He tried several legumes for soil improvement before he found the ones that did the most for his land. He tried varying rates and methods of fertilizer application, and he tried more than one tillage method. The combination of the conservation methods that he now uses is the formula which has put the maximum amount of life into his formerly "dead" soil and has opened it up to receive the rain that falls on it.

Mr. Harbers did not pattern his cropping system after those used on neighboring farms, as might be supposed. His conservation principles are derived from those used by corn growers in Iowa, by farmers he had met overseas while in the armed forces and of whom he had read. Although he had never seen these Iowa farms, he reasoned that if Iowa farmers could double corn production by good soil management cotton would respond to the same principles. In conversations with fellow servicemen on faraway shores, he learned the principles of conservation farming as applied to corn growing, and when he returned home, he applied those which were needed on the cotton farm he purchased.

Crops

He combined crops to feed, protect, and condition his soil with crops to produce a cash income. He did not expect to get cash directly from all crops planted. Any grazing or hay or seed harvested from the legumes was incidental. The pay-off came from his cash crop, cotton.

He used Hubam (annual) sweet clover to open up the subsoil and provide organic matter at greater depths to keep the soil open. While the corn farmer may have used bromegrass-alfalfa meadow for the same purpose, Harbers had to use a crop adapted to his area.

He used Willamette vetch to cover up the land when it would otherwise be bare following cotton and subject to damage from wind or rainstorms. He tried other sown crops for this purpose, also, but finally settled on this vetch as the best for his land, since it also provided additional nitrogen for his cotton crop. The corn farmer may use a small grain or ryegrass for his cover and residue-producing crop or leave large quantities of corn, grass, and weed residues on the land to provide a surface mulch and cover during the otherwise fallow season.

Under other conditions, it might have been necessary for Harbers to use other crops in his cropping system. Climatic or soil conditions might have required different crops to get the same results that sweetclover and vetch have achieved for him, and that a meadow rotation, winter sown crop, or crop residue management has for the corn farmer.

Under other hazardous soil-erosion conditions, Harbers might have had to add other crops to the three he now plants. If wind erosion had been a problem, he might have needed some tall-growing crops as a barrier against the sweep of the wind. Or, if the slope of his land had been steep enough to require additional protection from water erosion, he might have been forced to plant thick-growing sown crops in contour strips across his cotton land to slow down the flow of water and desilt it.

A single crop that remains on the land for a number of years without tillage will allow maximum rebuilding of the soil structure, enabling the individual soil particles to cling together in aggregates, or groups, and resist packing or cementing together in clods or dense layers. Such a crop is not used in Harbers' plan, but is represented by the meadow crop of corn growers.

This account of Harbers' experience should point up the fact that the selection of crops is based on the needs of the land for protection and maintenance of fertility and soil structure, in addition to the cash crops needed for the farming enterprise.

Crop sequence. By dividing his cropland into approximately four equal parts, Harbers was able to establish a four-year rotation plan on each part, staggered in such a manner that he has the same amount of cotton each year. Of course, he also has the same amount of other crops each year. His crop sequence is simple: Hubam sweetclover one year and cotton three years (followed each year by Willamette vetch planted September

15 in the cotton middles, whether wet or dry). Then the rotation starts over again with sweetclover for one year and cotton (vetch) three years.

His corn-growing teachers may have used an even more simple rotation: meadow (composed of a grass and legume) three years and corn three years, or they may have interposed a year of soybeans or oats between the meadow crop and the corn.

Both Harbers and his teachers based their rotations on these principles, as they were applicable:

(1) Deep-rooted crops precede crops which receive the most benefit from maximum storage of moisture in the soil or which feed deeply.

(2) Cover crops follow crops which leave the land bare and subject to wind or water erosion.

(3) Legumes are used to add nitrogen to the soil, to assimilate commercial fertilizers and deeply placed natural minerals in the soil, and to make these substances available to the nonlegumes used primarily for cash income. Harbers found that fertilizers were more effective when applied to the legumes than when applied directly to the cotton.

(4) Residue-producing crops are planted before a fallow period or before a clean-tilled crop. Both sweetclover and vetch produced large amounts of residue for Harbers. All of the crops, including corn, produced residues for the corn farmer.

(5) Crops used in a strip-cropping pattern must produce heavy residues or be followed by a cover crop. Harbers did not use this treatment, but many corn farmers and others do.

(6) Crops that remain on the land for a number of years, such as meadow crops, are used just before crops which permit the most erosion, since the land is then in its best condition to withstand erosion. The abundance of organic matter left in and on the soil and the great improvement in soil structure help the soil particles to hold together and resist erosion. Since

Harbers could not use such a crop, he improved his tillage methods to reduce soil disturbance to a minimum. Nationwide, the most common sequence in a conservation cropping system is (a) a legume or grass, or a combination of the two, (b) a clean-tilled crop, and (c) a small-grain crop.

Tillage

Tillage practices must be included in the conservation cropping system, since the value of the residues produced by the conservation crops depends on how they are used. Because Harbers uses plants to keep his soil open and residues to keep the surface soil from baking and crusting, his land does not require the usual amount of tillage. He has found that excessive tillage damages soil structure and either destroys organic matter or places it below the surface where it cannot provide a mulch to protect the surface. Minimum tillage therefore is a definite part of Harbers' plan. This practice has gained widespread popularity since the publication of Edward H. Faulkner's provocative volume, *Plowman's Folly*, in 1943.

Tillage practices are based on these principles:

(1) *The use of equipment which will work with a mulch and leave it on the surface, as nature would have it.*

In the fall, Harbers' land is chiseled, and beds are thrown up with a row disk. Then the chisel plow is used again. With fertilizer and small-seed attachments, the fertilizer is put on each side of the bed and below the vetch seed.

In the spring, the beds are undercut with sweeps to kill the vetch, and the vetch residue is chopped with a disk harrow, set straight. Afterwards, the row disk or a disk opener is run lightly over the beds to clear the surface and sweep the residue into the furrow. Cotton is then planted on the firm, undisturbed bed. Although he has a clay soil, Harbers is able to plant with this minimum amount of soil disturbance because the legumes keep his land in good condition. Later cultivations move the surface residue from the furrow back over the ridge and against the cotton rows.

The greatest progress made in recent years in the design of field equipment has been the perfection of tools which will give almost any type of desired tillage to the soil while leaving all plant residue in the surface. Chisels and sweeps can loosen the soil, kill weeds, or cultivate a crop while leaving all plant residue on the surface. Drills and row planters that can operate in heavy stubble have been developed.

(2) *When a cover crop is not used, enough of the current crop is left on the land to protect the soil during the fallow period.*

Harbers may leave the sweetclover residue on the surface during the winter with complete safety, but the cotton residue would not protect the land unless he permitted grass and weeds to make a good growth before frost.

Delayed fallow has proved profitable in increasing wheat yields and protecting the soil in dry areas where wheat is planted every other year.

The year's last cutting of hay crops is made early enough to leave considerable growth at the end of the season. Early removal of livestock from supplemental pastures is required for the same reason. Feed crops are often headed, leaving the entire stalk, with little or no grazing, to protect the land from wind and water erosion during the winter. Bundle feed or silage crops are cut high enough to leave protective residues in the field. Early lay-by of row crops to permit growth of wild vegetation will give protection to land where the regular crops do not provide sufficient residues.

Even where cover crops are to be established, the maintenance of all residues on the surface adds to the efficiency of off-season protection. With adequate amounts of residues on the ground, tillage can be delayed in the spring, since these residues will enable the soil to receive and store rainfall—which is the only reason for early tillage when the condition of the soil is such that planting tools can be operated efficiently. Then the later tillage begins, the better, since the residual cover will help protect the soil from spring rains and winds while increasing moisture penetration.

Of additional importance to the farmer is the reduction in the cost of tillage operations.

(3) *There should be no more tillage than is absolutely necessary for seed-bed preparation, planting, and cultivation.*

The reduction of tillage operations on Harbers' farm not only saves him money, but is beneficial for the following reasons: Every trip over the land tends to pack it and destroy its granular structure. And each stirring helps to burn up organic matter which is valuable in Harbers' farming operations. It is nature's way to use roots to open the soil, rather than the plow. It is nature's way to use a mulch to keep the surface open, rather than a cultivator or harrow.

The cost of making a crop is cut when the tractor is kept in the shed, and experience has proved that yields are generally improved when a minimum amount of wise tillage is employed. A High Plains farmer, referring to the excessive tillage which he and his neighbors have established as a common practice, said, "We are just farming too good." It was true in the sense that he meant it.

Definition

A conservation cropping system, then, is that combination of cropping and tillage practices necessary to maintain the soil in its greatest state of productivity. It means the best use of plants and their residues for the maintenance, improvement, and protection of the soil and conservation of its moisture. It calls for the regular use of all of the essential crops, in the proper sequence, with only the minimum amount of cultivation for seed placement and harvesting.

The term, "conservation cropping system," is used to steer clear of the misunderstandings which have been built up around other terms such as "cover cropping," "crop rotations," "soil-building crops," "fertility-building crops," "stubble mulching," and "crop-residue management." These are all parts of one essential practice, a conservation cropping system, and none is an end in itself.

There are similarities in all good conservation cropping systems, for all are based on the principles listed above. The systems vary because of the differences in types of farming, suitability of crops to the land and climate, equipment available, and the intensity of treatment required for each piece of land.

Harbers' conservation cropping system, combined with his drainage works, enabled him to produce 80,000 cotton plants per acre instead of the customary 40,000, and to increase production six times. Some systems double and triple yields of wheat, tobacco, corn, and many other products. Other systems provide for the addition of profitable side lines, such as livestock, to the farming enterprise. A conservation cropping system is the basic treatment for cropland.

Purpose of the Conservation Cropping System

The first aim of a conservation cropping system is to produce more and better crops at less cost. There is no substitute—no panacea—that will increase yields and reduce costs, other than nature's plan for soil and plant management. The second aim is to preserve the productivity of the land for our years and for the generations to come. These aims are both selfish and generous, and every farmer can subscribe to these motives.

To achieve these general aims, here are the standards to be reached:

(1) Use for cropland only that soil which can be maintained in economical production over a long period of time. The principles might apply to poorer lands which may produce for a while, but such lands are properly used when they are in permanent vegetation, and no conservation cropping system is designed to try to keep them permanently productive.

(2) Choose intensity of treatment in accordance with the needs and capabilities of the land. Poorer lands may need to be kept in sown crops with frequent use of legumes or meadow mixtures. The best land may require only an occasional planting of deep-rooted and residue-producing crops. Between these two extremes, however, there are many gradations of need and many combinations of treatment.

(3) Design the cropping system to provide maximum ground cover, both living and dead, which is nature's way of protecting the soil.

(4) Provide for the improvement of soil structure, which is achieved primarily by the root systems of plants. The roots must be deep and strong to loosen the soil; they must be mas-

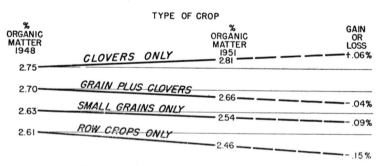

FIGURE 3. *Organic matter, the regulator of our soils. Three-year experiment, Texas Blackland Experiment Station, Temple, Texas.*

sive to leave large amounts of decaying roots below the surface. The chosen system should allow for a reduction in tillage, which tends to destroy soil structure. Tillage reduction is also accomplished when a meadow crop is on the land for several years.

(5) Use the large amount of residues produced above the ground on the surface for the purpose for which they were intended—the protection of the soil against the forces of erosion, extremes of temperature, and excessive drying or wetness, so that the soil may be a better habitat for the myriads of plants and animals, protozoa, fungi, yeast, and others that give "life" to the soil. With the careful use of residues, crops grown on the land are benefited.

(6) Maintain fertility through the beneficial effects of the soil-improving plants themselves, and by their assimilation of fertilizer additions and subsequent release of them to other crops. In these ways, losses through leaching and erosion are also reduced.

In summary, a proper cropping system is the most efficient and profitable conservation treatment that can be applied to land. Where any other conservation treatment is necessary, a conservation cropping system is likewise needed. A good conservation cropping system can often be substituted for other conservation measures when the erosion hazard is not great, but no other conservation treatment can be substituted for a proper cropping system.

2. SUPPORTING, SUPPLEMENTAL, AND SPECIAL PRACTICES FOR CROPLAND TREATMENT

Time was when the conservationist would tell the farmer that a certain mechanical practice, such as terracing, contour farming, or strip cropping, was the framework on which a conservation program could be built. Too often, the farmer constructed the framework but never completed a program. And too often, both the farmer and the conservationist were willing to let it go at that.

Because mechanical treatment usually precedes the establishment of a conservation cropping system, it has seemed basic to the program. But it is more accurate to say that the conservation cropping system, with all of the elements discussed in the preceding section, is the conservation program for cropland. It may need supporting and supplemental practices to provide adequate protection—to approach the care that nature gives lands with grasses and trees for protection.

Man disturbs the balance of nature when he removes the trees, plows the sod, and puts the land in cultivation, so it is man's duty to take the measures necessary to re-establish erosion control to replace the trees or sod. The use of plants in his cropping system is his first and most important measure, but this is adequate only on the best land. As the land becomes steeper, or more unstable, he must add other practices to supplement the use of plants. The more critical the erosion problem, the more intensive his use of plants and supporting practices must be. Finally, there are some lands which are so subject to erosion that soil scientists believe that they should never be placed in cultivation. These, Class VI and VII soils, should be returned to nature's permanent vegetation. But for those soils which can remain in cultivation, the intensity of treatment is planned according to the needs of the land for protection and improvement.

ELEMENTS OF THE CONSERVATION CROPPING SYSTEM

The Practice	*Where Needed*
1. Deep-rooted plants to keep the land "opened up"	All cropland
2. Crops to add organic matter to the soil, both above and below the surface	All cropland
3. Cover crops to protect the soil between regular crops	All cropland

4. Tillage methods to use and leave stubble on the
surface for soil protection and
moisture conservation   All cropland

The need for practices in addition to the conservation cropping system is determined by the effectiveness of the cropping program. On some lands a good cropping program is all that is necessary. If the crops planned, with their residues properly managed, cannot effectively protect the soil under any storm, then additional measures must be employed.

To bring the various practices used on cropland into some order, they will be considered in three categories: special programs, supporting practices, and supplemental practices.

Special programs include drainage, irrigation, and flood-control measures, which are applied as needed, practical, and available. The first two may be essential parts of a conservation program for a cropland field, but are not limited to use on cropland. They are all important enough for more detailed discussion, and other parts of this book will be devoted to these special practices.

Supporting practices are added to the conservation cropping system to improve the control of wind and water erosion. They are not ends in themselves, but are often part of a conservation program for cropland.

SUPPORTING PRACTICES

The Practice	*Where Needed*
1. Contour farming	All cropland on slopes where soil or moisture conservation is a problem.
2. Terracing	All cropland where water erosion cannot be adequately controlled with a conservation cropping system, contour farming, and strip cropping. Where outlets are available and soils are suitable for terracing.

3. Contour strip cropping	Sloping cropland where terraces are not necessary or practical.
4. Wind strip cropping	On lands subject to wind erosion— where wind damage cannot be controlled by the conservation cropping system.
5. Windbreak plantings	On lands subject to wind erosion— where wind strip cropping is not adequate or practical.
6. Diversion construction	Where there is runoff water from grassland, woodland, or other areas which should be intercepted and diverted from the fields.

Supplemental practices generally add to the basic conservation program for a cultivated field. They may correct a deficiency in the soil or environment or one which has developed as a result of improper use of the land. They may facilitate the establishment of the conservation program, as pre-treatment before beginning the cropping program or for the removal of obstructions. Or they may be designed as treatment for small parts of the field which will not be in regular cultivation.

SUPPLEMENTAL PRACTICES

The Practice	*Where Needed*
1. Subsoiling	Where compacted layers have developed below the surface and it is necessary to break them up prior to the establishment of deep-rooted conservation crops.
2. Deep plowing	Where there is a wind erosion problem and where adequate and suitable clod-forming (clay) material can be brought to the surface before the start of the

conservation program. To a limited extent, this practice is used to bring original topsoil to the surface when it has been covered with silt.

3. Fertilization and other soil additives

Where there is a mineral or other deficiency which would affect the growth of crops. In a conservation program, these are generally added to the conservation grass or legume crop.

4. Waterways

Where there is a problem of runoff water which must be taken down a slope and across a field. They may be constructed prior to terracing.

5. Obstruction removal or leveling

Where rocks, stumps, hedgerows, dunes, ridges, earthworks, or other obstructions, including gullies or ditches which must be filled, would interfere with the establishment of a conservation measure or the reorganization of field boundaries.

6. Emergency tillage

Where it is necessary to roughen the surface of the soil for temporary wind-erosion control. Should be needed only when there is a failure of a cover crop.

7. Treatment of odd areas

Where special treatment is needed for spots of thin or badly eroded soils, sand dunes, or spots subject to severe wind erosion which might cause erosion to spread to other areas; bluffs and steep slopes, wet spots, sink holes, slick spots, gravel, rock, small areas infested with undesirable plants such as bindweed—where any of these lie in a field in such a manner that they cannot be separated for more efficient land use, such as retirement to pasture, woodland, or wildlife.

59

8. Wildlife habitat development	Where wild insects are needed for the pollination of crops, or other wildlife may be valuable for the control of insects, or for sport, recreation, or food.
9. Planned pollination	Where pollinating insects are to be brought in (as a colony of tame bees) to assure a maximum set of seed.
10. Hedgerow planting	Where needed to slow the flow of water, for guide lines, field boundaries, to serve as living fences, or to provide food and cover for wildlife.
11. Fencing	Where needed as temporary or permanent field boundaries to assure proper land use, to provide rotation grazing, controlled grazing, or protection from grazing.
12. Channel improvement	Where needed to increase the capacity of the channel and prevent clogging of major water courses through the farm, or to prevent undue channel enlargement or bank caving.

A conservation program for cropland will be built primarily on a combination of the preceding practices, according to the needs of the land and the intensity of treatment necessary. The above practices, simplified somewhat by the arrangement, are the basic factors in any farmer's conservation plan for the control of erosion on cropland. The farmer who studies the needs of his land and recognizes the uses and limitations of all of the conservation practices will know how to combine them into an effective program. The supporting, supplemental, and special practices may be added to offset deficiencies in the conservation cropping system.

If only a slight erosion hazard remains after the conservation cropping system is set up, contour farming may provide the remedy. If, with contour farming, there is still some erosion hazard, a contour strip-cropping pattern may provide all of the additional protection needed. A slightly more difficult situation may require terraces, with proper outlets. This may, or may not, eliminate the need for strip cropping, although contour farming would still be needed.

Under other situations, erosion by wind, rather than water, is the problem. This might require only a strip-cropping pattern for wind-erosion control in addition to the conservation cropping system. In the High Plains, stubble-mulch tillage and summer fallow are relied on to maintain adequate vegetative cover on the soil to control wind erosion.

Where both wind and water erosion are to be dealt with and the cropping program is not adequate to control both, strip cropping with tall-growing plants (for wind erosion control) and contour farming (for water erosion control) may be needed. If this contour strip-cropping pattern controls wind erosion but still permits water erosion, terraces can be added to make the program completely effective. But if the contour strip-cropping pattern is not effective against wind erosion and placing the strips across the direction of the wind flow will permit water erosion, the problem is complicated because of the abandonment of contour farming.

The farmer cannot safely choose the method which will protect against the more severe of the erosion hazards and ignore the other. He must try to control both, and must look for other practices to add to his program.

He may decide to use trees, planted in a suitable pattern around and across the field, as windbreaks to control wind erosion, while he uses terraces and contour farming in the field for the control of water erosion. Or he may find that his wind erosion problem is due to mismanagement of the soil, which resulted in the finer (clay) particles in his surface soil being washed or blown away, and that he has a suitable clay material under the surface at a depth that can be reached with a plow.

This material may be plowed to the surface or mixed into the topsoil to change the texture and reduce its susceptibility to wind erosion to such an extent that a good cropping program, or a contour strip-cropping pattern, can control wind erosion and eliminate the need for tree windbreaks. The farmer will realize that good soil-management practices must be maintained to prevent the soil from again deteriorating into a wind erosion hazard, since deep plowing cannot be used on a field repeatedly.

In extreme cases, where no combination of these practices will control both wind and water erosion if an erosion-permitting crop is kept in the cropping system, it is necessary to substitute a crop which leaves the land less vulnerable. The weak link, in many cases, is in the cropping program, and adequate conservation requires a major change in the farming pattern. Under these conditions such a change should be seriously considered by the farmer. Often he will find that crop substitutions will be more profitable to him—certainly in the long run.

Under varying conditions all of the above practices may be used. Some are self-explanatory. Others require a second look.

Deep plowing may be used when poor material has been deposited over the original topsoil and the better soil needs to be brought to the surface. Subsoiling, or deep chiseling, may also be added to the conservation plan to break up a dense, compacted layer of soil below plow depth that restricts root growth and water penetration. This practice is properly employed when it is immediately followed by deep-rooted grass and legume crops to keep the soil open. Used in this manner, subsoiling is a pretreatment measure for the conservation cropping system. It is unwise to rely on subsoiling to keep the soil open year after year, since the plow sole is the result of damage to the structure of the soil, and improvement can come only from crops which will fill this zone with a great amount of roots.

Commercial fertilizers and limestone are important in the conservation program when they are necessary to secure maximum growth and development of grasses and legumes in the conservation cropping system. The following "cash" crops generally receive more benefit if fertilizers are applied in this manner rather than directly to the so-called cash crop.

Manures, compost, cotton burs, wood chips, hay, and other mulch materials benefit the land directly since they add organic matter and some fertility. When properly applied, soil conditioners and gypsum improve the structure of the soil and are therefore conservation measures in themselves. However, all of these are of rather limited application, and, regardless of how important they may be to small areas, they cannot be considered major conservation practices.

There are many special problems found on small portions of a field, and the treatments applied are so various that a detailed account will not be undertaken here. It is important, however, that the farmer recognize these problems and give special treatment to the small areas affected. Many times these spots, treated like the balance of the field, have continued to deteriorate until they are totally unproductive, beyond salvage, and often enlarged to damage better land near by.

Watercourses are the paths taken by runoff water as it flows unimpeded down a slope or across a field or farm. They should be adequate to carry the flow, protected to prevent erosion and gullying, and properly maintained. They may be natural drains that require only grass for protection. They may be outlet channels that are shaped and grassed to receive water from a terrace system and are, therefore, part of the terrace system. On many farms the larger watercourses may become choked with trees, brush, and debris, and they may become too small to handle the flow after large rains. If valuable bottom lands are being damaged by flooding, measures should be taken to enlarge and protect the channel and prevent it from deteriorating again. On

63

the other hand, channels that are deepening and widening too rapidly require restrictive measures—the application of the protective measures which would have kept the channel from enlarging in the first place.

Diversion terraces or dykes are also planned for a special problem. They may intercept and remove water which normally flows down watercourses through the field. They may remove water from an active gully or an eroding area, or protect an odd area which requires special treatment.

Rearrangement of fences may facilitate conservation treatment or the use of conservation crops, although fences are not in themselves a conservation measure.

Planned pollination and the development of a wildlife habitat in connection with cropland usually have a similar purpose. The farmer may rent several stands of tame bees to place in a field of blooming vetch, alfalfa, clover, or other crops to assure a maximum set of seed and make the crop more profitable. Or he may develop a suitable home for wild bees in a gully or other odd area, along a stream bank, in a fence row, hedgerow, windbreak, or similar place, so that the wild insects may serve him in the same beneficial way. Actually, wild bees are more efficient pollinating agents than tame honey bees.

Emergency tillage is patently not a conservation practice that should be planned. It is to be resorted to only when more desirable methods fail to control wind erosion. Cover crops or crop residues should be used to hold the soil down; but when sufficient stubble or other growth is not produced and cover crops fail because of drought or insects, then emergency tillage operations become a conservation treatment. Many farmers plan to control wind erosion by listing, chiseling, or other operations during the season of strong winds, but they fail to consider that cover crops or adequate plant residues would do the job better and cheaper, and at the same time help improve the soil.

Cropland Treatment

The special programs of irrigation and drainage the farmer can plan for himself or with the help of his neighbors. In either case, the conservation cropping system will be the foundation of his success as a farmer, although its application may vary considerably from methods used by the dry-land farmer. In fact, either program may lead to costly failure unless wholly adequate conservation cropping systems are used. This is discussed more thoroughly under "Drainage" and "Irrigation." Although the supporting practices are seldom needed under drainage or irrigation programs, many of the supplemental practices, such as waterways, subsoiling, fertilization, liming, treatment of odd areas, planned pollination, and even wildlife habitat development are important parts of a complete conservation program.

Flood prevention is becoming an increasingly important aspect of the conservation picture. The single farmer can seldom do much about it alone, other than adopt the practices listed under channel improvement. But this program can be undertaken on a watershed basis. Creek watersheds requiring attention may vary from a few thousand to several hundred thousand acres in size. The farmer will realize, however, that a good conservation program established on his farm and all of the farms in his community will help to provide flood control downstream and speed the day when the Soil Conservation Service can undertake the larger program of flood prevention. He can also help to develop community consciousness of the need and value of such a program, and he can work with his soil conservation district and other farm and community leaders to secure this assistance for his watershed.

Among the practices and programs listed in this chapter will be found the treatments which will enable every farmer to secure the maximum returns from every acre of cropland, and at the same time preserve it for his own time and for the generations to come.

Nowhere in the conservation farmer's creed will be found a suggestion that he take what he can get today by exploiting the land and let the future take care of itself. That view would be shortsighted indeed, since every farmer expects to have a future himself. By careful planning now, he can assure himself that his soil will not play out before he does, and that there will be something left for his children.

Therefore, he will not choose only one or two practices which will enable him to produce his cash crops a little better for the time being, but will also undertake those practices needed to prevent further damage to or deterioration of the soil, and will not ignore areas which are suffering more severely or have a special problem. It is true that certain practices will give profitable increases in yields and may even reduce the rate of soil destruction, but an adequate conservation program will improve production while controlling erosion and maintaining or improving the soil. This is the program that pays in both the long and the short run.

In some areas most farmers have adopted such a program. In other areas most farmers are trying to work out such a program. In a few areas many farmers seem to have little interest in such a program. But in all cases there is a reason why the land is not being given a complete conservation treatment. Seldom is it because the farmer wants to exploit the land, for after all, what he wants is increased income, which is best obtained by conservation farming.

In some areas, and for some soils, more experimentation and demonstration is necessary to discover and introduce the most efficient conservation methods. Here the farm agency workers have more work to do in research and education, but the individual farmer is under no less obligation to collaborate in experimenting, demonstrating, studying, and teaching.

All too often the individual farmer does not understand the principles on which an effective and profitable conservation program is built. It is the responsibility and privilege of the farmer to work these out himself, with whatever help is available—for there are not enough agricultural workers in all agencies to aid all farmers in reaching this understanding.

It is the purpose of this section to present the basic principles on which a sound conservation program can be built for cropland. The more important practices will be discussed in more detail under appropriate headings, and the conservation principles pertaining to the special practices and to grasslands and woodlands will be discussed in other sections.

The theme of this section is that a *combination* of practices is required for most lands. A sound cropping program must first be planned. Supporting practices should be chosen as needed, and the special programs should be included when they are appropriate. And the whole should be supplemented with practices designed to meet a peculiar problem, treat a particular area, or facilitate the establishment of another practice.

The whole must be worked out meticulously and carefully— perhaps not in a day, or in a year. It may take a lifetime. Perhaps the solution cannot be found in the use of standard and accepted methods, for these are being altered and improved each year, and some that were popular just a few years ago have been discarded now. Sometimes the farmer himself must experiment to find a crop or a method that fits his problem, but in this case his experiment should be worked out cautiously— with the help of conservation or agricultural technicians available to him—and the results carefully checked.

Perhaps the farmer will work out much of his plan alone or with his neighbors, for agricultural workers are few and very busy. Certainly he should have an important part in formulating any program designed for his land. He should check carefully the effectiveness of each practice—how it affects crop production, the land, and other practices. He should continually strive to improve his program. But he should consult a conservationist for technical guidance concerning the needs and capabilities of the land when he contemplates any major change. And he should always call for expert assistance when he is ready to establish any major practice.

3. TERRACES

Field terraces are becoming an increasingly important factor in the combination of conservation treatments given to cropland. Diversion terraces are used to prevent concentrations of water from entering cropland from woodland, grassland, or adjoining farms. Although field terraces are important only on cropland, they do appear on other lands when cultivation is used in connection with orchards or other tree plantings, or on grasslands when a sod is not desirable. They may be used, for example, when grass is planted in rows and cultivated for seed production. Other minor exceptions may be noted, but the point is that complete terrace systems are designed for cropland, and not for other land uses. This is not true for diversion terraces, which are more generally found on non-crop land. Their uses are many, but the discussion here applies to their construction and maintenance in any use.

History and Definition

The purposes and development of terraces as used in the United States may be discussed together. Homesteaders generally put their best land into cultivation first. They cleared out the trees and broke the sod along the creeks, leaving the higher land in its natural vegetation. While nature's protective cover remained on these uplands, very little rainfall runoff came down across the fields. But as the timber was cut or the grass overgrazed or burned, increasing amounts of runoff flowed across the lower fields.

Cropland Treatment

Farmers placed dams in the paths of natural watercourses that led into the fields, but where the runoff was great, these dams failed. A series of dams, often placed down the entire length of the watercourses and through the field, were built, but these also failed to give more than temporary protection.

Then farmers considered making the dams larger, cutting through higher places along the fence lines, and carrying the water to another disposal area without letting it enter the field at all. This was sometimes possible, and the practice became known as "hillside ditching." Since such ditches and dykes ran along the fences separating pasture or woodland from the field, no consideration was given to the "fall" or "grade" of the ditch, and severe gullying action usually developed.

From this experience the idea of the diversion terrace was born, when farmers sought means to establish these ditches on a grade which would carry the water but which would not result in gullying. When farmers, with the technical assistance available to them, learned the technique of regulating the grade and size of the ditch according to the quantity of water to be handled, they had developed the diversion terrace. This type of terrace was first used at the top of or above cropland. The native vegetation in the pasture or woodland above controlled most of the erosion and protected the channel of the diversion terrace from siltation and thus contributed to its success.

Gradually farmers began to adapt this principle to other situations. Some fields had relatively flat areas above steeper slopes. The more level land suffered little from erosion, but the steeper slopes began to erode. It seemed logical to build a terrace just above the steeper slopes to intercept the water from the flatter areas and direct it away from the slopes. If the level portion of the field was small and therefore did not shed a great deal of runoff, these terraces could be built up until they would carry the load. But, even then, erosion was seldom halted on the steep slopes, and the farmers began to add additional terraces below the first one until the entire slope had something resembling a modern system of terraces on it.

Sometimes the level area above was too large, and the runoff broke the terraces almost as fast as they were built, so the farmer also started adding terraces above his original terrace line until he could control the runoff from the flatter area.

Other farmers and agricultural workers saw the value of terraces and applied them in many ways—always with the idea of intercepting the runoff from rainfall and leading it off of the field slowly and in such a manner that erosion would be decreased and rainfall percolation into the soil increased, resulting at once in both soil conservation and increased crop yields.

Many mistakes were made in spacing and grade, in methods of construction and maintenance, in selection of soils which could hold terraces, and in attributing benefits to terraces which more properly belonged to contour farming; but much progress had been made by the time of the establishment of the first federal erosion-control experiment stations in 1930 and the organization, in 1933, of the federal Soil Erosion Service, which became the United States Soil Conservation Service in 1935.

Since those dates, terracing has come to be based on a sound technology, and its acceptance by farmers throughout the United States has been rapid. In fact, the demand for terraces has often got out of hand, for important as they are on some soils, they are not always a perfect solution. Farmers began to consider them as the one conservation treatment which would heal all the ills of their fields—that they could establish them and then forget them. Thus they demanded and often built terraces without adequate planning.

Many terraces had no safe place to spill the water, which often poured into gullies, aggravating the erosion problem there and even leading gullies back up each terrace channel. Water was spilled into roadside ditches to cause gullying and sometimes destroy public roads. Water often emptied into hastily built outlet channels before a sod cover or any other protection was established, or it flowed into fence-line channels on steep or poor soils where it would never be practical to establish adequate protection—and here again gullies developed, frequently eating back into the field and up the terrace channels.

Farmers were sometimes not ready to adopt a system of farming required for the "successful" use of terraces. Too often they plowed over the terraces, with no thought of safeguarding their height and channel capacity. They would list their row crops as they always had—right over the terraces—so that silt and runoff water flowed into the channels, filled them with silt, and broke gaping "windows" in the ridges.

In addition, farmers were often not ready to admit—and sometimes were not aware—that terraces are only supporting measures for a better system of farming on all the land, which is described in this book as a conservation cropping system. As the science of conservation farming has evolved, agricultural workers and farmers alike are coming to realize that the erosion conditions which indicate the need of terraces also indicate the need of cover crops, deep-rooted and residue-producing crops, tillage practices to secure the best use of crop residues, contour farming, other conservation practices, and sometimes even a radical change in farm organization and the types of crops grown.

Terracing is not *the* conservation treatment, nor is it a wonder practice. Vital as it may be on some lands, it is only a supporting practice. This is the modern concept of terracing.

Terracing is a practice designed to handle excess runoff water from heavy rains. Without terraces, some farm land may be eroded by light rains. Generally, however, contour farming, cover crops, and organic material incorporated into the soil or left on the surface should cause most of the water from light rains to enter the soil and protect it from the small amount of runoff. But for rains of great intensity or long duration, terraces are important devices for protecting soil that is already saturated. They lead the excess water slowly from the steeper slopes and intercept it, even on flatter slopes, before it concentrates in such large volume that it could scour or gully the land. They are guide lines for contour farming. Level and water-spreading terraces are important in water conservation.

The farmer who is interested in terracing should consider it in three aspects: planning the terrace system and its appurtenances, establishment, and maintenance. For each of these aspects, there is assistance available in nearly all parts of the nation. He should avail himself of this assistance by applying to his soil-conservation district office or some other agricultural agency. Technical assistance and usually financial assistance are his for the asking. He may avoid costly errors by getting trained conservation workers to help him lay out the system.

Types of Terraces

The farmer will want information on the type of terrace which will best suit his farming needs and soil conditions; he will want to know about equipment for building the terrace; and he may want to know the specifications which the technicians who supervise the construction of the terrace system will have to follow. With this information and the help of the conservationist, he should be able to make a sound decision.

Two principal types of terraces are generally recognized, and a third type is sometimes used under special conditions. The choice of types is generally determined by the slope of the land, although consideration is given to the amount of rainfall.

Channel type terraces. Channel type terraces emphasize the channel rather than the ridge. With equipment such as a bulldozer or grader with reversible blade, dirt from the uphill side is pushed down into the terrace ridge. Then the channel is plowed out and enlarged. The flow line on this type of terrace is below the natural ground level, and there is a flatter back slope to the terrace ridge, which is important in steeper slopes. The ridge of the channel type terrace does not need to be as high above the natural ground line as for other types, and therefore there is less fall from the top of the terrace ridge to the ground below the terrace. The ridge can be lower since the carrying capacity of the terrace is controlled by the size of the channel. On the other hand, if a ridge type terrace is constructed on steep land, some soil is moved from the area immediately below the ridge, thus increasing the fall from the top of the ridge to the bottom of the useless channel cut below the ridge.

The channel type terrace may be used on all but the flattest slopes. It is generally recommended on slopes above 3 per cent, and in some places it is required on slopes above 5 per cent.

Ridge type terraces. This type of terrace is built from both sides of the ridge. As much soil is moved uphill into the ridge as is moved downhill into the ridge. This type of terrace is better on flatter slopes, where channel capacity can be maintained without building the ridge so high that it interferes with farming operations. It is somewhat easier to maintain under certain types of farming operations. It is usable on slopes up to 3 per cent.

Water-spreading terraces. This is the type of terrace in which all the soil for the terrace ridge is moved from below the ridge. The use of this type is generally limited to slopes of 2 per cent or less, since its primary purpose is to spread the water as widely as possible above the terrace ridge, thus securing utilization of the rain which falls on the land or water which is diverted into the terrace system from an outside source. This type of terrace materially increases in-soak and is valuable in low-rainfall areas. It is also used on extremely flat land with a slope of less than one-half of 1 per cent, where it would be difficult to remove the water discharged from a cut channel.

With the ridge built entirely from the back or lower side, there is no channel to collect the water and concentrate it against the terrace ridge. The water, regardless of the size of the rain, will spread uphill to the maximum distance permitted by the natural slope of the land. On land sloping 1.5 feet in 100 feet, a nine-inch rain can be held by a properly built water-spreading terrace. Some farmers are experimenting with land leveling between the terraces to assure uniform distribution of the rainfall.

Water-spreading terraces are built to ridge-type specifications and are level from end to end. At the ends, blocks are thrown up to hold the water until it soaks into the ground. When crops are in danger of being drowned out, or when it is necessary to get into the field for tillage or planting operations, the blocks are removed and the water allowed to drain off into a prepared waterway.

Wesley John Underwood, co-operator with the Greer County, Oklahoma, Soil Conservation District, terraced fifty acres of his farm near Willow, Oklahoma, in this manner in early 1950. The soil was a fairly heavy clay loam on a gentle slope. On an adjoining field of the same slope and soil type, he had conventional channel type terraces. The first rain that fell was a five-inch downpour. His water-spreading terraces held all of the rain and spread it between the terraces. The channel type terraces drained most of the water off rapidly, and the field was drying up before all of the water had soaked into the ground between the water-spreading terraces.

A later two-inch rain was caught between the terraces. Since it was near cotton-planting time, Underwood removed the blocks from the ends of the terraces and let the water drain off. However, because the land covered by the water-spreading terrace was so wet, the planting of the cotton crop was thirty days late, while the land covered by the channel type terrace was dry enough for planting at the regular time.

74

Underwood was discouraged. The combination of the late planting and the unusually heavy rains seemed to indicate the impracticality of the new terrace system. When harvest time arrived, however, his attitude had changed. The soil with the additional storage of water proved more productive. The land covered by the water-spreading terrace produced one bale of cotton per acre, even with late planting, while the land covered by the channel type terrace produced only one-half bale of cotton per acre.

Underwood found that yields were consistently greater on land covered by the new terrace system, and he now plans to level the channel type terraces and replace them with water-spreading terraces. He also found that planting is not unduly delayed when there are normal spring rains. Furthermore, he believes that good soil management, including the use of wheat and stubble mulch in rotation with cotton, has improved the condition of his soil so much that heavy rains, such as those in 1950, would be absorbed by the soil more quickly and would cause less delay in planting.

Although a water-spreading type of terrace may be used in a regular system of field terraces, it has a use entirely different from the general concept of terraces for erosion control. One variation, known as the syrup-pan system, picks up outside water and directs it to one end of the top terrace, where it is released to the second terrace and led to the opposite end of the field. There it is released to the third terrace, to be brought back again to the near end. This process is continued until the entire field has been irrigated or the water dissipated.

Another variation of the water-spreading terrace is designed to divert water from a central channel through a system of gates or turnouts and into each terrace until it is filled.

In either case the terraces may be level or gently graded in the desired direction. Provision must be made for releasing the water before crops are drowned out and for carrying the waste water off the farm without causing erosion, as in the case of any irrigation system.

Such systems are designed for spreading water on gently sloping fields where the soil depth and permeability make the practice desirable. Expert assistance should be secured for the planning and design of such a system. The following guide points should be considered in determining need and feasibility:

1. Land on which water is to be spread should have a slope of not more than 1.5 per cent, and preferably less than 1.0 per cent, especially on slowly permeable soils. Soils that are too shallow to utilize the additional water properly should not be irrigated in this manner.

2. The area from which the runoff water is to be trapped should be not less than twice nor more than eight times the size of the area on which the water is to be spread, unless there are adequate controls to bypass the excess water.

3. The contributing watershed should have sufficient cover or be adequately protected from erosion, so that the runoff will not contribute large quantities of silt or have an extremely high rate of runoff.

4. Prior to construction, a plan should be developed by a skilled conservation technician showing specification for all parts of the system—the control gates, outlets, and terraces, which may need to be larger than normal size.

5. Provision must be made for the safe handling of excess water when it cannot all be retained in the system.

Diversion terraces. A diversion terrace is an individually designed channel constructed across a slope for the purpose of intercepting surface runoff water and conducting it to a safe outlet.

On cropland diversion terraces are used to reduce the length of the slope, especially where the land is nearly level and a complete system of terraces is not needed; to supplement strip cropping; to divert water away from bottomland; or to cut off outside water from a terraced field where the land above is not terraceable because of topography, land ownership, or land use. On land in any use they are employed to divert water out of active gully overfalls or away from farm buildings. They may be used to divert water into a farm pond on pasture land or to protect areas newly seeded to grass or planted to trees. They may be used in old orchards where a serious erosion condition exists, but where terracing is not possible. And they may be used as hillside drainage ditches on fields of imperfectly or poorly drained soils.

Diversion terraces should be designed and staked off by a trained engineer, since the drainage area, the quantity of water to be handled, and the velocity of flow determine the size and type of terrace needed. They cannot be standardized, as are field terraces. Diversions and their outlets are designed so that the velocity of the flowing water will not exceed that allowable for the type of vegetation, or lack of it, to be used in the channel.

The drainage area above the diversion should be in grass or trees, if possible. Otherwise, a filter strip of grasses is planted on the area immediately above the terrace channel to reduce the silting, which is the cause of most failures of properly constructed diversion terraces.

When used with strip cropping to reduce the length of the slope, the spacing of the terraces should not ordinarily exceed the width of three strips, but may vary according to soil type, location, width of strips, and the rotation used. They should not be used as permanent control on fields which can be terraced.

For the control of gullies, the diversion terrace should be placed far enough above the head of the gully so that the sloughing of the gully bank will not endanger the terrace.

When the outlet for a diversion terrace is to be on pasture or woodland, it should be designed so that the velocity of the discharged water will not be high enough to cause erosion in

77

the spill area. Waterways may be constructed and grassed for the disposal of water from a diversion terrace, as for any other type of terrace. Permanent drop structures may be used to lower the water from the spill end of a diversion terrace to a stable grade, if needed, but this type of protection is more expensive than the construction of grassed waterways.

Construction should often be delayed until the area above the proposed diversion is sufficiently well protected with grass or trees to prevent undue erosion from the watershed. The diversion terrace is built like a regular terrace, with all of the soil moved from the uphill side when possible. Equipment used for regular terracing, including farm equipment, may be used. Once started, the terrace should be built to specifications and completed without undue delay. An inadequate or poorly constructed diversion terrace may break and cause more damage than the runoff water would cause without it. All slopes should be flat enough to permit working, seeding, and mowing.

Protection of diversion terraces usually includes the following steps:

(1) Grassing. The entire disturbed area, including the channel, ridge, slopes, and an area at least twenty feet wide above the upper slope, should be planted to permanent grass to prevent silting and scouring.

(2) Mowing. The channel should be kept free of weeds, briars, and bushy growth which might obstruct the flow of the water and cause silting.

(3) Removal of silt. The channel may require maintenance because of silt accumulations. Small deposits of silt may be removed with a shovel or scraper. If the silt deposit extends the full length of the diversion terrace, the channel should be plowed out as in regular maintenance plowing. Excessive channel silting indicates inadequate protection of the watershed above the terrace or too much vegetation in the channel, or both. In either event, the channel must be kept silt free to avoid failures.

(4) Repairs. Breaks may occur for any number of reasons, but should be repaired immediately. Rodents may make holes which can cause breaks. If these are discovered in time, they can be repaired with a shovel. If breaks occur consistently at about the same place in the terrace ridge, this may indicate that there is a block in the terrace channel which should be removed. The assistance of conservation workers may be needed to find the block.

(5) Reseeding. When it is necessary to reseed the channel of the diversion terrace, the land should be plowed, with the plowed soil moved uphill to the top of the ridge and uphill on the upper side of the channel, so that a dead-furrow will fall within the channel. In other words, the channel is "plowed out." This increases the cross-sectional area, or carrying capacity, and deepens the channel. This dead-furrow runs the length of the terrace channel, and harrowing, disking, and other mechanical operations should also be done *with* the terrace, rather than across it. Reseeding should be done when the strip immediately above the channel is in hay or a permanent grass cover.

Planning

Some fields are so situated in relation to pastures or other protected spill areas that the planning of the needed terraces is simple. Other fields offer more complicated problems, particularly when the acreage is large or all of the farm is in cultivation and spills for the terraces must be shaped and protected.

The farmer can be assisted by the conservationist or other technician in a number of ways. The conservationist will determine the approximate location of the key terrace or terraces, by a survey or field inspection. The key terrace is often the top terrace if the field has only one slope pattern. However, if there are several slopes and ridges, the technician may see that several groups of terraces will be necessary. These must be fitted together into one pattern; therefore, he will want to locate the terraces which will fit into more than one group. He will want to know about how long the terraces must be. He will want to know if the terraces will reach a pasture spill without flowing too far in one direction. And if they will not all reach a pasture spill, he will tell the farmer where waterways should be located so that they may be shaped and protected before the terraces are built. If there are variations in land use to be considered, he must know how a terrace system would affect, or be affected by, them. For instance, land that is to be retired to permanent pasture will not need terracing, but if it lies above the area to be terraced, a diversion terrace may be needed below the grass to protect the field terraces below. Often the boundary of the grass planting will be adjusted to the location of the diversion terrace.

The farmer will usually have a choice of several locations for a waterway to serve a set of terraces. He may also have a choice in the type of waterway and the vegetation. When all the information concerning the terrace has been determined by the conservation planner, he presents the picture to the farmer, so that he can choose his course of action.

Sometimes, however, there is little or no choice, because of the strict requirements of an adequate terrace system. As will be explained later, terraces must begin near the high place in the field and must run either level or tipped only slightly toward one end or the other. The "lay of the land" determines their location. When they are moved too far downhill or given too much grade, the farmer will be in for trouble, and no dependable conservationist will assist him in the construction of a system that is doomed to failure, for such a course would only result in unnecessary expense and damage.

Grade of terraces. Field terraces are designed to be level from one end to the other, or slightly tipped toward one or both ends. The grade may vary or be constant.

Cropland Treatment

Level terraces are more effective for moisture conservation since the water moves off only as it develops a head (depth), and so has more time to soak into the ground. The level, water-spreading terrace is most efficient in this respect since it spreads the water to a maximum distance above the ridge. The regular ridge-type terrace is the second most efficient terrace if it is run level, and it is generally recommended for slopes of less than 3 per cent. The channel type terrace gives less spread to the water, but it also may be run level.

Level terraces are most satisfactory on permeable soils where the water is readily absorbed and will not drown out crops. They prove to be satisfactory on less permeable soils if they are laid out and built carefully, and if the farmer tills the land in such a manner that no blocks will be formed in the channel to impound the water.

Level terraces of any type, if built to proper specifications, will safely hold and carry off excess water, even when the terraces are long. They are safer under certain circumstances where silt fans or other blocks are apt to form in the channel to stop the flow of water, since the entire length of the terrace then becomes a reservoir to store the water until the blocks can be removed. If the channel becomes so full that water begins to flow over the ridge, it will flow over in many places and usually will not form concentrations that can break the terrace.

Precautions to be observed in connection with level terraces include (1) careful surveying and checking to assure that the terraces are actually level and (2) proper maintenance to keep them level. It has been argued that more water holes occur where level terraces cross natural depressions or gullies in a field than would be the case if the terraces were graded. This is not true since there cannot be enough grade on a field terrace to drain these holes. In either case, the holes must be filled up or allowed to silt up before they are eliminated.

Variable graded terraces have a lower end which has more

grade than the portion near the block end. As the graded terrace brings water toward its discharge end and this water is added to that which falls immediately above, the grade is increased to speed the water on to the end of the terrace. This change in grade is recommended on all terraces which are to have any grade at all, except very short terraces, which may be of constant grade.

The maximum grade generally allowed on standard field terraces is 0.25 foot per 100 feet, except that the last 100 feet may fall as much as 0.5 foot. A level section of terrace is often run at the upper, or block end.

For example, a variable graded terrace 1,800 feet long may have the following variations expressed in fractions of a foot per hundred feet: 300 feet level, 300 feet at 0.05, 300 feet at 0.1, 300 feet at 0.15, 300 feet at 0.2, 200 feet at 0.25, and 100 feet at 0.5. A more common variation would be the use of three changes for an 1,800-foot terrace. In high rainfall areas there might be 600 feet at 0.1, 600 feet at 0.2, and 600 feet at 0.25, while in a low rainfall belt the same terrace might be surveyed to have 600 feet level, 600 feet at 0.05, and 600 feet at 0.1 or 0.15. A reduction in grade slows the flow of the water and improves the chances for in-soak.

Allowance for cut. The engineer surveying the terrace line will allow for the estimated cut which the machinery will make in excavating the terrace channel. If the channel is to be cut 0.6 foot below the natural ground line, the surveyor will mark the place on grass pasture or grassed waterway at least 0.6 foot lower than the line he has been running, so that the water will flow out without impediment. If he has been grading the line at 0.2, he will mark this spot on the grass 0.8 foot lower than the last point in the field so that the grade will be maintained. If the water is to spill into a narrow outlet channel, he will add the depth at which the water is expected to be flowing when the terrace is discharging water. This is not an increase in grade at the end of the terrace, but an allowance to assure an uninterrupted flow of water from the terrace.

Blocking. When a terrace is designed to spill only at one end, the other end must be blocked. This may be done by increasing the grade or by placing a ridge of soil at the end to be blocked. If it is undesirable to have the water ever escape from this end of the terrace, it is better to increase the grade of the terrace end. But if water may occasionally escape from this end without damage, a small ridge of earth may be used as a block. Then, if a heavy rain threatens to break the terrace, the small block may be washed out or removed with a shovel.

Graded terraces should never be blocked on the spill end, regardless of type. It is usually inadvisable to block the spill end of level channel type terraces, but in areas of low rainfall it is not an uncommon practice to block the spill ends of level ridge type or water-spreading terraces in order to hold the water on the land longer and thus increase the in-soak.

Such blocks are of two types: the partial-closure and the closed-end block. The partial-closure block is approximately one-half the effective height of the terrace ridge. The closed-end block should be at least two-thirds the height of the terrace ridge, but should not be the full height unless the terrace ridge is sodded down or planted with a crop that would not permit the ridge to be damaged if the channel fills and water flows over the ridge.

The block should be narrow so that it will be weaker than the terrace ridge and thus break first if the terrace becomes overloaded, or be easy to remove in case sufficient penetration has been attained and crops are in danger of drowning out.

Terrace-end openings should be made the full width of the terrace channel and cut to the designed grade so that the water will flow out evenly and without restriction. When terraces are to spill onto pastures, the fence should be removed, or opened, so that construction equipment can properly open the discharge end. This is usually cheaper and easier than completing the opening in any other manner. Care should be exercised by the farmer to keep these ends open. This means he should not throw a furrow slice across the channel or allow weeds, trash, or other debris to collect and clog the ends of the terraces.

Outlet protection. Terraces should spill individually on well-protected pastures, meadows, or wooded areas, if these are available. If not, a suitable waterway must be provided, as discussed under "Waterways."

Spacing. Terraces are spaced according to the steepness of the land across which they are to run. On relatively flat land, rain collects and moves off slowly, and it can run a considerable distance before collecting in large enough quantities to cause erosion. On very steep land, the raindrops "hit the ground running," as one farmer expressed it, and can cause erosion before they run very far. Therefore, if all other factors that cause erosion are equal, the course of runoff rainfall must be intercepted by terraces more frequently on steep land than on flatter land. It is on this basis that the formulas for spacing terraces were developed.

The vertical spacing of terraces should usually be obtained by the formula "slope (in percentage) plus 2 and divided by 2" in areas where the average annual rainfall is thirty inches or more. In areas of less rainfall, the formula is given as "slope (in percentage) plus 3 and divided by 2."

If the slope falls 1 foot in 100 feet (or 1 per cent), the equation would be $\frac{1+2}{2}$ or $1\frac{1}{2}$. This would be the vertical distance between terraces. The horizontal spacing should therefore be approximately 150 feet. In lower rainfall areas, the vertical spacing could be 2 feet and the horizontal spacing 200 feet. Spacings on other slopes are calculated in the same manner.

A system of terraces based on the spacing formulas provides effective protection against water erosion, but this protection is most effective when used in conjunction with good soil-management practices, such as the use of cover crops, residue crops, and crops to keep the soil open. These formulas, however, do not provide terraces of adequate protection for the improvident farmer—the farmer who allows his terrace channels to fill with silt and his ridges to break. This farmer, who loses the protection of this expensive improvement, is generally the type of farmer who objects to the closeness of the terraces. The man who is really concerned with the protection of his land seldom objects.

Spacing the top terrace. The top terrace in a system should be spaced no more than a normal vertical interval below the top of the slope or below a diversion terrace. If it is necessary to exceed this spacing by more than one-third of the normal interval, the top terrace should become a diversion terrace and be designed to handle the additional runoff. If much erosion has been occurring on the land above this top terrace or if the area is too small for profitable cropping, it should be planted to permanent grasses or trees for grazing, wildlife, or other such uses.

With an understanding of the above principles, the farmer is ready to make the necessary decisions concerning a standard terrace system for his cropland. If protected spills are available, he is ready for construction to start. If he must provide spills for the proposed terraces, he should study the principles listed later under the heading "Waterways." If he is to build his own terraces, rather than employ a contractor, he will need to study the appropriate material discussed under "Terrace Dimensions" on the following pages, and he may need to consult with his conservationist or engineer concerning construction methods and the equipment he has available.

Surveying the terrace lines. By the time the farmer has

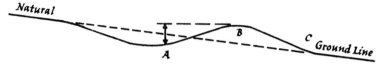

FIGURE 4.   A—*End of front slope of terrace. Also bottom of water channel.*
B—*Top of terrace ridge (measurement for height to be made 2 feet from center of terrace).*
C—*End of back slope at natural ground line.*

TABLE I

Slope %	Height above Bottom of Water Channel — Feet Vertical distance "B" above "A" on Sketch *	Channel Cross-Section Sq. Ft. †	Minimum Width Terrace Ridge Measured from "A" to "C" on Sketch — Feet		
			Short Terraces	Medium Length Terraces	Long Terraces
2 or Less	1.2	16	16	18	20
3	1.2	15	16	18	20
4	1.3	14	16	18	20
5	1.3	13	16	16	18
6	1.4	12	16	16	18
7	1.5	11	16	16	16
8	1.5	10	16	16	16

* Height may be decreased 25% for short terraces and 15% for medium length terraces except that the height must be at least 1 foot.
† The channel cross-section may be decreased 25% for short terraces and 15% for medium-length terraces.
The upper and lower slopes of the terrace should be approximately the same width.

worked with his conservationist in developing plans for his terrace system, he will have learned that a survey party is available at no cost, to mark the terrace lines for construction. A date book for this work will be set, when he will be in the field with the engineering party to assist with the work and mark the lines.

RIDGE TYPE TERRACE

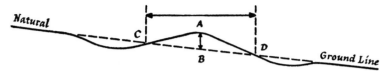

FIGURE 5.   A—*Top of terrace ridge (measurement for height to be made 2 feet from center of terrace).*
B—*Natural ground below center of terrace ridge.*
C—*End of front slope at natural ground.*
D—*End of back slope at natural ground.*

TABLE II

	Height above Natural ground —Feet—	Width above natural ground —Feet—			Cross-Section above Natural ground — Sq. Ft.		
Slope %	"A" above "B" on Sketch	Short Terraces *	Medium Length Terraces†	Long Terraces ‡	Short Terraces	Medium Length Terraces	Long Terraces
1	1.0	16	18	20	9	11	12
2	1.1	16	18	20	9	11	12
3	1.2	14	16	18	9	11	12
4	1.3	13	16	18	9	11	12
5	1.4	12	14	16	9	11	12
6	1.4	12	14	16	9	11	12
7	1.5	12	14	16	9	11	12
8	1.5	12	14	16	9	11	12

* Short terraces are those which drain not more than 600 feet in one direction.
† Medium length terraces are those which drain not more than 1000 feet in one direction.
‡ Long terraces are those which drain more than 1000 feet in one direction.
The dimensions given in the table may be decreased 10% for fully settled terraces.

After the survey party has marked stations along a line with stakes, mounds of earth, or bits of paper, the engineer will tell the farmer how to plow out the lines and how much liberty he can take in straightening out the line, for if the farmer straightens out the line by plowing under a marked point, the ground line of the terrace at that point will be too low and will have to be compensated for by enlarging the fill. If he goes above the marked point, the ground line will be higher and the channel must be cut deeper. It is generally more advisable to go under the marked point—a fill is easier to construct and maintain than a cut in the channel.

The marked line should be the flow line for the channel of a channel type terrace; therefore the center of the ridge will be some distance below. But the ridge of a ridge type terrace is usually built on the marked line.

Terrace dimensions. The accepted terrace specifications vary in different states. For the specifications required in one of our Western states, see Figures 4 and 5 and Tables I and II

Shape of terraces and fills. The terrace ridge should be wide based, with the slopes well rounded and as full as possible, as also should be the slopes of the channel. There should be no peak on the top of the ridge, since such a peak adds no effective height to the fill and sharp points are hazards in farming operations. The shape should be such that an automobile may be driven over or across the terrace ridge and channel, when settled, in any direction and at any angle without strain.

Fills should be full bodied and built to such height that, after settling, they will be above the normal level of the connecting terrace ridge. The ground on which they are built should be clean. The banks of any gullies beneath the site of the fill should be broken down and compacted before the fill is started. It is generally best to build the fills before the terraces are started. Terrace construction operations will blend the fill with the balance of the terrace ridge better than if the fill is added afterward. Also, the fill will be more compact. Special care should be given to making the fills the strongest part of the terrace ridge.

Terraces generously built to good specifications and properly shaped are not obstructions in the field and are least objectionable to the farmer. Most objections are to small ridges that

88

must be kept peaked and uncrossable if they are to give adequate protection to the field. The farmer should be able to plant crops on the slopes and top of a properly built terrace. The terrace job should not be regarded as complete until this can be done.

Construction and Maintenance

Methods and equipment. Although it is a long and tedious job, the farmer can often build terraces himself if he has a two-row or larger tractor and his equipment is in good condition.

Most machine shops can design and mount a bulldozer on the front of the farm tractor that will serve effectively in making the fills or in building the entire terrace. One-way and other disk plows have been effectively used, especially where they are equipped with a power lift. Moldboard plows tend to make the ridge too narrow, but an "island method" has been devised to make the building easier and to give greater width.

Several types of terracers on the market now can be operated with a good tractor. Some are disk type, and some are blade type. One consists of a fast-revolving augur which takes the dirt from a moldboard plow and throws it onto the terrace ridge. This type moves the earth efficiently, but it should be operated in connection with some other type of equipment so that the earth can be compacted in the terrace ridge. Farmers also use a rotary fresno for terrace construction, maintenance, and other types of earth work.

Conservation workers do not discourage the farmer from building his own terraces when he is properly equipped and willing to undertake the job. In fact, he will probably appreciate his terraces more and take better care of them when he has done the work himself. However, he should be warned that building a good terrace takes lots of work. He should complete each terrace started and build it to specifications.

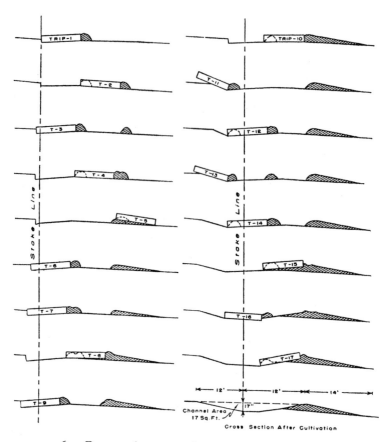

FIGURE 6. *Progressive steps in constructing a channel type terrace with a 12 foot blade terracer.*

Perhaps it is more satisfactory to most farmers to employ the work done with large equipment such as road patrols, bulldozers mounted on crawler-type tractors, and similar equipment. Contractors with such equipment operate under the supervision of conservation workers and must perform a complete job before they are eligible for the government's cost-share or payment for the farmer's share of the cost. While on the farm, they are available for other work which the farmer cannot do with his own equipment.

Terrace maintenance. When the farmer has established a terrace system, he has invested a considerable amount of money and work. He has installed one of the better physical improvements that can be made on the land. Its effectiveness will depend on him.

The specifications for terracing have been carefully developed and properly applied. With proper maintenance they should last indefinitely. Damage to them will come only from an unusually heavy rainfall, from rodents, or from improper farming operations. Infrequent intense rainstorms may not damage the terraces if the land is under a good cover and the terraces are in good condition. But even the damage from heavy rains can be repaired. Gophers or other rodents may tunnel under a terrace ridge and cause damage, but rodents can be destroyed and the damage repaired. However, the farmer who lists or plows over the terrace will seldom take the time to repair the damage he has done. In fact, such tillage methods aggravate the damage that might be done by a heavy rain—a rain that might not cause any damage on land that is properly tilled.

Terrace maintenance consists of three simple steps: Perform all tillage operations with the terraces; use cover crops and crop residues between the terraces to help control falling and running water; and plow systematically to maintain the capacity of the terrace channel.

Farming with terraces means farming on the level, more commonly called contour farming. This practice is discussed in more detail in another part of this book, but its relationship to terraces and its advantages should be emphasized here. Uphill and downhill farming across terraces will fill up the channel with the dirt that slides down-hill before the plow. It tears down the terrace ridge and reduces its effectiveness. It opens up many furrows down which runoff water and topsoil will be carried to the terrace channel from the area above. There it is deposited to reduce further the capacity of the channel and damage the terrace system. Continual around-the-field plowing will move portions of the terrace ridge uphill and portions down, causing blocks in the terrace channel and breaks in the ridge.

In contrast, contour farming with terraces keeps more water on the field for crops because every ridge, furrow, and row of growing crops forms a barrier to runoff water, causing it to move more slowly and allowing more to soak into the soil. It saves topsoil and the fertilizers and lime that have been applied. It reduces the amount of replanting made necessary by heavy rains and results in better stands and increased crop yields. It reduces siltation on lower fields by the simple process of keeping more silt out of the runoff water. Since it reduces the amount of runoff water, less damage results from runoff and floods.

It has been repeatedly pointed out by conservationists that most real soil protection results from the use of crops to give cover and protection and to add organic matter which enables the soil to resist erosion. Even the contour-farming pattern is secondary to the cropping program for soil conservation. Terraces are designed only to supplement these practices and give added protection to the land during heavy rains when some water must run off. They are not planned to replace a conservation cropping program. Likewise, proper cropping systems and tillage practices are not designed for the protection of the terraces, although they are essential if the farmer is to secure the best results from his terraces.

The method of plowing for the maintenance of the terrace is determined by the type of terrace. Since the channel, rather than the ridge below, is the part of the terrace that carries the

Cropland Treatment

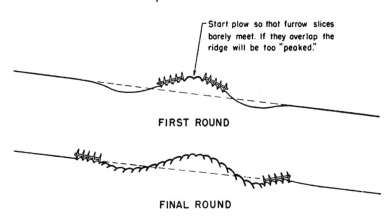

Start plow so that furrow slices barely meet. If they overlap the ridge will be too "peaked."

FIRST ROUND

FINAL ROUND

Vary width of land each plowing so dead furrow will not fall in some place repeatedly. Plow area between terraces as a separate land.

Note: If terrace should become peaked, start back furrow on back slope, one plow width from top of ridge.

FIGURE 7. *A recommended method of maintenance of ridge type terraces with disk plow.*

water, the farmer must keep the channel capacity adequate. On the flatter slopes, it may be more desirable to have a shallow channel, so that the water will back up a maximum distance from the terrace ridge to provide some irrigation effect. In this case, the ridge is accented, and maintenance plowing should preserve the size and height of the ridge, and thus the capacity of the channel will be maintained.

On steeper slopes where water cannot be effectively backed up to any great distance above the terrace ridge, the terrace is maintained by plowing out the channel. Its capacity is maintained by keeping it as deep and as wide as possible. A ridge is maintained only to give more depth to the channel. It is not desirable to build up a high ridge on steep land since that

93

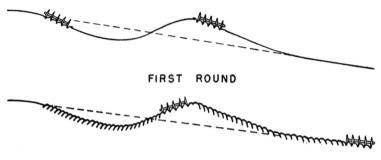

FIRST ROUND

FINAL ROUND

Rounds Should Be Spaced So That Width of Plowed Area Be-
low Terrace Is ⅓ More Than Width of Plowed Area
Above Terrace. This Calls For Overlapping The Rounds
Above Terrace.

NOTE: This Method Not Recommended For Continuous Use.

FIGURE 8.   *A method of maintenance of channel type terraces
with disk plow.*

increases the slope on the back side of the ridge, causing it to
be more difficult and dangerous to farm.

Therefore, for the ridge type terrace, plowing will lap the
soil onto the ridge from both directions, and the "land" laid
off for this plowing may continue up or downhill as far as the
farmer desires (see "Land Preparation" below).

For plowing a channel type terrace, however, the width of
the "land" must be smaller and should be laid off so that a
dead-furrow will fall in the upper edge of the terrace channel.
The terrace ridge will be one side of the "land," and the other
side will be twice the distance from the ridge to the upper side
of the channel. For example, if it is six feet from the top of
the terrace ridge to the edge of the flow line in the channel and
this flow line is ten feet wide, the upper side of the "land" that
is laid off for plowing out the channel should be thirty-two

94

feet above the terrace ridge. This will make the dead-furrow at the upper edge of the water channel, or sixteen feet above the terrace ridge.

If this type of terrace has gone several years without the proper maintenance and the channel is pretty well filled up, a double plowing may be needed. In this case, the first plowing should be shallow enough so that the second plowing will go under the loose earth first turned and pick up a fresh cut in undisturbed soil. But the last round, in the first dead-furrow, should be omitted or should be shallow. This will give greater width to the newly formed water channel and will also add more soil to the front slope of the ridge. Normal plowing operations will add enough soil to the back slope of the terrace ridge.

Adequate width for this plowed-out "land" should be emphasized. A "land" that is too narrow will increase the steepness of the front slope of the terrace without actually adding greatly to the channel capacity.

A common error in terrace maintenance has been to plow to the ridge of terraces on steep land, as outlined above, for the maintenance of ridge type terraces. Because of this plowing and the natural movement of soil downhill, the terrace channel may fill up until it is above the original ground level. To keep the terraces effective, the ridge must be built higher and higher, often to the point where it is impossible to farm them because of the steepness of the slopes. The terraces are benched and the field resembles stair steps. The farmer can remedy this situation by beginning the type of maintenance recommended above for channel type terraces. When he has developed an adequate channel, he can plow down a portion of the terrace ridge. When this situation exists, the farmer should consult a conservationist for technical assistance. It will sometimes prove cheaper and more satisfactory to level the old terraces and establish a new system. In any event, the redesigned terrace should be checked for adequacy.

4. CONTOUR FARMING

Contour farming is "farming on the level." For all practical purposes, each row is "located" on level ground, where it can hold the maximum amount of rain and increase absorption for crop use.

Contour farming saves moisture and reduces runoff and erosion. It is a pattern of farming used to supplement a conservation cropping system. At Marcellus, New York, yields have been increased from 11 to 31 per cent by the use of contour farming alone, in experiments that ranged over a period of from one to seven years. Contour farming and up-and-down tillage were practiced on identical plots of steep land, and the results were compared. Increases in corn yields on the plots under contour farming were 6.2 per cent in 1942, 17.7 per cent in 1943, 3.8 per cent in 1946, 23.8 per cent in 1950, and 26.3 per cent in 1953, an average increase of 15.6 per cent in five years.

Beans showed an increase of 31 per cent in 1953, and an average increase of 19.45 per cent. Hay showed an increase of 13 per cent in six years. Cabbage showed an average gain of 24.4 per cent in three years, in spite of the fact that one year the tables were reversed and contour planting showed a 10.1 per cent decrease. Wheat showed a 17 per cent increase the one year it was included in the experiment, and oats and barley showed a 13.6 per cent increase in a two-year trial.

Contour farming is used on short strips of gently sloping land without the support of terraces or strip cropping. On steeper land, strip cropping and terraces are needed to supplement contour farming in a conservation cropping system.

For guide lines the farmer uses terraces, permanent guide lines, and lines run each year and not marked. Permanent guide lines are marked with tree or shrub rows or a strip of perennial grass which does not concentrate water, but allows it to flow through the line freely. Ridges are not used to mark such lines unless they are properly built terraces. Small ridges or furrows would tend to concentrate water, but would not be able to contain it during a heavy rain, and the resulting break would cause severe erosion.

The farmer may realize the need of adopting a system of contour farming without being fully prepared to accept the major changes that will be required in his way of farming. He may not understand the methods necessary to make the system fully effective. Often there is no opportunity for him to have many simple contour farming procedures explained. The result is that the program seems unnecessarily difficult, point rows too bothersome.

The practices that come naturally to him often result in ridges on or against the strip that marks his permanent guide lines, in terraces improperly maintained, in dead-furrows placed in the same spot every year to enlarge and expose infertile soils below, and in crops damaged by turning on point rows.

The following suggestions are offered to help the farmer understand the contour farming system that he is about to adopt, in the hope that they will enable him to see the value of the terraces or permanent guide lines as divisions in his field and to make use of them as sub-field boundaries, and, likewise, to understand the reasons for maintaining his terrace system and keeping it functioning properly. He will not find the task too difficult if he will rid himself of some mental reservations, do adequate planning and study, and prepare to go the whole way with his new system.

Arrangement and Planning

Field Arrangement. The farmer generally is used to fields that are oblong and bounded by straight fences, or in other shapes determined by natural boundaries. These fields have been plowed in one or more lands, and the rows have run in a certain direction year after year. He has been able to determine exact acreages of the fields, and it has been no great problem to divide them into two or more smaller fields and determine the acreage of each.

Now he is going to change his tillage pattern completely and farm on the contour. His fields and his lands will conform to terraces or guide lines to a large extent. Therefore, he should consider the possibility of removing all interior fences or field boundaries and re-establishing them according to these lines. To do so may save trouble later. If he can do this, his whole job will be made easier, for he will not have to contour farm in rectangular fields, which is like fitting round pegs into square holes.

The boundaries of pastures, woodlands, and such natural obstacles as creeks, major gullies, and areas of nontillable soils cannot be changed, but fences, roads, and lanes can be moved and the smaller gullies eliminated. Such changes will often improve the total conservation plan and provide fields with a better functional value from the standpoint of farm arrangement.

For instance, farm roads and lanes may be placed under terraces or on enlarged broad-based terraces, where they will be drier, have perfect protection from erosion, are easier to maintain and are usually more attractive. Small fields near the farmstead used for supplemental pasture, calf lots, and feed lots should also be included in terracing and boundary rearrangement plans. The boundaries of the farmstead itself may also be rearranged, so that terrace ends can be extended into the farmyard to pick up water that is causing erosion there.

Some land-use changes may be advisable. Odd corners may be retired to permanent grass because of difficulty in farming them, or to avoid the construction of a lane, or to provide a permanent pasture area nearer the farmstead. Sometimes there is better land in the pasture that will fit into the terrace system. Such land can be put to cultivation to offset the loss of retired areas. The location of the terraces or permanent guide lines will govern such changes.

The resulting fields may be far more desirable in the farm plan. Certainly they will be more effective in helping to establish a complete erosion-control program for the farmer's lands.

When the farmer can visualize the lay of the lines on his land, he should begin to study possible changes in permanent field boundaries and the best use of each enclosure. Perhaps he will decide that he needs fewer permanent enclosures, and that he can more effectively use temporary or electric fences for pasture in connection with the conservation crops he plans to use in rotation over his land. Thus we approach the subject of subdivisions of permanent fields.

Fields within fields. If the farmer's permanent fields are large and he wants to subdivide them so that he can rotate his regular and conservation crops, he will again want to use the terraces or guide lines wherever possible for these temporary divisions. If any of the crops are to be grazed at any time, he will need fences and an access to permanent pasture or to the farmstead and to water. If more than one crop is to be grazed, and at different seasons, multiple divisions will be necessary. If none of the crops are to be grazed, or if the land for one is fallow while the other is in pasture, no fences within the larger field are necessary.

Occasionally one part of a field is planned for an almost permanent grazing crop, while adjoining areas cannot be grazed. This will occur when the soil is poor enough to require the continued use of sown hay and pasture crops, or on better soils when the most profitable use is for such crops. Fences for such areas may be of the permanent type, but often the farmer chooses to use temporary fences so that field boundaries may be changed at will, and because they are easy to remove for the control of weeds.

99

Such field boundaries may conform to soil type, but if possible they should conform to the permanent lines so that the contour farming pattern will not be broken.

This subdivision of fields poses two new subjects, the construction of the fences and the determination of acreages.

Acreage determinations. Often the farmer has not rotated his crops, has not used fertility-improving crops, or has not made other needed adjustments because of the fact that it was difficult to determine acreages on subdivisions of the larger field. Now he can take advantage of permanent guides to initiate crop-rotation programs.

In setting up such a program, he should consider the area between each two permanent lines as a "land," or minor subdivision of his field. He can ink in the approximate location of each line on his conservation plan map, or have his conservation office do this for him. Or he may secure a sketch of his farm with the lines marked. When he has learned the acreage between each pair of lines, he will ink it in on the map or sketch. Of course, the acreage above the top and below the bottom lines will also be shown. The total is the acreage in the field. This will provide the basic information for planning his cropping system each year. Note that it is not recommended that the field be divided into three, or four, or five equal parts, regardless of the type of rotation the farmer now plans to follow. The plan may be changed next year, and the farmer should be in a position to make adjustments quickly and easily.

This is how the plan works: The farmer finds that he has 5.5 acres above the first terrace, or guide line, 3.6 acres between lines 1 and 2, 3.4 acres between lines 2 and 3, 3.5 acres between lines 3 and 4, and 7 acres below line 4, which in this case is the bottom line. The total is 23 acres for the field.

Suppose that this year he wants to plant about one-third of the field in soybeans, one-third to corn, and one-third to oats. A logical division of the field would be on the second and fourth lines. Above the second line are 9.1 acres; between the second and fourth lines are 6.9 acres, and below the bottom line are 7 acres. This may be accurate enough for the division of crops on the field. If it is not, he may make his divisions halfway between lines 1 and 2, and three-fourths of the way down from line 3 (or one-fourth of the way up from terrace 4). This gives him 7.3 acres in the top field, 7.8 acres in the middle field, and 7.9 acres in the lower field. If the lines vary a great deal in length, a percentage division of the terrace interval would not be accurate, and the overlap of one crop into an adjoining terrace interval should be determined by counting the number of rows required to provide the desired acreage. Consult Table III, and use it in the following manner.

Show the length of each line, also in ink, on the conservation plan map, or overlay. Line 4 is approximately 2,000 feet long. By consulting Table III, it is found that it will take six and one-half 40-inch rows to make an acre. If you want to plant corn, for example, in the 7 acres below the line and want to extend corn above the line far enough to get an additional acre, you will be approximately accurate if you plant six and one-half rows, as shown above.

With a little practice, the farmer will be able to divide his field into any number of subdivisions with reasonable accuracy. If there are a larger number of lines in the field, and if the acreage in the intervals is smaller, he will have less difficulty in making the division.

Preparation of map or sketch. The conservationist will help as much as his time will permit, for he wants the farmer to be able to maintain these field divisions on the contour. If aerial photographs of the farm have been made since terraces or guide lines were established, these developments should appear on the picture from which the farm plan map is made. The farmer or conservationist will ink these lines in, and, with the use of a planimeter, he can determine the approximate acreage between each interval. If the farmer does not want his map marked up with these lines, he can prepare an accurate sketch, or overlay.

If the terraces or guide lines are new or if they cannot be determined from the available aerial photograph, the conservationist will help the farmer sketch them in on the map or overlay. Exact locations are not important, since neither the acreage nor the lengths will be measured from this sketch. If the conservation office has measured these lines, there may be a record of their lengths on file in the office. This will be added to the sketch. If this information is not available in the office, measurements should be made in the field.

TABLE III

Determining Number of Rows in an Acre

For row lengths shown in left column, the number of rows required to make an acre are shown for common row spacings:

If row length is:	(For row spacings given, the following number of rows make an acre.)				
	30 in.	36 in.	38 in.	40 in.	42 in.
50 feet	348.5	290.4	275.1	261.4	248.9
100 "	174.2	145.2	137.6	130.7	124.5
150 "	116.1	96.8	91.7	87.1	83.0
200 "	87.1	72.6	68.8	65.3	62.2
250 "	69.6	58.1	55.0	52.3	49.8
300 "	58.0	48.4	45.8	43.6	41.5
350 "	49.8	41.5	39.3	37.3	35.6
400 "	43.5	36.3	34.4	32.7	31.1
450 "	38.7	32.3	30.6	29.0	27.7
500 "	34.8	29.0	27.5	26.1	24.9
600 "	29.0	24.2	22.9	21.8	20.7
700 "	23.5	20.7	19.7	18.7	17.8
800 "	21.8	18.1	17.2	16.3	15.6
1000 "	17.4	14.5	13.8	13.1	12.5
1500 "	11.6	9.7	9.2	8.7	8.3
2000 "	8.7	7.3	6.9	6.5	6.2
3000 "	5.8	4.8	4.6	4.4	4.1
5000 "	3.5	2.9	2.8	2.6	2.5
5280 "	3.3	2.8	2.6	2.5	2.4

Cropland Treatment

With the use of a survey chain or other measuring device, each line is measured and its length carefully recorded, to be inked on the map later. These lengths are needed for determining acreage by row lengths (see Table III). They are also needed for computing the acreage between each pair of lines. Then the distance between each pair of lines should be measured in several representative (or average) places.

These distances (between pairs of lines) are totaled and averaged. The greater the variation in distances between lines, the greater should be the number of measurements taken, since the result should represent the actual average distance between the lines. When this is determined, the length of each pair of lines should be averaged. The average length multiplied by the average width gives the square feet in the interval. The number of square feet is then divided by 43,560 (the number of square feet in an acre) to get the acreage in the interval. Record this acreage to the nearest tenth of an acre between the lines on the map or overlay.

When this is done for all of the intervals, the total should equal the known acreage of the field. If it misses by more than a slight margin, a recheck should be made. For very irregular areas, the conservationist can help to determine a method for measuring.

An alternate and perhaps better plan is to secure the services of a qualified engineering party to map the field. They can use engineering equipment and methods designed for doing this work accurately, and their acreage calculations will be dependable. Such work is not a part of the services ordinarily rendered by the conservation office, but surveyors may be available for the work.

Land Preparation

The ordinary plows move slices of earth to one side, out of its natural position. For this reason they tend to make undesirable ridges and dead-furrows. This situation is aggravated in long, narrow fields or lands between terraces or permanent guide lines.

The answer to the problem, of course, is to change the pattern in plowing or use tillage implements which do not move the soil out of place. Subsurface sweeps and chisel-type implements, often supplemented by disks and harrows, are replacing the one-way disk and moldboard plow because they do not displace the soil, and do leave a protective cover of crop residue on or in the surface of the soil.

A third choice is to use a two-way moldboard or disk plow which can be operated to move the soil in only one direction —uphill. This offsets the natural sloughing and movement of soil downhill. The two-way plow has two sets of plows mounted on power-lift attachments on the tractor. One set of plows throws the soil to the left, the other to the right. When the plowman reaches the end of the field, he turns around and starts back with the wheel in the furrow he has just plowed. He lifts the set of plows he has been using and lowers the other set. With this type of plow he does not lay out a land around which he plows, throwing the soil uphill on one side and downhill on the other, as with the conventional one-way plow. With the one-way plow he must either plow uphill on one end of the land and downhill on the other, or he must drive this distance with his plows out of the ground. With the two-way plow there is no plowing uphill or downhill or driving empty. And the result is far more satisfactory than land preparation with the one-way plow. There are no dead-furrows, unless they are intentionally made in the terrace channel. There are no unnecessary ridges. There is no soil plowed into the terrace channel. In fact, the soil is always plowed away from the channel, and thus the channel capacity is maintained.

The use of such equipment as that listed above is more satisfactory for preventing undesirable land shifts. But if the conventional, one-way plow or moldboard disk plow is to be used, the farmer can avoid the development of the dead-furrows or ridges if he will change the width of his land frequently, making the dead-furrows fall in different places each year. This he may do by plowing a land around the terrace ridge, as recommended for the maintenance of a ridge-type terrace, halting this operation when he has plowed twenty to thirty feet each way from each terrace. Then the unplowed areas between each terrace can be plowed in another land. He can alternate this method with a similar method based on the recommendation (above) for the maintenance of a channel type terrace. Or, thirdly, he may plow out from each terrace ridge until these lands are about twenty feet from each other in the closest places. At this time the farmer should follow recommendations given below under "Problems in plowing and planting terraced fields."

The farmer who observes the effect of his plowing pattern and changes that pattern to move the dead-furrows will have little trouble operating in a terraced field, although it is admittedly not as easy as plowing around the entire field in one land.

Planting. Since each terrace line is approximately on the contour, it will be the guide line for planting. Rows should be laid off above and below the terrace until they approach the center of the interval. The bottom row of the land on one terrace and the top row from the land centered on the terrace below should be not more than twenty feet apart at the closest place before the point rows are planted. These short rows, made necessary by variations in the width of the terrace intervals, should fall near the center of the terrace interval. See "Problems in plowing and planting terraced fields" for the remaining steps.

Point rows are avoided when the farmer plants a sown crop for hay or grain in strips between strips of row crops. If this effect is desired, the row planter should be stopped when the two crop lands, at their closest point, are at least the width of the drill, but preferably twenty feet apart to allow for the turning of the drill. This method will put all of the rows most nearly on the contour and will leave the remaining strip between terraces to be sown.

An alternative is to center the row crop land on every other (alternate) terrace. Rows are laid off until the upper row comes just under the terrace above the point where the terraces are closest together, and the bottom row clears the channel of the terrace below. Then the point-row areas are sown, and finally the terrace ridge is sown.

Problems in plowing and planting terraced fields. Point rows provide the most serious objection to plowing and planting in terraced fields, generally because the farmer does not know what to do with them. Too often he solves the problem by plowing or planting over the terraces, making all of the rows and lands the full length of the field. Or, if he begins with any of the methods listed above, he plows or plants until the rows meet in the narrowest part of the terrace interval. Then he must turn on land that has already been plowed or planted.

The simplest solution is to leave an unplowed or unplanted area, large enough to turn on, where the lands meet. It should be approximately twenty feet wide for larger equipment, although smaller equipment will require less room.

When this much space is left at the narrowest place in the terrace interval, the odd-shaped areas, caused by bends or curves in the terraces, are planted or plowed. In all cases the plowing and planting ceases when the area is reduced to the space originally left for turning. After all of these odd spaces are worked, the farmer will have an even-width strip running the entire length of the terrace interval, or land, and he has not turned on plowed or planted land. He can then complete the operation by plowing or planting this longer strip.

This method will not work for cultivating row crops, since

Examples of conservation farming. ABOVE: *Terraced field of oats in foreground, contour and terraced field of soybeans on right, terraced outlet grass waterway in middle, with complete conservation practices of farmstead windbreaks, terracing, contouring, and strip cropping in background.* BELOW: *Effective use of contour strip cropping.*

Examples of terracing. ABOVE: No terraces, no contour farming—but a heavy loss of soil and rapid runoff. BELOW: Proper use of terracing and related conservation practices increases yields and protects the soil.

turning would have to be done on planted areas when the point rows are worked out. Of course, this problem does not exist when sown strips are used, as outlined above, to eliminate point rows, or even when the strip originally left for turning is sown or planted to a permanent grass for this purpose.

Harvesting crops. Harvesting sown crops, especially with a combine, presents no problem if the land is not too steep and the terraces can be cut over. In this case, the cutting is done around the field in the usual manner. If the terraces are not crossable, it may be desirable to open a cut near the center of the field, following a terrace, and then cut up and down from there.

When row crops are to be harvested with large machinery, the process recommended for plowing or planting is reversed. The long rows which were planted last (on the original turning area) are cut first. Then the point rows are worked out, with turns being made on the original turning strip. Finally the longer rows along each terrace are harvested. This sequence is important since the point rows will bend into the original turning area, and the crop cannot be properly harvested without first clearing this strip for turning during the harvesting operations.

The same procedures apply to land preparation and planting and harvesting crops on the contour, where guide lines rather than terraces are used.

Guide lines for contour farming. Plowing operations should not form a ridge on the guide line, however, since such a ridge would tend to concentrate water, causing breaks and increased erosion below. If ridges are desirable, a complete terrace system should be established.

For contour farming without terraces, guide lines should be run every year or marked with some device which will not cause water to concentrate, such as trees, shrubs, or a grass strip. If a contour strip-crop pattern is to be followed, with the strips alternated between row crops and sown crops, with the sown crop taking up the point rows, guide lines should be run each year.

If permanent strips are to be established, with a perennial grass crop to occupy the intervening area, including the point rows, the cropland area should be laid off equidistant above and below the guide line, leaving the desired area for the grass crop. Then the contour strip is marked, and a guide line is not necessary until a change is made in the pattern.

5. WATERWAYS

In its broader sense, a waterway is any way, course, or route in which water is concentrated as it flows from its place of origin on its way to the sea. This covers both large and small waterways.

In conservation farming the term "waterway" is limited to those protected watercourses which are used primarily for the purpose of transporting water. Therefore a gully or a swale in a field which is plowed and planted is not a waterway, even though water is concentrated there when rainfall provides the runoff. Gullies with steep banks are not waterways, although they are watercourses, for there is no place in conservation farming for a gully or an unprotected watercourse.

Waterways, then, are shaped or natural channels which are in some way protected from erosion. They are used for the safe disposal of excess water which runs across a farm, from fields, from terrace systems, or from irrigation systems. Waterways that conduct water across cropland are the ones of interest here.

The need for waterways exists when there is runoff water, from whatever source, that causes erosion. A conservation cropping system or a strip-crop pattern of farming may eliminate erosion caused by runoff water. Water may escape from the field by running across the surface or seeping from the soil, but if there is no erosion, there is no need for a waterway. If there are channels where erosion is active, waterways are needed. Waterways may be simple and easy to establish. The farmer may plant grass in these watercourses and thus eliminate the erosion, and he has satisfactory waterways.

But if there are too many of these watercourses in the field, the farmer may desire to concentrate the water in one or two places by the use of diversion terraces or a system of field terraces. If the water cannot be spilled onto a grass pasture or similar area where adequate protection against erosion exists, the farmer must have one or more waterways of adequate size and shape, with sufficient protection to handle the runoff from these terraces safely. And in most cases, the waterways should be prepared and protected before the terraces are built. It is difficult, and sometimes impossible, to shape the channel or establish vegetative protection after the channel is actually carrying water from a terrace system or from an outside source.

In some areas conservation authorities recommend that all natural drains in a field be planted with vegetation, with or without reshaping, to serve as outlets for terraces or the natural flow across the land. In areas of less rainfall, one or more natural drains may be chosen to serve as waterways and the others closed by extending terraces across them. In a few cases, the waterways may be located along a field boundary or in some other favorable site which is not a natural watercourse.

As a general principle, however, waterways should be located in natural drains. There the soil is usually better for the establishment and maintenance of the vegetative cover which is generally relied on for protection. The grade or slope is usually less and more constant. The capacity of natural drains generally is larger. A final important factor is that natural drains do lead to a watercourse where the waterway may be ended, and the discharged water may leave the farm in its proper course.

In laying plans for his waterways, the farmer will usually consult with a conservation technician and consider the following items:

(1) Use. Although the primary use of a waterway is to carry excess water safely from a field, the secondary uses are important. Runoff water demands its right to cross fields below it. The farmer who does not recognize this right suffers inconvenience, damage to his land, and loss of income. Gullies and eroded areas produce little or nothing of economic benefit and cannot be used as terrace spills. But the farmer who recognizes this basic right of excess water and who provides a protected and controlled waterway can prevent further damage to his land and can maintain or increase his income by securing pasture, hay, or seed from the plants used to protect the waterway. He takes advantage of this excess water and uses it to irrigate these grass or legume crops.

A waterway near the pasture may be easily fenced with it. In another location, or on better soils, plants that will produce hay may be preferred. Seed crops are often valuable. The farmer will have his preference of the plants to be used, but may find that he will have to use a sod which will give better protection even though less desirable for hay or pasture, or he may have an opportunity to locate the waterway on a gentler slope or deeper soil, where both needs may be adequately served.

This secondary use may be very important. Often the waterway is the most profitable hay or pasture area on the farm. It may be widened and established to a sod to serve as a lane and may replace a narrow, eroding lane.

(2) Places of beginning and ending. The waterway must extend from the highest point where water collects in dangerous volume to a safe disposal area. The upper point is usually located at the mouth of the top terrace or at the field or farm boundary where a volume of water enters. The lower point may be on grassland, woodland, or in a stable natural drain. If a gully condition exists where the water must be released, supplemental measures such as an erosion-control dam, a diversion terrace, or a sod flume may be needed.

(3) Complex slope conditions. One part of a field may slope to the north and another part to the south, with a ridge, or divide, running across the field between the slopes. In this example, it is obvious that two waterways would be needed—one for each slope. There may be several slope units, each requiring a separate waterway. On other occasions, a careful engineering survey may show that a waterway may be planned to serve more than one slope.

Suitable pastures or woodlands may serve some terraces on complex slopes or serve one end of long terraces, and they should be taken into account in the planning stage.

These slope units indicate the natural flow of the water. It is often advisable to plan enough waterways to permit all runoff to leave the field or farm in its natural course; this would be an important factor in determining the number and location of the waterways. But sometimes the water may be brought from one watershed or one slope to another and concentrated in a single waterway.

(4) Length of terraces to be served. There is a limit to the distance which terraces may be expected to carry water in one direction, because of soil, slope, type of terraces, the rainfall belt, and other conditions. If the length is greater than the safe maximum distance, waterways may be provided at or near each end of the field or as needed, so that the terraces may spill at both ends. A waterway near the center of the field may serve terraces running in both directions away from the waterway.

(5) Efficiency. Finally, any waterway planned must meet a set of conditions that will assure its successful performance, whether it is in a natural drain or is to be a shaped channel.

Size: The cross-sectional area must be large enough to handle the flow without permitting water to escape from the channel and damage adjacent cropland.

Depth of flow: When water runs deep, its cutting power is greatly increased. When it is spread out and runs shallow, its velocity and its erosive powers are reduced. On steep slopes the waterway is widened to reduce the velocity of the water. On flatter slopes the waterway may be narrowed and deepened to increase velocity and get the water away. In either circumstance, velocity and depth of flow are controlled by channel width and the grass to be used.

Vegetative protection: The farmer may have a choice of a narrow channel with a more effective type of sod-forming vegetation or a wider waterway with a less efficient grass or legume. Or he may have a choice of locating a waterway where the more desirable plants will perform satisfactorily because of the slope, depth, and fertility of the soil, or of locating it where it is most convenient to him but, because of less favorable conditions, will require a more efficient sod. Obviously the soil must be good enough to provide the protection needed, even though fertilization, manuring, or other soil-improvement measures are necessary.

Other protection: Concrete or masonry overfall structures are more effective than vegetation on many soils and must be used in lieu of vegetative protection under favorable conditions.

Construction

Shaping the waterway. In cross section, a waterway is flat-bottomed, saucer-shaped (parabolic), or V-shaped. The first provides the maximum spread of water. The second, in the shape of a broad arc, concentrates small flows in the center. The third is usually used on very flat slopes to increase the velocity of the flow.

In designing a waterway, conservation engineers carefully

determine the shape, width, and depth which will move the water freely while controlling its erosive powers during both the small and heavy flows resulting from light and heavy rains. Shaping operations should accurately follow the design.

In general, the waterway will be made as straight as possible. If turns are necessary, they should not be sharp, but gentle, and slightly banked like a modern highway on a curve. Auxiliary waterways may enter a principal waterway at right angles, but the engineer will allow for this situation in his design.

The farmer who shapes his own waterway should be careful to maintain the staked width in his construction, especially when the waterway enters a steeper area. Natural drains should be straightened as much as possible, and high places should be removed, even though considerable moving of earth is required.

Equipment. Any waterway which does not require an excessive amount of earth moving can be shaped with farm equipment. Small waterways down regular slopes or in small drains are not difficult. Small hummocks or irregularities in the course of the channel may be corrected with a bulldozer mounted on a farm tractor or with a fresno. Personnel of the conservation office will give the farmer adequate assistance in the use of this equipment and in supervising the construction.

In many areas experienced contractors operating heavy equipment may be employed for the construction of large and small waterways. The hiring of these contractors has been greatly facilitated by the purchase-order program of the Agricultural Conservation Program, which provides for the government to bear a share of the expense of construction, to be paid direct to the contractor on completion of the job. Waterway programs have been greatly accelerated and improved where contractors of this type are available.

Replacement of topsoil. Since the design of most channels calls for the removal of soil to a depth of from six to twelve inches, and sometimes, in the removal of hummocks or other irregularities, to an even greater depth, the saving and replacement of topsoil in the waterway may be an important factor in aiding the establishment of a vigorous growth of protective grasses.

This is a difficult task with average farm equipment, especially when building shaped channels on regular terrain. In natural drains where the watercourse is to be widened, the job is not so difficult.

Here is the procedure to follow where the course of the channel is relatively flat from side to side and the finished channel is to be six inches below the present ground level. If the depth of the topsoil is not sufficient for the top six inches to be removed and still leave enough fertility to produce the protective crop, a six-inch cut of topsoil is removed from one side (one-half) of the waterway and piled on the second or undisturbed side. Another six-inch cut (making a total depth of twelve inches) into the soil is made, and the dirt is moved to the outside of the waterway to form the berm. The first cut of topsoil is now moved back into the excavation, and a six-inch cut of topsoil from the second half (other side) of the waterway is piled on top of the first cut of topsoil. Another six-inch cut of soil is removed from the second half of the waterway to form the berm on that side. Now the topsoil is spread from side to side of the completed waterway, making a level channel six inches lower, but with the same six inches of fertile topsoil. If the waterway is to be lower in the center than on the sides, the subsoil should be removed accordingly, so that when the topsoil is spread evenly on the excavated base it will conform to the desired design.

If one side of the waterway is higher than the other, the topsoil may be moved to the higher side, while the excavated subsoil is placed on the lower side as the berm. When the topsoil is replaced, the higher side will provide the confining bank, and a berm is not needed.

Cropland Treatment

In a natural drain the topsoil is often deep enough that it is not necessary to save and replace the topsoil, but if it is necessary, the process is much simpler than that for the waterways mentioned above. The topsoil is bladed, or pushed, to either side, beyond the limits of any cutting or sloping required. Then the channel area is smoothed to specifications, and the sides are properly sloped. Gullies are filled, and high places removed and that soil spread in low places—all with the subsoil remaining in the channel. Then the topsoil is brought back in and evenly spread.

Protection and Maintenance

Waterway protection. As has been previously pointed out, waterways are now almost universally protected with permanent or semipermanent vegetation. However, there are slopes and soils where vegetation cannot be expected to give adequate protection, and drop-structures of masonry or concrete are built to carry the runoff water safely in these cases. Such structures are, of course, much more costly, but they have their place in waterway protection. They require special care in design, layout, and construction supervision; this assistance is available from conservation engineers, who should be consulted when this solution seems to be needed. Other uses for concrete or masonry structures in connection with waterways will be mentioned below under the heading "Protecting the end of the waterway."

For vegetative protection of the waterway, certain preliminary steps are necessary: land preparation, fertilization and manuring, and selection of the best plants for the soil, climate, and job to be done.

Land preparation may include deep plowing or chiseling to break up compacted layers of soil, thus permitting better storage of moisture and the entry of roots. This will also improve the bond between the replaced layers of topsoil and the subsoil beneath. It will include other tillage operations for the establishment of a proper seedbed for the crop to be planted.

If it is available, barnyard or poultry manure should be spread in the waterway, particularly if the topsoil in the waterway is not deep and fertile. If manure is not available, a straw mulch or other organic matter should be worked into the soil with fertilizer and lime as needed. The amounts of these amendments should be determined by soil tests or experience. Ten to twenty tons of manure per acre should be plowed into the soil with fertilizer and lime. After land preparation and seeding, a light coating of manure or straw will help in protecting against erosion, conserve moisture, and aid in germinating the seed.

Dense, sod-forming grasses and legumes, such as those used in lawns are most desirable for waterway protection, but any thick-growing grass is satisfactory if the channel has been designed for its use. In Pennsylvania a desirable mixture is composed of twenty-five pounds of bluegrass, twenty pounds of redtop and two pounds of white clover for each acre. In areas where it is adapted in the southern part of the nation, Bermudagrass is used extensively because it makes a dense sod. In the West, the wheatgrasses are ideal. In the selection of the best plants for waterways, the local conservation officials should be consulted.

Protecting the end of the waterway. The area below the lower end of the shaped waterway should be inspected to determine whether it is adequately protected by grass or trees against gullying, and whether it is of sufficient size and shape to handle the expected runoff. There should be no abrupt fall at the end of, or immediately below, the shaped waterway. There should be no material narrowing of the watercourse unless there is grade enough to maintain the velocity of water leaving the waterway and unless there is also sufficient protection, as mentioned above, to prevent erosion.

Greatly increased water velocities with insufficient protection may cause gullying action to occur, and such gullies are apt to eat back up the waterway and destroy its usefulness. Greatly reduced velocities may cause siltation which can kill the vegetative protection in the spill area and in the waterway, and result in eventual gullying and the loss of production from the grassland so affected.

The most common difficulty at the spill end of a waterway, and the one which requires the most care to assure protection, is the discharge of water into a gully or over a steep bank of a stream where vegetative protection cannot halt the advance of the gully up the waterway. Even though this gully head is some distance below the end of the shaped waterway, the hazard should be considered, and plans made for halting the gully head immediately, or, at least, before it advances to the waterway. Four general methods are used for the protection of this area:

(1) Diversion terrace. If the flow from the waterway is not too large, a diversion terrace may be used to carry the discharged water to a safer disposal area. Sometimes the diversion terrace can carry the water each way from the waterway and spread it on a well-grassed portion of pasture where it will not hit an abrupt overfall or gully when it again enters a natural watercourse. Occasionally water can be carried into the drainage area of a farm pond if the additional water is needed. But a safe spill for the terrace must always be available, for there is no permanent gain in starting a gully at another place.

(2) Sod flume. The head of the threatening gully or the bank over which the water must run may be sloped and planted to a vigorous-growing sod grass. This method is generally effective only on small gullies where the banks are not high, where an effective width can be maintained to the bottom of the watercourse, and where the flow is not large or of long duration.

117

The slope should not be more than 20 per cent, or 5 to 1, and less if possible. For this reason, high banks are seldom sloped, although banks of three to five feet are effectively treated. It is better if the flume enters the gully at right angles, so that an effective width can be maintained. It is obvious that if the flume enters the gully at its head, the width at the bottom will be no greater than the width of the gully. This condition would greatly increase the velocity of the water and endanger the success of the project. Since the safe width of a planned and shaped waterway is determined by the quantity of water to be carried, the slope of the channel, and the effectiveness of the grass cover, it is apparent that a sod flume on a slope steeper than that of the waterway should be wider, or the cover far more effective. The planning engineer will consider these factors in making his recommendations.

The flume is normally protected until the earth work is well settled and the sod well established, usually by a temporary diversion of the water flow. Extreme care should be taken in the planning, shaping, protection, and sodding of a flume.

(3) Overfall structure. This is a concrete or masonry structure designed to let the water fall from the grade of the waterway to the grade of the watercourse below. Construction is most economical when the drop is only a few feet and the quantity of water to be handled is not great. Under such conditions the conservation engineer can plan and stake out the structure, and the farmer can build it at a reasonable cost. Considerable labor is involved in even the smaller structures since trenches must be excavated for wing walls and foundation, and the gully floor must be shaped so that the spill apron may be properly installed. When the quantity of water to be handled is great and must be dropped for several feet, the costs mount rapidly.

There are places, however, where no other type of protection is adequate. A combination of sod flume (2) and overfall structure (3) is employed when the banks are sloped, and concrete is used in place of sod for protection. If properly planned and built, this type of structure is satisfactory.

(4) Drop-inlets and erosion-control dams. An erosion-control dam may be used with or without a drop-inlet spill, although the two are more frequently used together, and for that reason are discussed under the same heading. The drop-inlet must have some type of retaining earth fill to be effective, although the fill may be more on the order of a dyke than a dam. An erosion-control dam may not include a drop-inlet spill if a satisfactory spillway of the type used for an ordinary dam can be provided.

The purpose of the drop-inlet is to let water escape through a tube into a gully without permitting erosion or an extension of the gully. When water falls freely over the banks or head of a gully from a height of several feet, it undermines the soil on the canyon wall, causing it to slough off. If the water is let down through a pipe, enlargement of the gully is halted. The tube must be firmly anchored. It must be large enough so that almost all of the water from the storage basin above the dam or dyke will be forced through the pipe, even during heavy rains. A spillway or diversion terrace must be provided to handle excess water which cannot be forced through the tube.

An erosion-control dam without a drop-inlet tube differs from a dam used to create a farm pond in only two important respects. It would be located as near the head of the gully as possible so that the smallest, rather than the largest, storage basin would be obtained. The spillway would be placed as high as the lip of the overfall, or at approximately that elevation, so that when the storage basin is full of either silt or water, the fall would be eliminated and no bank caving or gully enlargement would result. It is desirable that the basin fill with silt rather than remain for water storage, and this is the reason why a large storage basin is not planned.

It is evident that after the basin is filled with silt the dam and spillway would be no more effective than a diversion terrace. Therefore a diversion terrace should be used in preference to such a dam whenever conditions warrant. In either case, the spillway, or outlet end of the diversion terrace, should be capable of handling all of the flow.

However, the very presence of a gully indicates that the soil is erosible at this point and that an adequate spillway for a dam would be difficult to establish. It is under these conditions that a drop-inlet spillway, properly designed and built into the dam, will take most of the water safely through the dam. In very heavy rains some water may have to escape around the spillway during the period when the rain is falling at its greatest intensity, but when the flow is reduced the outlet tube will again handle the water. If the spillway is damaged during the heavy rain, it can be repaired. The farmer will be warned by the planning engineer that the spillway is relatively unsafe and that some maintenance may be necessary. To make the basin and pipe large enough to handle occasional high-intensity rains would be much more expensive than the type of maintenance required and would be an unnecessary expense under normal conditions.

The erosion-control dam with drop-inlet will be designed by the conservation engineer, who will stake it out, supervise construction, and report quantities to the county Agricultural Stabilization and Conservation Service office when it is to share in the costs.

The engineer will determine the quantity of water to be handled by the structure. He will survey the site of the dam and basin to find the size of the basin in the gully below the elevation of the lip of the gully head, and also to determine how large a basin can be created between this elevation and the elevation of a suitable spillway. From this information he will plan as effective a structure as possible. An example might be helpful.

Cropland Treatment

It has been determined that the engineer will want the pipe inlet to have approximately the elevation of the lip of the overfall, if possible. He will also want this pool to fill up as rapidly as possible after a rain starts. Then he will want a reserve (detention) pool, above the height of the inlet end of the pipe and below the spillway, which will store all additional water long enough to allow it to run through the drop-inlet tube. If these conditions can be met, the structure will work perfectly.

The engineer might find that a severe storm, such as occurs probably only once in ten years, would produce at its highest intensity 435 cubic feet of runoff during a period of fifteen minutes, which would then decrease to a safer rate. He wants to design the structure so that it can safely handle this peak flow. Should he have below the lip of the overfall a basin which would hold one acre-foot of water, he could safely put the inlet end of the pipe at basin height, and this pool would fill in less than two minutes. During the fifteen-minute period of heaviest flow a total of nine acre-feet of water would reach the dam. If it is economically feasible to build the dam high enough to hold eight additional acre-feet of water in the reserve pool, it could absorb the initial shock without depending on any of the water to run through the pipe. Then the problem, in that event, would be to design a pipe large enough to take care of the flow resulting from the rest of the rain, which might be expected to last for several hours.

As an alternative, the flood pool could be built to hold only six acre-feet of water, but if the pipe could be designed to carry two acre-feet of water through the dam in the fifteen-minute critical period, the dam would still function satisfactorily. If the dam could hold only five acre-feet and the pipe could not be designed to carry more than two acre-feet in fifteen minutes, one acre-foot would have to go over the spillway.

It is evident that several variables may make it difficult, or even impossible, to design a structure to work satisfactorily. If the gully is large, deep, and in a flat area, the storage area below the lip of the overfall may be large, while that at a higher elevation is negligible. In this case, an erosion-control dam may not be practical. A drop-inlet pipe installed in a dyke built above the gully head might be the answer. Of course, the lower end of the pipe should extend to the bottom of the gully or be supported by cantilever trusses to discharge the water past the gully banks.

Other practical considerations include the cost of installing dams and pipes large enough to meet the needs. The engineer must consider all of these variables in designing a structure capable of safely moving the water from the field elevation to the bottom of the gully.

Maintenance of the waterway. This includes several do's and several don't's. The negative recommendations concern practices which damage the vegetative cover or alter the size and shape of the planned waterway.

Among the most common errors is the practice of using the waterway as a farm road, which is a result of inadequate planning or the unwillingness of the farmer to leave room at the block ends of his terraces or in other locations for the necessary roads. The farmer will be happier and wiser if he makes provision for the necessary roads when his terrace and waterway system is being installed. Don't drive up and down the waterway regularly. To do so may destroy the grass and cause the gullying that the waterway is designed to avoid.

Similarly, don't drop plows or other implements in the waterway to damage the vegetation or make any kind of mound or pit which will interfere with the smooth flow of the water.

Don't encroach on the waterway by plowing or planting in a manner that makes it narrower each year. Leave the waterway as wide as it was originally, even though it seldom fills to

A *study in contrast.* ABOVE: *Inadequate and unprotected waterway; when these terraces were emptied into an unprotected roadside ditch, it was cut out to a depth of 25 feet and the gullying progressed back into the field up each terrace channel as much as 100 feet.* BELOW: *In use since the country was settled, this native-grass waterway has never broken out.*

ABOVE: *Cutting through a good stand of Indiangrass and big bluestem.*
BELOW: *Plants showing excellent range condition.*

capacity. Remember, it was planned for the large flows which occur at irregular intervals of ten years or more.

For adequate protection, waterways should not be overgrazed or mowed too frequently or too close.

On the positive side, do the things necessary to maintain the proper functioning of the waterway and the structures included in the outlet system. Fertilize and renovate the vegetative cover when necessary, replace sod when necessary, and mow or spray for weed control. If tall plants are used for the vegetative control, mow them, when necessary, to keep them functioning properly.

Control ant hills and exterminate rodents which may damage the waterway or structures. If damage has occurred, it should be repaired. Expensive concrete and masonry structures have been lost because of the failure of land operators to watch for burrowing animals which tunnel around or under the structures. When water begins to flow through such holes and enlarge them, the structure is endangered. The soil should be dug out for the entire length of the tunnels, and then carefully tamped back in place. Cracks or breaks that occur in concrete or masonry structures must also be repaired.

The waterway or water disposal system is as important to the farm as the terraces, fences, or other improvements, and it should be just as carefully maintained.

IV: Grassland Agriculture

AMERICA'S BILLION ACRES of grasslands contain the most versatile and the most indispensable plants in the country's agriculture, but this phase of husbandry is at once the least understood and the poorest managed.

Grass is the cheapest crop that the American farmer can produce, and because of its former abundance, especially in the western half of the nation, it has been the least appreciated. The seven hundred million acres of native grasses west of the Mississippi were ravaged and depleted in less than a half-century after settlement began. The plow and oversized herds of range cattle, sheep, and horses made waste of nature's bounty. Plows ate into millions of acres of land not inherently suited to cultivation, while growing herds were crowded into the diminishing range and pasture areas to gnaw the more productive grasses into the ground and leave the grassland remnants full of invading low-order grasses and weeds.

World War I created a demand for cropland products that lured opportunists into plowing up marginal lands for the few seasons of crops they were able to produce. The drought of the thirties, with the accompanying depression, made it unprofitable to till these marginal lands, and they were left to wash and blow away. Poor grass growth during the dry years, coupled with a continued increase in numbers of livestock, brought range and pasture conditions to their lowest point in history and was partly responsible for the huge dust storms that frequently spread across the country.

The cycle was repeated during and after World War II. There was more breaking out of the sod and more concentration of livestock on the remaining acres to take advantage of high prices and quick profits at the expense of the grass and the land. For more than ten years, livestock raisers put cattle on grasslands with little regard for the ability of the range to stand up under the load. Deficiencies in available food were made up by supplemental feedings, and the grasslands were abused again. The drought of the early fifties caused some reduction in cattle numbers but little improvement in grassland management. Again the poor growth of the grasses brought about a condition in which any but the lightest grazing was too much for the survival of the grasses. Ranges which had made some recovery in the late thirties and early forties were again reduced to a low ebb of productivity.

But during all this time farmers, ranchers, and agricultural leaders were learning that there is no security in such opportunism, that there is no stability in a farming operation based on the abuse of natural resources. They were learning that proper stocking and management of grasslands, whether tame or native, lead to security for the operator, for then his grass reserves can tide him over depressions and droughts. They were also learning better methods of re-establishing depleted croplands and grasslands to grass, and for this purpose researchers developed and introduced better grasses and legumes. During this period the golden era of grassland farming was born. The center of livestock production moved from west to east as farmers established poor lands to permanent grasses and introduced grass rotations into their farming pattern for better lands.

The more humid areas of the nation, where erosion had long

threatened the very existence of agriculture, have made great strides in rebuilding the rural economy with grasses, and they now look forward to a stability never offered by cotton, tobacco, and other row crops. Much work remains to be done in these areas, for there are still millions of acres to be developed into productive grasslands and managed for sustained production.

The more arid, western areas face a great program of reconstruction. True, there are some ranches and some localities where the principles of range management were respected and where the grasses are in good condition and capable of continued production. By and large, however, land operators succumbed to the temptation to make fast profits on high-priced cattle and now find their native grasslands in as serious a state of depletion as they were in the thirties.

These grasslands must be rebuilt. Although small acreages of range may be overseeded, the key to the rebuilding is sound management which will enable the existing grass plants to regain vigor and spread until once again the rangelands are luxuriant and profitable. On millions of acres of poor soils which have been in cultivation, range grasses and tame grasses must be replanted. This is the problem to be faced in rebuilding the basis for sound agriculture in the Western states.

The humid areas of the nation will continue to establish and manage introduced grasses for grazing and for hay. The West will have to rebuild largely on the basis of the native grasses now present, using only such introduced grasses as are adapted to arid conditions. Although methods vary considerably in the two regions, the principles are the same, therefore the development and management of grasslands in the two areas will be discussed together, with important differences in methods pointed out.

1. GRASSLAND DEVELOPMENT PLANNING

Good planning for grassland agriculture affects every acre on a farm or ranch and every farm enterprise. Grassland rotation can be planned for cropland without the addition of livestock to the farm enterprise, but more profitable uses can be made of the forage for grazing, hay, or silage if some type of livestock is kept. Because annual acreage and sometimes total acreages devoted to cropland use are reduced, plans must be made to increase the yields of the remaining acres or reduced income from so-called cash crops must be expected. In other words, the entire farm program should be adjusted to the potentialities of a grassland farming enterprise.

Planning should be based on land capability. First, the poor soil which is limited in its potential should be planted to a permanent grass cover. Better soils that are to remain in cultivation should have a planned rotation which includes grasses and legumes in accordance with their needs for protection and improvement.

Land capabilities, when interpreted by a trained technician with a knowledge of local grass, will indicate the type of grasses best suited for each site and the methods of establishment and management. A high-yielding grass is desirable on all land retired from cultivation, but fertility and moisture factors may limit the choice of pasture plants that will survive and give satisfactory returns. And intensity of use may largely be predetermined by land-capability surveys.

Then, in planning for the type and number of livestock for the farm enterprise, the opportunities for developing a year-round grazing program should be carefully considered, and pasture plants should be chosen to give as long a grazing season as is practical. They may include perennial warm-season plants in one pasture and perennial cool-season plants in another, sup-

CROP	COW-DAYS OF PASTURE PER ACRE						TOTAL
	MAY	JUNE	JULY	AUG.	SEPT.	OCT.	
JUNE GRASS OR BLUEGRASS (good - perm.)	15	30			2	3	50
ALFALFA - BROME (average – 3 yrs.)	15	30	30	30		15	120
2nd YR. SWEET CLOVER (average)	15	30	30	15			90
2nd YR. RED CLOVER-TIMOTHY (average)	15	30	15	15	15		95
JUNE GRASS - WHITE CLOVER (permanent)	15	30	15	15	10	5	90
REED CANARY GRASS (average - 10 yrs.)	20	40	40	40	40	20	200
SUDAN GRASS (average)			30	45	30	10	115
OATS (average)		40	20				60

FIGURE 9. *Michigan pasture calendar.*

plemental pastures for summer use on cropland, and cash-crop small grains for winter grazing, also on regular cropland, or fertility-building and cover crops planned for the conservation crop rotation. Of course, any gaps must be filled in with feed grains, hay, or silage, which should be produced on the farm if possible.

When the plans have been completed, the farmer should know which grasses to use on any acre concerned, and should be sure that the grasses are suited to the land and to his livestock program. He should also know which feed, supplemental pasture, and rotation crops should be used to benefit his cropland and to supplement the grasslands. These plants will not only be fitted to the farmer's land and needs, but at times his farming enterprise will be remolded to fit the needs of the land and its capabilities to produce.

In this planning, the farmer should seek the advice of his

PASTURE PLANTS		WINTER	SPRING	SUMMER	FALL	ACRES PER COW FOR BEST GRAZING SEASON		
		DEC JAN FEB	MAR APR MAY	JUN JUL AUG	SEPT OCT NOV	BOTTOM LAND	NORMAL UPLAND	POOR UPLAND
CULTIVATED PASTURE	WINTER SMALL GRAIN					1 - 2	1½-3	
	VETCH					1 - 2	1½-3	
	MADRID SWEETCLOVER 1st. YEAR					1 - 2	1½-4	
	MADRID SWEETCLOVER 2nd. YEAR					½-1½	1 - 3	
	HUBAM SWEETCLOVER					1 -1½	1½-2	
	SUDANGRASS					1 -1½	1½-2	
	JOHNSONGRASS					1- 1½	1½-3	
CULTIVATED OR OVERSEEDED PASTURE	RESCUEGRASS					3 - 6	4 - 8	
	BUR-CLOVER					4 - 8	6 - 12	
	BLACK MEDIC					4 - 8	6 - 12	
	RYEGRASS					3 - 6	4 - 8	
	DALLISGRASS					OVERSEED IN BERMUDA		
PERMANENT PASTURE	BERMUDAGRASS					2 - 4	4 - 8	
	NATIVE BLUESTEM					3 -10	6 - 20	12-40
	BUFFALOGRASS					6-20	10-30	20-50
	KING RANCH BLUESTEM					3 -10	6 - 20	12-40
	WEEPING LOVEGRASS					3 -10	6 - 20	12-40

BEST GRAZING PERIOD
LESS FAVORABLE GRAZING SEASON
DO NOT GRAZE IF SEED ARE TO BE HARVESTED

FIGURE 10. *Guide to grazing periods for pasture crops in the Dalworth Soil Conservation District.*

conservationist, county agent, vocational agriculture instructor, or other competent local authority. He can learn much from other farmers who are engaged in this amazing transformation to grassland agriculture, but there are many fine details of land capability that will escape his notice unless he secures an expertly drawn land-capability map of his farm, along with the interpretations that only local experts can give.

With this planning behind him, the farmer is ready to begin the establishment of grasses, with or without associated legumes, on land that is retired from cultivation or in rotation on cropland. Although the establishment of perennial grasses and legumes on land to be permanently retired is the principal object of discussion here, the same principles apply in establishing perennial plants for crop rotations.

Preparing the Land

When the land has been cropped, it has generally suffered from one or a combination of the following ills: sheet erosion, gullying, wind erosion, siltation, scouring, fertility depletion, or damage to the structure of the soil. The causes of these troubles should be alleviated or removed as much as possible before planting the vegetation which is expected to occupy the land permanently. The pasture plants themselves will do much to correct adverse conditions, but it is usually necessary, or at least desirable, to make some improvements in the characteristics of the land before planting the grass.

Smoothness. Obstructions should be removed from the field and the land shaped as nearly as possible as nature would have it. Gullies may be sloped in or leveled, when the water which caused the gullying action can be removed temporarily. Old terraces and gully-control dams should be leveled, leaving only enough protection to control erosion during the time required to establish the permanent grasses. On the other hand, gullying and erosion conditions that might create a severe handicap to the establishment of the pasture may be controlled by the construction of a few diversion terraces.

Smoothing the field before planting will give the best distribution of the remaining topsoil, avoid concentrations of water which might become erosion hazards, and allow for better distribution of water over the contemplated pasture so that it will be more available to the grass plants. Even diversion terraces or other temporary earthwork will eventually become a handicap to the established pasture, since they will divert, detain, or remove water which is needed by the grass. Therefore they should be kept to a minimum, and plans should be made for their later removal.

Tilth. Soil is composed of sand, clay, silt, or other inorganic particles, plus organic matter resulting from vegetation which has grown or has been deposited on the land. When the organic matter content is very low, the soil tends to crust, pack, form dense layers, and resist the entrance of water and air. Plants do not grow well in a soil that cannot receive and store water and in which air cannot move—which, in other words, is not aerated. All tillage practices are designed to improve these conditions of the soil—to allow water and air to move into it more freely. When grasses are established in a permanent pasture, tillage operations can no longer be depended on, and organic matter in and on the soil must serve to keep the soil open.

But poor soil conditions exist on most land to be retired to grass, and the tilth of the soil should usually be improved before the planting of grass. This pretreatment is often accomplished by planting fast-growing and deep-rooted legumes, by chiseling or deep tillage, by planting crops which die and leave large amounts of residue in and on the surface, or by a combination of these practices.

Fertility. When fertility is very low and soil structure is poor, a program for soil improvement may require one to four years before the land is ready for permanent vegetation. In one instance, the land is heavily fertilized and seeded to Singletary peas in the fall. In the spring a top dressing of fertilizer is applied, and when full growth is achieved, it is disked into the surface of the soil. The process is repeated until a measure of fertility is restored and enough organic matter is added to the soil to improve the soil structure. Then, in this case, the land is sprig-planted to Bermudagrass and overseeded to Dallisgrass and such clovers as are desired.

Other soils may be seeded directly to the desired pasture plants with subsequent normal applications of fertilizer. When native grasses are used, pretreatment may be given to improve the fertility and tilth, but fertilizers are not added during the planting because most native grasses, being slow starters, would not get much benefit from the fertilizer and annual grasses and weeds would be fed, thus adding to the competition that the good grass must withstand. The fertility in the soil must be sufficient to get the native grasses off to a start, but measures should also be taken to retard competing plants. Then, after the grasses are established, fertilizers may be added.

Seedbed. The land should be clean and well prepared for tame pasture plantings. After pretreatment to increase the fertility level and to add organic matter to the soil, the field should be plowed or chiseled deeply, then worked down to a smooth, firm seedbed. Limestone is added during this process, and fertilizers may also be added at this time or at the time of seeding if suitable equipment is available.

Native grasses may be planted on a clean seedbed if the soil is not subject to severe wind or water erosion and has reasonably good tilth. However, since these grasses will not develop rapidly enough to give good soil protection for a year or two, a trashy seedbed is usually preferred.

A trashy seedbed is one with a great deal of plant residue on the surface of the ground. The residue should consist of dead plants, such as annuals grown the year before. They should not have made seed to volunteer and provide uncontrollable competition for the planted grass, and they should be long-lasting plants which deteriorate into a mulch that will remain on the ground.

A heavy growth of low-order grasses could provide the surface mulch; however, care must be exercised in using such grasses. These grasses may be perennials—or they may be plants whose seeds could sprout and cause competition not easily controlled. A heavy weed growth may make a satisfactory trashy seedbed if regrowth is controlled with a 2-4-D spray. Both of these covers are used when the land is subject to dangerous erosion and it is not advisable to till the ground for the establishment of a more desirable type of cover. In both cases the land should be well disked to tear the perennials from the ground before the seeding is started. If wild grass or weed competition is allowed to return, the growth of the good grasses will be much slower, although usually a satisfactory stand is eventually obtained.

When it is possible to work the land that is to be established to native grasses, it is desirable to take the measures mentioned above for smoothing the land and improving its fertility and tilth. Then an annual crop such as sudangrass or cane is sown. It is mowed high to prevent the formation of seed heads, and unless the hay is badly needed on the farm, it should be allowed to fall to the ground to help form a more effective litter. This thickly seeded crop and the mowing help to prevent the growth of weeds and the development of weed seeds which may form competition after the grasses are seeded the following year. At planting time, this residue is disked, and the grass seeds are broadcast or drilled into the litter.

This type of seedbed is also used for tame pasture grasses and legumes on soil subject to severe wind or water erosion, for plants that are slow starters and for plants that do not require cultivation.

Advantages of the trashy seedbed are many. The litter holds rainfall, increases water absorption, and protects the soil from erosion. It reduces the drying and baking effects of the sun and wind, conserving moisture and aiding the growth of the grass plants. It maintains a more even soil temperature, keeping it twenty degrees or more cooler in the summer. And finally, it can be a start toward the development of a permanent surface mulch, an all-important factor in grassland management.

Land clearing. This includes the removal of brush, vines, trees, or other growth that would hinder land preparation and planting operations or the growth of the grass. Large areas, especially of sandy lands, may be covered with scrub oak or shinnery. Other land, where the operation of farm equipment is impossible and pasture plants have little chance to grow, may be infested with mesquite, sassafras, briers, and similar growth.

Various weed-killer sprays are effective in arresting the growth of this brush, and any remnants of native grasses in these areas will return if the brush is kept under control. If grasses are to be planted, it is usually necessary to remove a part or all of this growth. Heavy equipment, such as root cutters or bulldozers for tearing the larger plants out of the ground, is often used. Smaller brush can be handled with hammermill-like stalk shredders which pulverize the plants and leave the residue on the ground in the form of a beneficial mulch.

After removal of the brush, the land should be prepared as outlined above.

Drainage. When needed, drainage should be established before land preparation gets under way.

Denuded areas. Where the soil and all vegetation have been eroded or otherwise removed special treatment is needed. Such spots often exist in eroded fields which are to be returned to grass, and failure to treat them often results in continued erosion and enlargement of the worthless areas.

Soil may be moved onto these spots if it is readily available in sufficient quantities. If any subsoil remains, it may be worked up and covered with a mulch of any type, and then seeded with the desirable grasses. The mulch should be tied down with soil, woven wire, or brush. If the area is large enough to be significant, it should be protected from fire and grazing, and all vegetation should be encouraged until nature can build back enough soil to support a usable grass population. Such areas, in a lifetime, will probably be valuable only as a wildlife shelter, but should be treated to prevent the spread of damage to adjoining areas of better soil.

Planting

Seed. The farmer should make arrangements to get the seed he will need as far in advance of the planting date as possible. It is cheaper to buy seed in the field at harvest time, but the purchase should be conditioned upon satisfactory results from a seed analysis to be made later, unless the plant is of a type in which there is little variation in quality of seed.

Seed-test results can be compared to a standard by referring to tables such as those found in *The American Grass Book*, where average purity and germination factors for each commonly used type of grass and legume seed are given. The tables can also be used to determine the amount of seed needed, based on the live pure-seed count, to secure the desired number of germinable seeds per square foot.

Seed testing, then, is the basis for determining the quantity of seed. Cheap seed is sometimes expensive if purity and germination factors are low. The price should be based on the percentage of live, pure seed (which is determined by multiplying the purity percentage by the germination percentage, and then dividing by 100), and the farmer's choice should be guided by these same ratios.

Equipment. Planting equipment is usually specially designed to handle the various types of seed commonly planted in the area. Separate boxes may be required to handle two types of seed and spread fertilizer at the same time, and perhaps the equipment should be adjustable to handle widely varying types of seed, from the very trashy seeds, like native bluestems, to the very fine, clean seeds, like lovegrasses. Since planting rates may vary from one-half pound of the very fine seeds to ten pounds of the very fluffy and trashy seeds per acre, the drills must be versatile. But even so, they are seldom well adapted to the farmer's normal requirements for a drill that will plant small grains and legumes on cropland.

As most farmers will have only a limited need for these special drills or planters, it is not practical for each farmer to purchase this equipment for himself. Therefore, the special drills are generally made available by soil conservation districts and occasionally by chambers of commerce or similar organizations. When this type of equipment is to be used, the farmer should notify the handlers of the equipment well in advance so that they may plan to make the drill available to each farmer on schedule. Several farmers who have large acreages to plant may find it desirable to purchase such equipment jointly so that they will be sure of having it when it is needed.

Many drills or cultipackers are equipped with seeding attachments which work satisfactorily for many types of seedings. The manufacturer of one fertilizer spreader offers a seeding attachment to handle fine seeds, while the trashy seeds are spread through the regular fertilizer box. Grain drills have also been adapted to handle many types of grass and legume seed.

When no equipment is available, the farmer can usually do a fair job of broadcasting the seed by hand. Even the seed of the lovegrasses, which are so small that there are one and one-half million seeds to the pound, can be broadcast at the rate of two or three pounds per acre if one part of seed is mixed with ten parts of corn meal, cottonseed meal, or even fine sand.

Airplanes have been used successfully in broadcasting the seed of native grasses where large acreages are involved or where farm machinery cannot operate on the land surface. Some planters who have used this method have calculated that costs are lower than when ordinary planting methods are used. If equipment can be operated on the land, it should be disked after the seeds are spread. If there is a cover on the land that will provide natural lodgment for the seed, successful stands have been obtained without follow-up tillage. Some success has been obtained by spraying the brush "to set it back" and then seeding the land by airplane, with no further treatment other than later sprayings to keep the brush under control. This seeding method is used primarily for native grasses, rather than introduced grasses, since the former are in their natural habitat and can germinate and develop from the surface of the ground.

Most seeding equipment, however, is designed to place the seed in the ground at a depth of about one-half inch. Packer wheels or drag chains should be used to assure coverage of the seed and to firm the soil around the seed.

Planting methods. Grasses are generally drilled in rows eight to twelve inches apart. There are exceptions, however, including those grasses which require cultivation for proper development. These are planted in rows of varying widths, depending on the equipment to be used for cultivation. When the primary purpose of a grass planting is seed production, a single variety of grass is planted in rows and cultivated. When the primary purpose is grazing or hay, mixtures of species are generally planted together. Associated legumes may be planted with the the grasses, either before or after, according to the requirements of each for proper development.

Bermudagrass, for instance, is often grown in association with reseeding crimson clover in the South. The grass may be established from a planting of seed in the spring, or from sprigs and chunks of sod. It is allowed to develop throughout the summer; then in the fall a light working is given the land, and the clover is seeded with the necessary fertilizers. Bermudagrass is a warm-season grass and should be planted at the beginning of its normal growing season. Crimson clover is a cool-season legume and should be planted at the beginning of its growing season, which is fall in the South.

A dallisgrass–white clover association, on the other hand, would normally require the clover to be planted in the fall with the grass overseeded in February or March in the Gulf states, and a little later farther north.

A blue panic grass–sweetclover association in the Southwest would be planted on a well-prepared seedbed from April to June. The grass would be cultivated one to two years until all weeds are thoroughly controlled, and the sweetclover would be overseeded in the fall. Both are warm-season plants, but since sweetclover can survive in the Southwest and South if planted in the fall, this time is chosen because it would be difficult to secure a stand of the legume in the spring when the grass is making a vigorous growth. An alternate method is to plant the seeds in a mixture and cultivate together.

Competitive growth of weeds or annual grasses can be avoided to some extent by late plantings—after the first seed crop has come up and been destroyed by a final working of the ground. This is important in drilled plantings which cannot be cultivated for weed control.

Plantings should be made on the contour. It may be some time before perfect ground cover is obtained, and the contour rows will help to control erosion.

Farmers who use commonly owned planting equipment, such as the drills provided by soil conservation districts, must co-operate with their neighbors so that everyone will have a chance to use the equipment. The failure of farmers to co-operate in this respect has often discouraged district supervisors from trying to make such special equipment available. For example, if it is too dry or too wet for anyone to plant, the farmer may be justified in holding the drill for more favorable moisture conditions, but if others are willing to plant, he should take the drill to the next on the schedule and wait until it is rescheduled to him.

Most grass and legume seeds, especially those requiring special equipment for planting, have varying periods of dormancy and do not require optimum moisture or temperature conditions for planting. Plantings which are "dusted in," or which are made very early, have succeeded quite as well as those which were made under more ideal conditions. If the seeds are properly covered so that they will not wash or blow away, they will remain until moisture and temperature conditions are favorable for their germination. In fact, usually a sizable percentage of the seeds must lie dormant for weeks or months before conditions permit them to germinate. The naked seed, when stripped of its husks and appendages, has a hard coat which protects the seed germ until conditions are right for sprouting. This is true of the seed of most pasture plants. Sand lovegrass, one of the tiniest seeds planted, has lain in the ground a full year before sprouting and coming up to a good stand. Bluestems planted in December will not germinate before April, and have been known to come up for more than a year after planting. Sweetclover seed has been plowed under and remained buried for eight years before it was plowed again to the surface, where it germinated and made a good stand.

Because of this natural ability of the seed to take care of itself, it is possible for district officials to schedule a long planting season for grass and thus make the drills available to many more farmers. The farmer can safely follow the advice of his local group in grass plantings. This does not mean that he can plant any seed at any time and expect a successful stand, but that the risks have been calculated and checked through experience and that when the drill is scheduled to a farmer, he is not being asked to take unnecessary risks.

Exceptions to the general rules concerning grass planting methods will be explained by local specialists, who should always be consulted in connection with all plans for the establishment of grasslands.

Development of the Planting

The farmer has not assured himself of a successful pasture after he has made the necessary land and seedbed preparation and planted the seed, or even after this seed has come up to a good stand. He must now develop the planting. Here there are some things which he should and should not do.

First, he must give the grass time to grow and spread. Few perennial pasture plants will grow off rapidly and produce pasturage as quickly as an annual pasture crop, such as sudangrass or the small grains. And even with these grasses, the farmer knows that the pasture should have several weeks for development before livestock are permitted to graze. With annual plantings, the farmer may turn in his cattle a little early, if necessary, because he does not have a great deal to lose. When the crop has been grazed out, he can work the ground again and plant another crop. But if he has decided to establish a permanent pasture on a field—because of the needs of the land, because of the expense of annual tillage and planting, or because he wants a type of pasture not available from annual supplementary pasture plantings—the farmer has a great deal to lose if he does not let the grass develop into a productive pasture.

In the latter case, he should keep livestock out while the grass is young and not fully developed. This period varies from a few weeks to one to three years. In the case of some of the introduced grasses, such as tall oatgrass, blue panic, and others which develop rapidly, it may be only a matter of weeks, but in the case of most native grasses it may require as long as three years. In the past farmers were slow to accept native grasses for pasture plantings because after a full season's growth the plants were so small and spindly, if they could be found at all, that they seemed to offer little promise of ever developing into productive pasture. As a result many good plantings were plowed up.

140

During the weeks or the year or more that the grasses are in their infancy, they are almost helpless against grazing animals, insects, and competing plants. If protected, however, they will develop large root systems which spread out to find plant foods and go deep to get moisture during dry seasons. Too early grazing will result in many plants being pulled up or damaged and in insufficient development of the root system. The small returns from early grazing are not sufficient compensation for the total loss of a stand of grass or, at least, a greatly reduced yield throughout the years.

Then, after this very early stage when the plants are struggling for survival, there comes a period when limited grazing is possible, but some protection must be continued if maximum growth and development are to be achieved. In the case of many introduced grasses, this second stage occurs in the first month or two of the second growing season. For most native grasses, this stage occurs in the second to fourth years, when limited grazing is possible in the winter or for short periods during the growing season. In either type of pasture planting, the grass should be allowed to make seed and most of its topgrowth left for the entire growing season. The green topgrowth manufactures the foods necessary for plant growth and the development of the root systems. The seed is often needed for volunteer plants to improve the stand. The part of the plant which dies after the growing season falls to the ground to start the development of a mulch or litter. This organic ground cover is almost as important in adequate pasture development as the usable growth above the ground, for it traps the falling raindrops and increases the penetration of moisture into the soil, reduces soil temperature, encourages the growth of earthworms, and facilitates the spread of bacteria, fungi, and other organisms which live in the soil and improve it.

For proper pasture development, the farmer should allow time for adequate development and spread of topgrowth and root systems, and for the decay and decomposition of the organic litter which will form on the surface of the ground when a large amount of topgrowth is left at the end of the growing season. After the planted pasture has passed through these two stages, the farmer may give it full use, observing, of course, the principles of management discussed in the following section.

Avoiding competitive growth. If the farmer wants a pasture of low-order grasses, weeds, or brush, he should allow them to come in naturally, for nature will establish some type of cover on bare land when sufficient soil and fertility are available. Actually, that is exactly what nature tries to do when the soil is disturbed in order to plant grass, but the farmer must keep the wild growth in check or it will rob the young grass plants of moisture, plant food, and sun.

Weed and brush control is usually accomplished by mowing or spraying with 2-4-D spray. Mowing should be done early to prevent the development of invading plants, unless it will damage the tall grasses excessively. If the pasture plants have not been mowed early in the growing season and as a result the weeds have made a large growth which shades the young grasses, mowing should be postponed when the weather turns dry and hot. To remove the weed cover at this time could result in damage to the grass seedlings. Weeds should always be cut before the growth becomes heavy enough to form a thick mat over the grass.

A weed spray, if not made too strong, will kill the weeds without damaging the grass, but it cannot be used if legumes are planted in the mixture. Spraying is particularly valuable when the weed competition is of the low-growing type which cannot be controlled by mowing. Of course, 2-4-D solutions are not effective on wild grass, but spraying for weed control has proved more effective than mowing. Spraying kills the weeds, while mowing leaves stumps that may send out new shoots and continue to grow. Some weeds cannot be controlled by mowing, but are effectively controlled with a spray. Neither spraying nor mowing, however, has much effect on most of the wild grasses that grow voluntarily in planted pastures.

Cultivation. Certain grasses require cultivation for proper development, and all plantings do better with some cultivation. Both those grasses requiring cultivation and those grown primarily for seed production are usually planted in rows sufficiently far apart to permit the use of available tillage equipment. A row-crop farmer may plant the grasses in rows of the same width as those of his other crops, or he may use rows of half the width and adjust his cultivators accordingly. Chisel points will keep the surface soil mulched and help to conserve moisture. Sweeps will do the same, and will also help to control weed and grass growth in the middles. Even a harrow, with teeth set far back, can be dragged over sown plantings after the grass has developed enough root system to keep it from being pulled out of the ground.

Fertility. The fertility level of the soil must be maintained according to plan. To fertilize most effectively, a plan should be developed on the basis of soil tests and correlated with the needs of the pasture plants. Most tame pastures in the higher rainfall belts require regular applications of fertilizer. Nitrogen is generally used to improve the growth and quality of the grass and phosphate for the legumes. A high fertility level will help most pasture plants maintain a good growth and crowd out less desirable plants, while on poor soils only low-order plants may survive and the better grasses and legumes may die.

Planting and Care of Bermudagrass

The methods of land shaping and seedbed preparation listed above are applicable to Bermudagrass plantings, but the methods of planting and care may differ. Bermudagrass may be established by sodding or seeding. In areas of high rainfall and mild winters the grass may be established by seeding. In the Southwest, seed is produced under irrigation. Farther north, Bermudagrass seedings are sometimes killed during the first winter after planting because they cannot develop root systems sufficiently deep and extensive to withstand the cold. In this area plantings can often be saved by bedding the land with a turning plow in the fall, thus covering much of the grass with additional soil for protection from the cold. In the spring the beds are again leveled, and by the second winter the root systems are usually well enough developed to survive the cold. In this case, the grasses and legumes which are to be associated with the Bermudagrass are not planted until after the land is leveled during the second spring or in the following fall.

Most Bermudagrass is planted in the form of sprigs or underground runners. This type of planting usually makes better growth and survives the winters about as well as established stands.

The planting material is harvested in many ways. An old stand of the grass may be spaded or plowed up and the dirt removed by beating or shaking. Where a considerable quantity of roots is needed, it is wise either to use special harvesting equipment or to buy roots from a commercial source.

For machine harvesting, a well-developed stand should be located on sandy land or mixed soil. Before growth starts in the spring, all topgrowth and weeds should be burned off. The harvester equips himself with a chisel type field cultivator or a spring-tooth harrow with extra-strong teeth and a rake of some sort—preferably a side-delivery rake. The land *should not be plowed.* The operator pulls the toothed implement across the plot to be harvested until he has covered it in one direction. Then he turns and chisels crosswise to the first operation. He continues the process until the soil is thoroughly loosened four to six inches deep and many roots and runners have been torn

144

loose from the sod. Then he rakes the land to bunch the roots and runners, which are subsequently loaded and hauled to the planting field. The cross chiseling and raking is continued until the yield of planting material appreciably decreases, and then the harvester moves to a new area. The plots should be kept small. An area one hundred feet square will usually yield several truckloads of planting material. The best material comes with the third or fourth working.

The roots and sprigs should be collected, hauled, and planted immediately. A few minutes' exposure to the hot sun and drying wind may kill the roots unless they are well filled with sap. If there is to be a delay between harvesting and planting, the roots should be covered with soil or a tarpaulin. If they are to to be left overnight, they should also be wet down, if possible.

Furrows may be opened and the roots and sprigs dropped by hand immediately behind the furrow opener and covered at once for moisture conservation. The land should be packed— the tighter the better.

Several devices have been improvised to lessen the labor required in dropping the roots and to make the operation more efficient. Now available in many districts is an automatic planter, which, pulled behind an ordinary farm tractor, opens a furrow, drops fertilizer and roots at predetermined rates, closes the furrow, and packs the soil in one operation. One man so equipped can plant three to five acres a day if he is kept supplied with roots. This machine, developed by the Soil Conservation Service, is now available on the market.

A good manure spreader, set on a notch filed between "Off" and "1," does a fair job of spreading Bermudagrass roots, but it is difficult to cover the material properly with plows or disks, and much of the planting material is left on the surface to die.

The precaution against permitting cattle on new grass plantings is not applicable in the case of sprig-planted Bermudagrass. The cattle cannot get enough of the low-growing grass to damage it, and even their grazing seems to flatten the grass and facilitate the spread of runners. Trampling seems to help this type of Bermudagrass planting, and cattle help to remove a good deal of the competition from other grasses and weeds. This does not apply to seeded Bermudagrass plantings or those overseeded to other grasses and legumes.

Bermudagrass is a cultivated crop. It becomes root-bound after a few years and must be loosened up. Plowing or other tillage at any stage will not damage the stand if it is done at the beginning of the growing season when there is adequate moisture to start the growth again. For that reason the farmer should not hesitate to work the sod in preparing an adequate seedbed for overseeding other grasses and legumes.

The recommendations made earlier for the control of competing vegetation and the maintenance of fertility in newly established grasslands likewise apply to Bermudagrass. Since shade is particularly damaging to Bermudagrass, tall weed or shrub growth should be checked.

Cost of Permanent Grassland Plantings

It may appear that more time and money are required for the establishment of permanent grasslands than for annual pasture crops. This is frequently true, and for several reasons.

First, the land planted to grass is likely to be eroded and depleted and thus requires more effort to develop a satisfactory level for the production of any crop. In some areas of the South, much of the land that is now worthless can be developed into productive permanent pastures capable of supporting one animal per acre almost yearlong, and farmers have proved that it pays to establish this land in permanent pasture, although the cost may run from $25 to $75 an acre for materials and labor.

Good land, of course, may require no more shaping or preparation than that normally expended on making a crop. The care will amount to little more—and often less—than the cultivation of a regular crop. But even if the cost of establishing the permanent grass is greater than that of an annual crop, the long-term cost will be less, for once grass is established the upkeep will be very low. The farmer invests heavily in establishing the crop, but saves thereafter.

2. MANAGEMENT OF GRASSLANDS

Basis of Management

The goal of grassland management is to maintain the highest possible production of the plants which will provide the most grazing, hay, or silage. Basic in all types of grassland management are the principles of proper use and protection and an adequate supply of plant food elements and water. These principles are important in all grassland management, although the methods used in their application vary widely according to the type of grassland, the climate, and the soils on which the grasses are grown. When the farm or ranch operator understands these principles, he is better able to judge the value of methods recommended to him, or he may devise methods which better fit his own needs.

Proper use is the most important principle of grassland management, and is usually the most difficult for the farmer to accept. Historically, the failure to apply proper stocking rates has been the principal cause of the loss of productivity of grasslands. Overgrazing has ravaged the great natural grasslands of the Western states and lowered their potential to a fraction of what it should be. The benefits of high-producing grasses and legumes are often reduced to a minimum by the practice of taking too much of the growth and leaving too little for protection and maintenance of the sward.

"Take half and leave half" is a catchy phrase that expresses the principle of proper use for permanent grasslands. The half that is taken by grazing or mowing is the marketable product of the range or the pasture. If more is consistently taken, the more profitable pasture plants will be reduced in vigor and numbers and will be able to produce less and less abundantly, until finally the pasture or range will be filled with low-order plants. Moreover, profits will be greatly reduced, too.

To understand this principle, the operator must clearly understand one thing: The green growth above the ground is the manufacturing plant which converts raw elements into a form which is usable by the plant in its growth, development, and maintenance. This wonderful process, called photosynthesis, occurs in the leaves or blades when sunlight acts on the green coloring matter, called chlorophyll, in the presence of raw plant food elements and water obtained from the soil and the air.

If the green growth is removed by grazing or mowing, the process stops. Then the plant calls on the reserves stored in the roots to start growth again. If the topgrowth is removed as fast as it is formed, the plant continues to draw on the foods stored in the root system until this reserve is exhausted. Then the plant dies.

Knowledge of this principle aids in the control of bindweed, Johnsongrass, and other vegetative pests on cropland. Sweeps are used to cut off the plant above ground, and for seven or eight days thereafter a drain is placed on the root system. When the plant begins to manufacture its own food in sufficient quantity to maintain its growth and replace food reserves in the roots, the farmer who wants to control it will cut it off at ground level again. He continues the cutting at regular intervals through the growing season. The roots shrivel and the lower parts die. Finally the weed plant is killed or is so reduced in vigor that the farmer can make use of the land again.

The farmer or rancher unintentionally does the same thing to his valuable pasture plants when he overgrazes or mows too heavily. He may not do it so quickly, and he may do it to only the best plants in his pasture mixture. Or he may allow enough growth each year to maintain all plants, but in a greatly reduced state of productivity. And when the better plants are not vigorous and strong, less desirable plants can invade the field and multiply. In any event, overgrazing costs him dollars.

There are also positive values in this half of the forage left on the ground each year. These advantages accrue to the three important parts of a good pasture or range, the living ground cover, the dead vegetative residue, and the root system.

The root system will be deep and extensive when there is enough green growth above the ground to maintain it and keep it from drawing too heavily on its reserves. With an adequate root system, the plant is not restricted in its search for plant food elements and will go deep for moisture. When dry seasons come and available moisture is deep, the strong plant will continue to produce pasturage since it can tap this supply. But if the plant has been overused for a period of time, its shallower and poorer root system will become dormant if it cannot reach moisture. Growth will stop, and the farmer will find that he is short of pasture when he needs it most.

The dead vegetative residue or mulch which forms on the ground beneath the living plants in a well-developed pasture is quite as valuable to the grassland as the root system or the topgrowth, although none of it may be used for forage. This mulch helps to protect the soil from erosion and catches the falling raindrops and holds them to increase the insoak, letting the surplus water trickle off slowly without causing erosion. The mulch also keeps soil temperatures more normal. Tests have shown that bare soil under a burning summer sun may reach a temperature of 135 degrees when the air temperature is 95 degrees. But under a good pasture mulch, the soil temperature may remain as low as 80 degrees. The more favorable soil temperature results in greatly improved grass growth. In

TALLAHATCHIE RIVER BASIN, MISSISSIPPI		CONCHO RIVER BASIN, TEXAS		
PINE FOREST, BARE			RANGE IN GOOD CONDITION	RANGE IN POOR CONDITION
0.38	0.18			
.11	.19	ABILENE SILTY CLAY LOAM	0.22 / .57 / .53 / 1.02	0.10 / .13 / .09
.56	.13			
.06	.10			
.85		REAGAN SILTY CLAY LOAM	2.64 / 2.09 / 1.20	.09 / .13 / .25 / .21
.53	.10			
.17	.11			
.15	.17			
.32	.14	MERETA CLAY LOAM	0.29 / 1.81 / 1.36	.15 / .16 / .15
TOTAL 3.13	1.12	TOTAL 11.73		1.46
AVERAGE .35 INCHES	.14 INCHES	AVERAGE 1.17 INCHES		.15INCHES

FIGURE 11. *Inches of rainfall penetration per hour.*

the winter the mulch insulation keeps soil temperatures higher and reduces damage from frost. Of course, a good mulch protects soil moisture against evaporation by drying winds and the sun. Another significant value of the mulch is that temperature and moisture control improve the activity of microorganisms, such a bacteria, and the larger forms of soil life, such as earthworms, which aid plant growth in many ways. For example, certain bacteria aid legumes in taking nitrogen from the air and fixing it in the soil for use by other plants, thus increasing their growth, palatability, and protein content. Some nitrogen is created by bacterial action even though there are no legumes present in the grassland. Earthworms and other elements of the "soil life" improve the structure and permeability of the soil and aid in making plant foods available. The mulch, or litter, is always considered to be an important part of the grassland by grass specialists who recommend that a conscious effort be made to develop and improve it, and to protect it from damage by fire. The litter, of course, is maintained by the unused portion of the plant growth.

The topgrowth in the pasture or range may include a large percentage of weeds and low-order plants which the livestock will not relish. It is not enough to count this growth as part of the half which is to be left. Actually, one-half of the principal forage plants should be left when grazing animals are removed from the pasture. To determine when one-half has been taken, the farmer or rancher must learn to recognize the best plants, know how much each produces when not used, and develop a standard for gauging how much use each can stand. He may follow the example of grass technicians and make weight measurements until he can readily recognize the amount of use. It is better to clip and weigh a plant which has reached full growth and compare its weight with that of a clipping from a plant in his own pasture than to guess and make a mistake which will result in reduced productivity in the future.

This useful but unused portion of the grassland, aside from being the source of the material which makes the valuable mulch, is important for other reasons. It catches snow and rain and adds to the total moisture trapped on the field, it serves as an anchor for the residue lying on the surface of the soil, it prevents the winds from sweeping the ground surface and drying or damaging the soil, and, finally, it may be used in an emergency when the stockman is short of feed. In this last sense, it is a reserve feed supply which may occasionally be used without permanent damage to the pasture. The farmer or rancher should not depend on this reserve and should not use it any more than is absolutely necessary, for some temporary damage will always occur. If the reserve is used before the end of the growing season, there will be less food reserves stored in the root system—reserves needed to get the plants off to a good start the next growing season, to make new buds or to otherwise improve the stand or growth of the grass. Using the reserves reduces or eliminates seed production which may be an important factor in the maintenance of the stand. The taking of this grass reserve at any time reduces the ability of the grassland to trap and hold moisture and resist erosion. Grassland that is overused one season should receive compensation the next season by reduced use to allow for the recovery of the root system, the topgrowth, and the ground litter.

Grazing control is a means of protecting the grassland from its natural enemy, the grazing animal. In like manner, mowing, which can also be destructive, must be limited to keep from damaging the stand. There are other protective measures which must be taken, when needed, against other enemies. Weeds, brush, and other invading plants must be kept under control. When properly used and maintained, native grasses and some types of introduced plants are able to resist the encroachment of these invaders. When the planted grasses are temporarily overused, the invaders get a start, but a rest will usually permit the better plants to regain strength and control again. Some assistance from the farmer, in the way of mowing or spraying, will retard or destroy the undesirable plants, releasing plant food, moisture, and room for the return of the stronger and more desirable ones. In some types of grasslands, the undesirable plants are the stronger and must be kept in check to permit adequate growth of the preferred pasture plants.

Measures may be needed to control other enemies, such as insects (the grasshopper is often very harmful) and burrowing animals.

Plant food elements, if not naturally available in the soil in sufficient quantities, or if not made available (as in the case of nitrogen) by legumes or organisms in the soil, should be supplied. In general, nitrogen is applied to benefit the vegetative growth of the grass plants or to assist in seed production, phosphates are added to encourage the growth of legumes and improve the quality of the forage, and other plant foods are added to offset deficiencies and improve both the quality of the forage and the opportunities for survival of certain plants.

Limestone is used to neutralize acid soils, to permit the growth
of legumes, and to make an improvement in the forage, which
may be reflected in the health of the grazing animals.

Minerals should be added according to the needs of the soil,
as determined by soil analyses, and correlated with the needs
of certain plants. In certain areas, where exhaustive soil testing has established specific soil deficiencies or experience has
shown the value of established amounts of fertilizers and limestone on the types of pastures, applications may be made without testing of the soil in individual pastures. Where these needs
have not been definitely established, soil testing should always
precede the applications on each field.

In all areas there is much to be learned concerning the proper
use of pasture plants and the methods for encouraging desirable
plants, discouraging the undesirables, and protecting grazing
lands from their enemies. Therefore the greatest source of
knowledge of management of pastures and ranges is to be
found in working with Soil Conservation Service and Forestry
Service employees, county agents, vocational agriculture teachers and other leaders, and neighbors—in exchanging information and experiences concerning the still developing science of
grassland agriculture.

Managing Native Pastures and Ranges

Native grasses and grasslands vary from the true prairies and
tall grasses to the mixed prairies of both tall and short grasses
to the short grass and brush country.

Beginning at the western edge of the timber country, from
eastern Texas through the Dakotas, bluestems, Indiangrass,
and switchgrass, and small amounts of other tall grasses pre-
dominate. Farther west is found the middle and short grasses,
little bluestem, blue grama, buffalograss, sideoats grama, curly
mesquite, and sand lovegrass. To the north and west are the

wheatgrasses, the wildryes, and some of the bluegrasses. Everywhere there are many grasses of lesser importance which help to make up the pasture population and which have been established or have invaded lands used for grazing.

With the wide variation in types of plants and the mixtures in which they are found, with variations in the productivity of the soils on which they are grown and the climatic factors which affect their production, there are many pasture or range conditions which must be understood before proper treatments can be recommended. Furthermore, some grasslands have been relatively well used and now produce near their maximum potential, while others have been subjected to various degrees of abuse or misuse and their productivity lowered until some are almost worthless. This complicates the problems of planning for sustained or increased production or for rebuilding the variations of site, plant population, and damage through intensity of use, and within a state hundreds of these combinations will exist.

But guides and standards of management must be established for the benefit of farmers and ranchers who want to maintain and improve this important natural asset. On a local basis the problem is attacked in this manner.

Classifying the ranges. Within each soil conservation district, the climate is approximately the same, so there remain two principal variables, the soil type and the damage, or lack of it, which has resulted from previous use or misuse.

Each soil type originally produced the same type of plants and required a certain number of acres to carry an animal through the grazing season. Bottom lands produced more vigorous plants, made more forage, and required less acres to furnish food for a cow than ordinary uplands, steep slopes, broken lands, shale hills, or any other type of site found in the area. This was true for the original state of the land, or the *climax* condition—before man caused the grass to be damaged.

For each soil type in a certain area, the original conditions are determined as accurately as possible. One area, of specific soil type and location, is called a *range site*. The treatment for one range site cannot be the same as that for another range site. Since any two range sites differed in their ability to produce, the climax plants of one range site were inferior or superior in quality and quantity to the plants of another site.

The next important variable to be considered is previous use. One pasture may have been lightly used and still maintain its original population of plants, and is therefore about as productive as it ever was. Another pasture, on the same type of soil or range site, may have been so misused that most of its climax plants have disappeared and have been replaced by a combination of low-order plants of varying values. If the land was badly abused, only bare ground may remain. Between these extremes are many *range conditions* for each range site.

Range condition is generally determined by comparing the present plant population with that of the original or climax plant population, regardless of whether the range is now over-grazed. If the better plants are there, they will come back and give the production indicated by the range condition classification, even though the pasture is temporarily under too heavy use. The range condition, then, is the potential of the range site, as determined by the difference betwen the climax and present plant population. Rest and good management may be required to offset temporary overuse and bring production up to the level indicated by the range site and condition classification. Each site falls into one of the general classifications of range condition. These classifications are:

Excellent—if 75 per cent or more of the plants are climax plants.

Good—if 50 to 75 per cent of the plants are climax plants.

Fair—if 25 to 50 per cent of the plants are climax
plants.
Poor—if less than 25 per cent of the plants are climax
plants.

There is one qualification to the method of classification. If
the climax vegetation contained plants that are practically
worthless for grazing, they are not considered in the count.
If lower-order grasses were mixed with high-producing grasses in
the climax plant population, no higher percentage can be
counted than was in the original mixture. In one district, for
example, heavy upland soil originally contained 15 per cent
blue grama, 5 per cent hairy grama, 10 per cent buffalograss,
and the balance was composed of the higher producing bluestems, Indiangrass, and switchgrass. Now these pastures contain almost 100 per cent blue grama, hairy grama, and buffalograss. Although the grasses are making a good sod, the pasture
cannot be considered to have more than 30 per cent of the
climax vegetation, since 70 per cent of the original plants are
gone and the remainder are not as productive as the taller
grasses that were once present. The classification, therefore,
is "fair."

The various range sites within each soil conservation district
are identified, and guides are set up for determining range conditions. With this information, each acre of native grassland
can be classified, and each variation within a pasture can be
ascertained.

Using the range classification. Classification is the scientific
method of determining productivity and planning treatments
needed to maintain or improve the productivity.

Since proper use is the key to range management, stocking
rates are determined for each variation in site and condition.
In one district, six general sites are recognized: (1) bottom
land, (2) deep sand, (3) heavy upland, (4) medium-textured

upland, (5) red shale hills, and (6) gyp soils. The safe stocking rate, expressed in acres required to furnish grazing for one cow for an entire year, is listed in Table IV, which is a guide for technicians working with ranchers in the area.

TABLE IV
The Safe Stocking Rate, Expressed in Acres Required
to Furnish Grazing for One Cow for One Year

Condition	Site 1 Acres	Site 2 Acres	Site 3 Acres	Site 4 Acres	Site 5 Acres	Site 6 Acres
Excellent	11–12	14–16	14–16	14–16	20–24	24–30
Good	14–16	18–24	18–22	18–22	30–35	35–40
Fair	20–24	35–40	24–30	24–30	40–50	45–60
Poor	30–40	45–60	35–50	35–50	60+	70+

Site 1: bottom land; Site 2: deep sand; Site 3: heavy upland; Site 4: Medium-textured upland; Site 5: red shale hills; Site 6: gyp soils.

Note that as each site on this table is down-graded from excellent to poor the number of acres required to maintain one mature animal yearlong increases rapidly. Note also that some sites deteriorate more rapidly than others and that there is some spread in the stocking rates, especially in the categories below "good." When site 2, for instance, has just a little over 50 per cent of the original vegetation, 18 acres are required for each animal. If site 2 has just under 75 per cent of the climax plants, 24 acres are needed. Or the presence of certain other valuable grazing plants might indicate a stocking rate of one animal for 17 acres, the number between the ranges of "good" and "excellent."

Another important factor in determining stocking rates within in the prescribed range for the site and condition is rainfall. If rain does not fall during the growing season or if the subsoil moisture at the beginning of the season is below normal, grass production will be lowered and a lower stocking rate must be used.

Because of yearly variations in rainfall, many stockmen are tempted to discard a planned system of grazing management. When there is adequate moisture they feel that they have not used all of the forage which might have been taken without damaging the grass. In dry years, however, even the lower stocking rates may not prevent the range from becoming denuded. The farmer or rancher must learn to calculate and adjust to variables. If he consistently follows a planned program, he will find that the reserve forage, the increased vigor in the plants, and the deeper root systems developed in favorable years will tide him over for a while when drought comes. This is insurance against dry years—as good as silage in the silo or corn in the crib.

In a series of dry years, when the ground litter begins to disappear, the farmer or rancher is warned to reduce the grazing rates still further, until the rains come and the grass can again produce a surplus and re-establish good ground cover.

Small native pastures present different problems in management, and methods often vary from those used on large ranges. The principles of maintaining adequate growth, vigor, and ground litter are the same. Site for site and condition for condition, the stocking rates are the same. The per-acre loss from overuse is just the same on a 20-acre native grass pasture as on a 1,000-acre range. A certain site, with the grass in good condition, may be capable of producing a profit of $10 an acre. On the 1,000-acre ranch the total would be $10,000, while on the 20-acre pasture it would be only $200. When overused to the extent that the grass is down-graded to "fair" or "poor," either plot may be capable of producing only $5 in profits per acre each year. This loss is serious to the rancher, and even the smaller farmer does not want to throw away an income of $100 a year. That is not good management. Of course, erosion will occur and the grassland will become less and less productive. Important as this aspect of soil conservation is, the most important thing to the farmer is income.

Consider the farmer who wants to carry ten animals on a small pasture. His pasture could provide year-round grazing for two animals. Certainly he expects to make up the feed deficiency with supplementary pasture, grain, or hay. The animals are kept on the small pasture all year so that the extra feed will cost as little as possible. In a year or two the pasture will not produce enough for more than one animal, so the feed bill is increased. Later the pasture will produce even less, and, in addition, the farmer will find a serious and costly erosion problem on his hands. If he has a farm pond in the pasture, it will begin silting up, and this expensive structure may be lost. There is no bright side to this type of management.

The wise farmer, however, keeps his cattle on the small pasture only long enough to get his share of the grass yield, leaving the part necessary to maintain the grass. Then he puts his livestock on supplementary pastures or in the feed lot. He continues to get his $200 a year return from the pasture instead of perhaps $250 the first year, $150 the second, and eventually $50 or less per year. He can graze the pasture during a short season when the grass will produce best for his animals and actually increase the per-acre profit if he will then give the grass the rest of the season to produce for the next year.

All this still adds up to the maxim: Take about half of the year's growth and leave about half for the maintenance of the grassland. Ranges that are now depleted should be grazed so that the grass can restore itself. When pastures are in normal production, there is no substitute for proper grazing control, whether they be large or small. There are, however, a few methods of grazing control which are worthy of special mention.

Seasonal grazing is perhaps most advantageous to the farmer

or rancher. Every plant has its season of greatest palatability and food value. Little bluestem, for example, will generally produce best from about May 1 to July 15. Usually it has not made enough growth before May, and in midsummer it loses much of its protein content and growth has slowed down. April grazing will reduce the amount available for the rest of the season, since the plant will have less chance to grow vigorously if it is continuously grazed off while it is trying to get a start. In August, the plant will not furnish much of nutritional value, although there is plenty of bluestem forage available. This is not a fault of this plant, but a limitation characteristic of many grasses.

With *seasonal grazing* a range that is predominantly little bluestem can be stocked more heavily for two to three months and yield more profits; but the farmer must use other feed for the balance of the year and must remove the livestock from the range so that the grass will have the rest of the year to recuperate. If the pasture has been grazed heavily, he should not let the animals continue to run on the grass for roughage even with supplemental feeding.

If the grassland is pretty well divided between bluestem and sideoats grama, which has a later season of palatability, the farmer may leave livestock on the range for a longer season, provided his stocking rate is lower than in the case cited above. When the bluestem is most palatable, cattle will graze it first since it is larger and more easily available. When the bluestem becomes less palatable, the animals will begin to reject it and search for the grama plants. Like the quills on a porcupine, this reduction in palatability is nature's way of protecting its own. The stockman is cautioned, however, that heavy stocking will upset this seemingly ideal arrangement. The grama plants are also palatable while the bluestem is good, and if the taller grass is grazed down, the shorter grass will also suffer. If heavily grazed early in the season, the grama will not provide sufficient pasturage after the bluestem loses some of its quality.

Other plants found in native pastures have different seasons of use. The stockman should learn these plants of his own range. Seasonal use of pasture plants will lead him into providing other permanent pastures or supplementary pastures for other seasons of the year, as well as to take advantage of the differences in the plant populations of his grassland. For example, the stockman may have an area that is heavily covered with cool-season grasses. This is not a natural condition of the grassland since overgrazing, siltation, or some such destructive force reduced the climax vegetation and allowed the "winter annuals" to invade the site. However, this type of grass may provide good grazing from March to June, depending on the size of the area, the number of livestock, and weather conditions. If he fences this area separately, he may use it during this season as profitably as any other part of his grassland. Heavy grazing is usually not discouraged on winter annuals, but if the pasture is to be maintained, they must be allowed to make seed. This type of pasture should be fenced separately from the better native grasses to protect the latter when they begin their growth.

Rotation grazing may be based on the principles of seasonal grazing, but is not to be limited to them. When seasonal pastures can be provided for the entire year, the farmer is assured of the most economical feed available. When introduced grasses can be established to supplement the native range, this ideal condition may be approached.

In much of the range area, all of the grassland is of about the same composition, and thus one part of the pasture will seldom have a seasonal advantage over another part. But the farmer must depend on this grassland for some grazing throughout the entire year. And he must not overgraze certain plants,

such as the bluestems, while less desirable plants are not well used and are thus allowed to increase. Less desirable plants, if permitted to increase in this fashion, tend to crowd out the better plants and replace them with those of less value. Also, the stockman must not permit one area to be overused while another is underused.

To prevent such a situation, he provides cross-fences to divide the large range into smaller units, and within each unit he changes water, salting, and supplemental feeding areas as often as necessary to prevent overuse and trampling of the grass in one spot and to entice the livestock to other spots which are being neglected.

In adopting a rotational grazing program, the stockman will schedule the time when each area is to be grazed. One rancher in Texas, who divided his range into four units, found that one unit was in much poorer condition than the others because of overuse, and he scheduled it for two years of complete rest. He grazed the best unit, Pasture Number 1, for the first six months of the year, Pasture Number 2 for the second six months, Pasture Number 3 for the first six months of the second year, and Pasture Number 1 again for the second six months. Then, Pasture Number 4, which was originally the poorest pasture, entered the picture and was scheduled for grazing the first six months of the third year. Pasture Number 4 had made a satisfactory recovery, and each pasture subsequently supported an equal portion of the rotation schedule. Another rancher made three divisions of his range and used the poorest pasture only during the four winter months for several years until it made full recovery. He alternated the grazing seasons between the other two pastures.

One of the simplest, and perhaps the most effective, rotation plans was inaugurated by a rancher in the Panhandle of Oklahoma. Four divisions of his range were about equal in productivity. He rotated grazing over them in periods of four months each. Thus each pasture had a complete rest of twelve months between use, and there was a lapse of two years between the times that one pasture would be grazed during the same season. That is, Pasture Number 3 was grazed during the fall grazing season of the first year, but would not again be grazed during the fall until the third year. This type of rotation gives each pasture rest during its growing season and its seeding season in two of every three years. It averages dry and wet years together to provide grass for each year more satisfactorily than most systems of continuous yearlong grazing.

In the one-pasture system, in dry years, when little grass is produced, all of the forage is taken. None is left for winter use, none can make seed, no litter is maintained, no strength is stored in the roots for later production, and the better, more palatable grasses are greatly abused. Regardless of weather conditions the next year, the grass gets off to a slow start because of the reduced moisture and plant food reserves. It cannot recuperate because it is again in use. It will have a lower carrying capacity, and the stocking rate should be but seldom is reduced. Perhaps the greatest damage occurs to the more palatable, higher-producing grasses, since in a near barren grassland they will be sought out by grazing animals.

In the rotation system, on the other hand, one pasture may be overused in the course of a dry season. This is a warning to the rancher that he should then provide supplemental feeding—perhaps put his cattle in a feedlot—since his livestock have already harvested their share of forage production for the period. It is not a notice that he should abandon his rotation system and move his cattle to the next pasture ahead of the grazing schedule, for to do so would jeopardize the future production potential of both pastures and certainly reduce the pasture reserves that he will need the next fall, winter, and spring. Any temporary alteration of the rotation schedule must be made with full knowledge of the dangers involved, and with specific plans for providing greater amounts of supplemental feed during the next regular grazing season. And even this precaution may not work out as planned.

For example, the stockman has his grazing schedule worked out as follows: Pasture 1 for the winter months of November through February, Pasture 2 for March through June, Pasture 3 for July through October, and Pasture 4 for the next winter period. But the spring months have brought insufficient rainfall, and grass growth is poor. Pasture 2 is badly used by the first of June. He considers moving the cattle to Pasture 3 at this time, hoping that his feed crops will develop by August so that he will have plenty of feed by that time. Of course, the growth in Pasture 3 is poor for the same reason that it is poor in Pasture 2, and it will probably be depleted in two months or so, missing, in addition, this all-important rest period. Because of the rainfall deficiency, the feed crops are also likely to be poor. By August or September, the farmer will have to move his cattle again—to Pasture 4, which had been grazed the previous fall. The pasture will be damaged because for two years in succession it has not had an opportunity to produce seed.

What about the feed situation? His own feed did not produce, so it is likely that no one else will have a feed surplus. And finally, when he is completely out of grass, he will have to buy feed on a very high market or sell his livestock. His profits for the year are gone, and his prospects for the next year are poorer because his pastures have been damaged; at least their productive potential for the next year has been reduced, simply because they have not had their scheduled rest and cannot build up reserves for future grazing. His rotation system is gone, and it will take more than one year to get it effectively re-established again.

He might find a better procedure. When the spring pasture is well used, the livestock are in good condition, and the stockman might market some of them profitably. Or, realizing that grass production would not be normal, he might plant more feed, if land is available. But he should also foresee that feed production may not be normal on account of lack of moisture. Further, he should know that failure to maintain some grass reserves will leave him in even worse shape in the fall and winter than at present. If he decides to hold to his rotation grazing schedule, sell some of the animals that can be marketed profitably now, and purchase feed for the rest, he will probably find that hay can be bought cheaper now than at any other time of the year, because less provident neighbors will still be trying to get by on their grass and hoping for timely rains to make the feed crops. His herd will remain in good condition and make steady gains. When the next grazing season comes around, he will have the maximum growth in Pasture 3, as planned. If rains have come and the grass is near normal and feed prospects are good, he can buy some feeder cattle and make full use of his pasture and feed. If the rains have not come, he will be safe, his grass reserves will be properly protected, and he can look forward to better years.

Rotation grazing on rangeland offers security to the cattleman who can read correctly the signs of the seasons, who will adjust in time when the signs are bad, and who can expand quickly and wisely when the seasons are good. This is a scientific way of using half of the range and leaving the half which is needed for maintenance. Rotation grazing is more effective than seasonal grazing since it averages the good and bad conditions of two or three years together and gives the rancher more time to make adjustments. It gives all of the grass varieties a chance to rest and improve while it forces seasonal use of the poorer varieties. In comparison, yearlong grazing in the one-pasture system encourages the animals to overgraze the better varieties and, unless the range is overstocked, to neglect the less desirable ones. For example, when livestock are kept in the same pasture throughout the year, year after year, the bluestems, switchgrass, Indiangrass, sand lovegrass, the wildryes, and many valuable native legumes and forbs may be completely eliminated, while less desirable plants may be so lightly grazed that they will increase in numbers and vigor. This could hardly happen under a good rotation program. Usually the opposite is true. The better grasses are normally more vigorous if given an even chance and increase at the expense of the poorer plants.

Spotty grazing may result when animals are lured to one section of the pasture for water, salting, or supplementary feeding; when parts of the pasture are difficult to reach because of brush thickets, steep slopes, or gullies; or when, in a site protected from the wind, insects are annoying. When spotty grazing occurs, the cause should be determined and measures taken either to eliminate the cause of rejection or to lure the animals to the unused portions.

Brush screens may be removed, but steep slopes cannot be improved. Better water distribution may be secured by the addition of ponds, cleaning springs, or piping water to unused portions of the pasture. It is easy to move salting facilities into unused areas, and feeding locations may be placed in the rejected sites if they can be reached by the rancher in his truck. Certainly feeding and salting areas should be moved with regularity to avoid excessive trampling of the grass. They should always be located in the best grass cover accessible to the rancher's equipment, even though he experiences some inconvenience and in spite of the fact that there is some advantage in salting and feeding near the water supply.

These are tools in grazing management which will contribute to better grazing control, better grass utilization, and protection of sites which are subject to excessive abuse.

Other range management practices. All of the discussion so far in this chapter relates to grazing management and the utilization of the half which can be taken and the protection of the half which range plants need to maintain their stand, vigor, and production.

Few other practices are applicable except on small pastures or on small areas of the larger ranges, but where they are practical and needed, they may contribute materially to the production of the native grassland.

Control of competing plants includes mowing or spraying for weeds, brush, or tree control, removal of trees with heavy equipment, the use of certain types of livestock, (i.e., goats) to help control woody plants, and similar measures.

Harry M. Elwell, soil conservationist of the Guthrie, Oklahoma, Experiment Station, reports that the average yield of grass on fully cleared virgin land was five times that on land 90 per cent shaded.

Chemical spraying with 2-4-D or 2-4-5T by airplane or ground equipment has proved successful for ordinary weeds, blackjack and oak shinnery, and mesquite. A proper mixture has killed annual weeds without damaging valuable perennial legumes and forbs. Stronger mixtures used for perennial brush and trees will kill or damage the native legumes and forbs, but in many cases there is no other way to secure successful brush control. Generally the purpose is to kill some of the brush, to retard the growth of the rest, and to give the grass a chance to compete for the sunlight, moisture, and plant foods. Repeated applications of chemical spray are generally needed to keep the brush under control. Complete rest from grazing may be needed for a year or two, and adequate grazing management practices must be followed if the grass is to return to good production.

In addition to spraying the foliage of brush, applications of chemicals to the bark, stumps, and soil have proved effective. Basal bark treatment requires the complete wetting of the bark around the lower part of each tree in bands twenty to thirty inches wide. Early tests indicate that winter applications are best—from December 15 to March 15.

The use of ammonium sulfamate, applied during late summer in axe incisions around small oak trees less than ten inches in diameter, has resulted in good kills. Five pounds of this material in a gallon of water has proved effective.

Ester of 2-4-5T, five pounds to one gallon of water, has proved effective on spraying the stumps of larger trees. The entire stump must be thoroughly wetted.

The mowing of weeds and brush is not generally as effective as spraying, but is used where escaping spray may damage a near-by broad-leaf crop, especially an annual such as cotton. The "drift" from the sprayed field has damaged cotton, but failed to hurt the perennial alfalfa. Mowing should be done during the fast-growing or blooming stages of the weeds. Mowing does little good after the plant has matured and made seed. Goats have been used to retard certain types of brush.

Fertilization has not been tried extensively on native grass pastures, but early experimental results at the Red Plains Conservation Experiment Station at Guthrie, Oklahoma, indicate that the addition of fertilizer has some value. In a two-year test, grassland, cleared of brush and fertilized at the rate of 100 pounds of superphosphate and 33 pounds of nitrogen per acre annually, showed a gain of 49 pounds of beef per acre. Untreated plots produced 84 pounds, while the fertilized plots produced 133 pounds of beef per acre annually. Fertilized plots of reseeded native grasses at the same station have shown comparative increases, but more experiments and field trials are needed before valid conclusions can be reached.

Pitting or chiseling to increase insoak of rainfall may be valuable to help bare rangelands start on the road to recovery, but this mechanical practice should not be substituted for good range management which will develop a mulch to do the job more effectively.

Water spreading pertains to the diversion of water from flowing or intermittent streams to spread it on relatively flat areas of grassland, usually in valleys adjacent to the streams. The water should be silt free, or nearly so. Surplus water should be returned to the stream or again diverted to other grass areas, in a manner that will not cause erosion.

Overseeding better species of grass on a native grassland is practical when the higher-producing grasses have been destroyed, when the grass is of such a nature that it will survive, when other competing plants are controlled, and when grazing is rigidly controlled for the benefit of the new grass species.

A special word of caution is needed here. Many grasslands seem to have lost their best grasses because they have been overused and the more desirable plants have not been able to make any growth. Rest and weed control results in their return on most pastures, while generous reseeding without rest and weed control produces no beneficial results. The advice of a grass specialist should be obtained before this practice is attempted, and the farmer or rancher must be prepared to give the pasture at least as much protection as he would a field retired from cultivation and seeded to grass.

Managing Tame Pastures and Meadows

Tame pastures and meadows are composed of introduced grasses and legumes, grown singly or in mixtures, as opposed to native grasslands discussed in the preceding section.

Although the bases of management are the same, slightly different emphasis is given to certain practices. For example, vigorous growth and maximum production must be based on proper grazing control, but, unlike the native sward, the introduced plants are not able to maintain their dominance without supporting practices. Ecologists believe that a native rangeland, however badly abused it might be and however badly infested with invading plants, will return to its climax condition, with the better plants in complete control, if given enough time and if seed plants are still left. On the other hand, it is thought that most of the introduced plants in a tame pasture will finally give way to the native trees, shrubs, or grasses if long neglected. Variations in emphasis on certain practices will be seen in the discussion of pasture management methods listed below.

Grazing control. Proper stocking rates, pasture rotation, supplementary pastures and feed, and rest periods are accomplished much in the same manner as for native ranges, with one addition: proper utilization of the forage for some types of these pastures is being accomplished by total elimination of grazing.

Since the plants in these pastures are chosen for specific purposes, the tall, meadow-type grasses and legumes may often be planted in place of grasses that can better withstand the trampling of the grazing animals—if the farmer wants to "take the pasture to the cows," as one writer puts it. In this practice the animals are kept in the feed lot, and the forage is cut in the field with a field chopper and hauled directly to the feeding troughs or bunkers once or twice a day, as needed. During the lush growing season only a small portion of the field will be used, but this portion will be harvested completely without loss from rejections and trampling. The remainder of the pasture will grow without disturbance, and when it is ready to be cut, the surplus will be stored in silos or baled for hay. In general practice, the early growth will be ensiled since it will have a predominance of grass, and if it provides enough silage, later cuttings will be baled for hay. If the farmer plans to use all of the production from his grasslands, he may ensile all of the surplus. Stored with a preservative, silage is more practical than hay because it is better able to retain all of its food values. Also, there is less danger of loss as a result of unfavorable weather when the hay is drying. If the surplus is to be sold, however, hay can be handled and shipped more economically.

ABOVE: *Sod renovator tears up root-bound Bermudagrass so that it may be overseeded and fertilized.*
BELOW: *Milk production increased by use of kudzu on Class VI and VII land.*

Selective Cutting—
Continuous Production

Your Nation Needs
Woodland Products

Clearcut - Out of Produc

Profitable Work in Farm Woods

Pulpwood From Thinning Dense Stand

ABOVE: *Our forests, one of our most
important natural resources.*
BELOW: *Partially completed pattern of windbreaks.*

Moreover, the farmer may let the cattle graze on only a part of his grassland, perhaps on areas of poorer soil, where the higher-producing, tall plants cannot be grown successfully, or on part of a meadow-type planting. The rest of the grassland is ensiled or made into hay during the lush growing season. After this period, the farmer may rotate his livestock over the balance of the grassland. That portion which is grazed during the time that the pasture plants are growing rapidly and producing their maximum, while the farmer is withholding part of the grass for hay or ensilage, may be fenced into one field or into several fields which are rotated and treated in the usual manner, as follows:

Rotation grazing calls for subdividing the grassland into pastures small enough to assure maximum utilization of the growth within a period of ten to twenty days. This prevents livestock from selecting the more desirable plants and rejecting others, which would cause a loss in the grazing potential.

Immediately after livestock are moved to another pasture, the first pasture is mowed to clip all of the rejected plants and spread the droppings in order to prevent other spots from being rejected when the cattle are returned to the pasture. The first pasture is then allowed to grow, undisturbed, until time for its use again. Each pasture is treated successively in the same manner.

In the rank growing season, only part of the pastures is used for grazing, and the rest is cut for silage or hay. The management plan may call for a longer period of grazing for each pasture during this season, with shorter periods of grazing when grass growth is slower. Or it may call for quick rotations over all of the pastures during the early part of the season to secure maximum use of the early grass growth, followed by clipping to allow the grasses and legumes to come together for hay or silage production.

One Virginia farmer subdivides 70 acres of grassland into 14 pastures, averaging 5 acres each. From them he secures adequate grazing for nine to ten months each year and all of the ensilage and hay that he needs for the rest of the year, for a herd that grosses $16,000 a year from milk sales. This dairyman, C. T. Rice of Oakton, has no cultivated acres.[1]

Successful grazing management of tame pastures always calls for some type of use, followed by rest and renewal. The single-pasture system with season-long grazing is not satisfactory because it results in excessive damage to some types of plants, trampling, rejection of certain plants, and accumulation of droppings which increase the amount of the rejections.

Most successful, from the standpoint of getting nearly 100 per cent utilization of all forage and absolute control of the "take," plus no damage from trampling, wallowing, or droppings, is the use of the field cutter to take the forage to animals kept in feed lots. This method also saves time and money required for fencing and moving the cattle, and prevents roaming or other unnecessary exercise which may reduce milk or meat production. It gives the cattleman better control of the ration by enabling him to mix grass, protein feeds, or supplements with the chopped feed from the field, in accordance with its quality. Such controlled feeding should reduce loss from bloat and contribute to the health of the herd. In addition, pasture renovation is needed less often.

Maintaining the desired plants. Any number of the above steps in grazing control will increase the use of all plants and prevent excessive overuse of certain ones, therefore helping to keep the desired plants strong and thrifty. However, some refinements are needed.

Seed production of certain reseeding annuals and biennials, such as the lespedezas, crimson clover, sweetclover, and the ryegrasses, is necessary. Stocking should be light when the flower buds begin to form, and livestock should be removed

[1] Sellers G. Archer and Clarence E. Bunch, *The American Grass Book*, 146.

during the flowering and seeding stages. If the pastures all contain the same mixture, the livestock must go to the feed lot, or supplemental pastures must be planned to carry the herd at these times.

Renovation is needed on most tame pastures every three to five years. The plants become root bound, and some plants begin to disappear because they have run their cycle or been overused, or because other plants have begun to dominate the seeding. Tillage may be accomplished with plows or some type of spiked implement. After thorough working, the land is disked or harrowed smooth again.

At this time, the seeds of plants which have become depleted or which did not make a seed crop before renovation must be sown again. This is done by broadcasting and rolling, or with a cultipacker with seeding attachment. Liming and fertilization usually accompany renovation, and applications are made in accordance with soil texts and established practices.

The cattleman uses these indications to determine when a pasture needs renovation: (1) Certain plants, such as Bermudagrass or intermediate wheatgrass, have become root-bound and need cultivation to regain their vigor. (2) A certain type of plant, such as tall fescue in a fescue-ladino clover mixture, has become dominant at the expense of another which is needed to keep the quality of the pasture at a maximum. (3) The vigor of all of the plants is reduced, and mineral fertilizers or lime, or both, cannot be effectively added without tillage. (4) There are weeds and grasses which cannot be controlled by mowing or other management practices.

Complete renovation may not be necessary in certain instances. Bermudagrass or similar grasses may have crowded out other plants desirable in the mixture, but at the same time may not need renovation for its own good. Fortunately there are seeding and fertilization implements on the market with which the farmer may add the needed seed, fertilizer, and lime without greatly disturbing the sod. These planters are used annually to plant vetch, ryegrass, and similar cool-season grasses in the fall, or lespedezas, sweetclover, and similar warm-season plants in the early spring.

Some farmers find it more profitable to graze this type of planting heavily, not allowing the annuals to make the seed needed to maintain themselves, but replanting and fertilizing each year.

Discouraging undesirable plants. As has been pointed out, weeds, brush, and unwanted native or invading grasses will, if not kept under control, return in a tame pasture planting. The taller plants can usually be kept under control by mowing, and, if the pasture contains only grasses, the broad-leaf weeds can be killed with a herbicide such as 2-4-D or 2-4-5T. Some hand grubbing or cutting is often practical in controlling isolated clumps or plants.

A recent innovation in such control was developed by Reuel W. Little, of Madill, Oklahoma. He uses a sharp-pointed injector which he stabs into the base of trees ranging from a few inches to one hundred inches in circumference. With the point in place in the bark of the tree, a trigger releases a mixture of 2-4-D and 2-4-5T in solution in a penetrating agent. The poison is carried into the roots and kills an elm in two days, a post oak in two weeks, and all other trees on which it has been tried within six weeks. The "gun" resembles a bazooka and weighs eleven pounds empty and only a little more when filled. Mr. Little uses it selectively, to kill undesirable trees and brush, but he leaves ornamental and shade trees. He reports that his process will kill a large tree as quickly as a small sapling of the same variety, and that the cost of using the injector and fluid runs from $4 to $5 an acre. The labor cost for application is less than for any other type of spraying of the herbicide—generally not more than a total of $25 per acre for normal infestations. The method has the advantage of being usable on trees or brush in legume pastures, where normal spray operations would kill or damage all broad-leaf plants.

The maintenance of a good stand and vigorous growth of the desirable plants by proper grazing management will prolong the useful life of a pasture planting and defer the time for renovation. Overgrazed pastures fall more quickly to invading plants than those in which plantings are kept strong and vigorous.

Hay making. Pastures make the highest-quality hay when they are growing vigorously and the legume is entering the blooming stage. As the plants mature and growth slackens, as much as 20 per cent of the feeding value of the hay may be lost. Early grass growth should be grazed, ensiled, or clipped and allowed to fall to the ground. To avoid picking it up later, it is best to use a stalk shredder which will chop the undesired old growth and allow it to filter to the ground for quicker decomposition.

Hay should be cut and hauled immediately to a dryer, if one is available. The saving of leaves and preservation of color and food nutrients make immediate processing profitable. In addition, the farmer, by processing the hay immediately, avoids the risk of exposing it to unfavorable weather or floods while it is down and wilting.

Late cuttings are undesirable. The hay is lower in quality, and the grass and legume plants are subject to damage. Late cutting will also prevent the storing of plant foods in the roots, which are important for early and vigorous growth the following spring.

At the end of the season, pastures and meadows should have sufficient growth to protect the ground adequately through the winter, hold snow, and provide a mulch for the germination of seeds and prevention of drying and baking which would result on exposed soil. The mulch cover maintains more desirable soil temperatures for soil life and for seedling emergence in either winter or summer.

V: Farm Forestry

NEITHER the extent nor the economic value of farm woodlands is generally recognized. Partly for these reasons and partly because forestry planning, planting, and management practices take much longer than crops or pasture programs to bring cash income, woodland resources have continued to dwindle, even after the great orgy of timber hogging was stopped.

Everywhere the acreages of pine and other desirable tree species are declining, while acreages of less desirable hardwoods, brush, and abandoned land are increasing on privately owned farmlands. An enormous potential still exists on the 165,000,000 acres of woodlands on private farms, but the U. S. Forest Service states that only 4 per cent of the acreage is properly managed and judiciously harvested for maximum and sustained yield, the management of 23 per cent is fair, but that of 73 per cent is actually poor or destructive.[1]

Mississippi in 1949 received an income from wood products second only to cotton, in spite of relatively poor harvesting and management. But what of the future? Such income can be maintained or increased, but as in all wooded areas of the nation, income is declining and the basic resource is being destroyed.

[1] A *Reappraisal of the Forest Situation in the U. S. Miscellaneous Publication No. 688* (1948). U. S. Forest Service.

Alabama is 60 per cent wooded. Nearly 8,000,000 acres of its total area of 33,000,000 acres is in farm woodlands, with the balance in large private or governmental holdings. In addition, 10 per cent of the state's total farmland is idle—no longer suited to cropping—and should be planted either to trees or pasture.

Of North Carolina's 19,000,000 acres 62 per cent is forested, with nearly 6,000,000 acres in farm woodlands. But the state has less than 5,000,000 acres in both cropland and pasture land, and over 1,500,000 acres are idle. Between 1936 and 1947, the acreage in cropland decreased by 2,200,000 acres, idle land increased by 1,000,000 acres, and forest increased by over 2,-000,000 acres. At the same time, however, the pine acreage was decreasing while the acreages of undesirable hardwoods and damaged areas were increasing. With poor to fair management on the remaining pine lands, the potential was also decreasing. The picture is not good. It is estimated that more than 1,000,-000 acres in North Carolina should be planted to pine trees.

Woodlands appear to some extent on farm lands in all parts of the nation, ranging from a little more than 1 per cent (2,-000,000 acres) in the northern Great Plains to more than 43 per cent of the farm land in the Southeastern states, or 29,-000,000 acres. In the Northeastern states, where forest production early gave way to cropping, more than 10,000,000 acres of cropland were abandoned in the period from 1915 to 1935.[2] More than 165,000,000 acres of the nation's one billion acres of private farm lands are in forest.

Of the commercial private forest land of the United States, 139,000,000 acres, or 40 per cent, are within the boundaries of 3,250,000 farms. The remaining 26,000,000 acres of woodland on farms are not considered commercial forest land, which means that they are not harvested for saw timber, pulpwood,

[2] Arthur H. Carhart, "Root, Grass—or Die," *The Rotarian* (August, 1953), 29.

stumpage, firewood, Christmas trees, decorative wreaths and cones, telephone or similar posts, or fence posts. Much of the timbered areas serve other useful purposes, such as homes for wildlife, insect habitats, protection for stream banks, windbreaks, and recreation areas. Many acres have been planted for erosion control alone. However, much of the woodland is practically worthless and occupies land that should produce commercial trees or grass.

Farm forestry is perhaps the most difficult branch of silviculture, the art of producing and tending a forest. It involves educational, technical, and financial aid to the millions of farmers who have woodlands or should integrate woodland enterprises with their total farm operations.

1. PLANNING

In farm forestry, perhaps more than in any other part of the farm business, long-time planning, based on sound land use, is necessary for success. And this is doubtless the reason that farm forestry has been so badly neglected.

Crops may be planted in the spring, and, barring drought or insects, the harvest comes in the fall. Pasture or range grasses may be planted with reasonable assurance that within a period of from a few months to two or three years a harvest of hay or grazing can be obtained. But a tree planting may require longer for development than a farmer's normal tenure on the land.

Crop yields bring a high return for each acre. Pasture income is often as profitable as cash crops because of the reduced planting and management costs. Of course, profits from the original harvest of native stands of commercial timber were good, and returns are still reasonable from properly managed plots, although per-acre income may be less than that from good cropland or pasture land and payday may come less often. The 4 per cent of the nation's farm woodlands poses no serious problem to the forester or conservation worker. But as woodlands grade downward, with less and less promise of profit unless more and more work is done to improve the stand of marketable timber, the problems increase. When undesirable trees have almost completely replaced the commercial species, the problem is at its worst, and it is perhaps even more difficult than the re-establishment of forests on abandoned and idle land.

In any case, an adequate plan of woodland management, integrated with other phases of the farm enterprise, is a must for the farmer. His planning should be done with the skilled assistance of technicians from soil conservation districts, the Forest Service, state departments of forestry, extension services, or similar agencies, or sometimes of representatives of the lumber industry who furnish the markets. Adequate, long-time planning should follow the general steps listed below.

Survey of Resources

As in most other operations, the first step is to survey and assess resources. In this area the farmer will want competent advice on two important items which will form the basis of his planning: (1) He will want to know the potential of the woodland now on his farm. Can a feasible system of management be adopted that will protect this basic resource and improve his profits? He will need recommendations concerning the management practices involved, an estimate of the cost in labor and money, and an estimate of the returns that may be expected. (2) He will need to know the soil resources of his farm if there is any question of other uses for the land. Perhaps some land which is badly deteriorated or damaged woodland is suitable for crop or pasture production, and the alternatives should be considered. He will need to know which acres that are now in other uses should be returned to forest trees or used for either trees, pasture, or crops. These are determinations of land capability and are part of the planning assistance given through soil conservation districts by the Conservation Service.

In addition to this basic information needed on all farms are specific recommendations concerning the use of specialized types of woody plantings to meet specific needs. This includes the use of windbreaks to reduce wind erosion on cropland or to protect farmsteads and the establishment of post lots in non-wooded areas to provide for farm needs, erosion control, and wildlife plantings. Advice should be sought on the need for such plantings and the suitability of soils on the farm for such use.

Practices to Be Considered

As in every type of farm enterprise, there is a combination of practices—and no single practice—which will give maximum returns. After the farmer has received the basic information detailed above, he will formulate his own plan of action based on the recommendations available to him. His plan will generally include one or more of the following specific practices.

Planting. Plans must be made for each type of planting desired, whether for production of woodland products, for control of erosion on eroded lands or gullied areas, for stabilization of sand dunes, spoil banks, strip mine areas, or similar sites, for post lots or windbreaks, or for underplanting or interplanting of existing woodlands.

The types of trees to produce the desired products or protection must be chosen with due regard for the soil and climate. Planting materials, whether seedlings, seeds, or cuttings, must be decided on and arranged for well in advance of planting time; and if planting equipment is available, it must be reserved.

The pattern of the planting and the spacing between the

rows and within each row must be determined, or the plantings may be cross checked. In the case of a windbreak, rows of different varieties of trees are chosen because of height, or the protection they afford at different levels, and the best arrangement determined. Some plantings should be made on the contour, and guide lines must be established. Other variations in the planting pattern may occur.

Land preparation may include leveling, diversion terraces, or other measures to prevent excessive accumulations of rainfall runoff, removal of undesirable vegetation, and plowing or other seedbed preparations, depending on the needs of the land and the planting equipment to be used.

Care of the new planting should include the control of competing vegetation and regular cultivation. Disk or harrow-type equipment is best, especially after the root system begins to spread. Hoeing may be necessary to remove weeds close to the trees. Pests, such as rodents, are sometimes a problem and may be poisoned or otherwise discouraged. Dead trees should be replaced with good stock. This type of cultivation and care is usually continued until the trees start to form a canopy over the ground and interfere with continued cultivation.

Natural reforestation. Woodlands that have only a minimum of desirable species can be improved by discouraging the undesirable trees by cutting the older trees back and cleaning out young growth. The desirable trees will increase after the removal of this competition if the parent trees are allowed to seed and open spots are treated to encourage the development of seedlings. Although the process may be slow, the farmer can work on the project as he has time, and it is the only practical method by which many types of depleted forests can be improved.

Stand improvement. Under this heading are several practices used to maintain or improve the production of fair to good forests.

(1) Pruning. Remove limbs, living or dead, to improve the quality of the standing tree.

(2) Release cuttings. Judicious cutting in a stand past the sapling stage improves the composition and character of the stand. This may mean the removal of desirable varieties as well as weed trees, but it allows the remaining trees to develop better. Ammate may be used to kill the undesirable trees.

(3) Salvage. Trees that have been damaged by fire, insects, disease, lightning, or other disasters should be removed before decay begins so that the salable products may be salvaged.

Woodland protection. The greatest danger to woodlands is fire. Prevention is the best protection, and under this heading come the construction of fireguards and the removal of inflammable material by controlled burning and other methods. Fireguards should be clean and sufficiently wide to prevent ordinary fires from leaping across them. Controlled burning means using fire according to a planned procedure—when conditions are not right for an intense fire and its area can be adequately controlled. This will not only reduce the fire hazard by removing inflammable material, but may improve the quality of the land cover and habitat conditions for wildlife. This practice should be used with caution, under strict supervision, and when conditions are best for control.

Even after the best methods for prevention are installed, fires sometimes do start. In preparation for fire fighting, access roads should be provided, if possible, into all parts of the forest. Community groups should be organized and equipped for a quick attack on any fire that breaks out. Watching service should be established and arrangements made for alerting the fire-fighting group.

Protection of woodlands from livestock damage is an important factor in good timber production. Woodland pasture is generally poor, and returns from grazing seldom offset the loss from damaged trees and killed seedlings.

Disease and insects take a toll on woodland. The farmer should learn the danger signs and methods of treatment. This information is often made available seasonally by extension and conservation personnel and by lumber companies.

The methods of management and protection discussed above apply to plantings as well as to old stands of timber.

Harvesting. Farmers often defeat the purposes of a good management program and hurt their future incomes by careless or misguided marketing and harvesting methods, which have been important factors in the deterioration of farm woodlands.

The farmer should curb the desire to sell undeveloped timber products in order to get a greater immediate income when it will mean damage to the stand and a reduction in later production. This natural and understandable inclination has been the principal cause of poor marketing policies.

There has been a lack of understanding and appreciation by the farmer of the true value of the timber products belonging to him. The natural stand was produced without cost to him, and generally he has regarded a sale as a windfall. The buyer set the price—as low as he could, naturally—and farmers who did not know the value of their woodlands accepted what was offered. Since the buyer wanted all he could get at each place and the farmer wanted to sell as much as he could, immature trees were taken. The buyer wanted to get the most accessible timber, and even after the farmer had had his timber cruised and marked for cutting by a trained forester, substitutions were permitted.

Because of a lack of regard for the value of his timber resources, the farmer sold by the "border" or acreage, allowing the cutter to take whatever he desired. The buyer was an expert and estimated the true value of the cutting, including immature trees. The farmer was not an expert on timber values and took what was offered. The buyer often had little interest in the continued productivity of the woodland, and so, in addition to taking all that he could use, he carelessly damaged or destroyed much young growth. The farmer, showing as little concern for the future of his woodland, permitted this rape of his timberland.

Today the picture is brighter, but it is far from satisfactory to foresters and woodland conservationists who are attempting to salvage the remnants of the nation's great forest empire and establish woodland production as a basic farm enterprise. Ethical and farsighted sawmill and logging companies realize the need for sustained production, are harvesting more selectively, and are even helping farmers to learn the value of their woodlands and to adopt methods for the protection and improvement of their forests.

The rising price of timber products has induced farmers to take a new interest in planting, protecting, managing, and marketing their woodland resources. Public agencies give assistance to the individual owner in the form of education and technical services.

Harvesting and marketing recommendations are listed below:

(1) Do not sell by "border" or acreage, thus allowing the cutter to take whatever he desires.

(2) Market each type of product separately, whether it be saw timber, pulpwood, stumpage, firewood, Christmas trees, posts, or decorative material.

(3) Sell saw timber by the board feet in individual trees. This requires expert assistance in cruising and marking the stand which is available.

(4) Permit no substitutions and allow the buyer to take only the marked trees.

(5) Insist on the protection of young trees.

(6) Learn to estimate quantities and values of products and sell by units, as outlined for saw timber.

2. *CRUISING AND MARKING*

Cruising and marking means the accurate determination of the board feet of lumber available in mature and marketable trees, with due regard for the maintenance of the timber stand and its continued production. This is the only dependable, accurate way for the farmer to learn what he has for sale. It is comparable to the weight measurement of his cotton and cottonseed, and the bushel measurement of his corn, oats, wheat, and other products. In addition, this method assures continued yields and protection of woodland property values.

In a standing forest, an expert is required for making this determination. Marketing associations may employ such an expert, but most farmers depend on the assistance of foresters from the Forest Service, Extension Service, state divisions of forestry, and county agents and conservationists with the Soil Conservation Service. Lumber companies provide this service in some areas.

One of these experts, with the assistance of the owner, can mark, tally, and compute 50,000 board feet a day in marketable stands that average 250 feet per tree. Since this totals only 200 trees, it is apparent that a very large staff of these experts is required for this phase of marketing. Without the cumulative tally system which was worked out by the Lake States Forest Experiment Station, marking, tallying, and computing would be even slower.

Woodland conservation, like all other phases of conservation, has as its ultimate objective maximum sustained production of vegetative products. It is based on sound land use, adequate soil protection, and moisture conservation. To work out the most successful program and integrate it with his other farm enterprises, each farmer should obtain expert help familiar with local problems. This is available in every county or parish where farm forestry is important in the agricultural economy.

VI: Nature's Acres, or Wildlife on the Farm

EARLY SETTLERS in North America found fish in the streams and game birds and animals in the forest and on the prairie. This game provided recreation, food, and furs and leather for sale or trade for clothing. Today the decrease in numbers of many species of wildlife is not due to the increased hunting and fishing pressure, but is a result of the destruction of food sources and habitat conditions favorable to their survival. In highly developed agricultural areas, hunting has become merely an excuse for hiking, and fishing is poor except in well-managed ponds and lakes. Yet there are more hunters and fishermen today than ever in history.

The rapidly developing science of wildlife management is pointing the way to a return of conditions favorable to the farmer and the sportsman. Yet, to the farmer, wildlife development must mean more than an increase in the number of game birds, animals, and fish, for many forms of wildlife are beneficial to him, and the farm plan should contain measures for their encouragement.

Insects are necessary for the pollination of legumes, cotton, fruits, and other crops for good yields of seed or fruit. Bees can increase the seed yield of alfalfa more than all the fertilizer that can be hauled to the field, and for this purpose the wild insects are far superior to tame bees. The ladybug has been

ABOVE: *This quail feeder supplies
food for wildlife during severe weather.*
BELOW: *Bobwhite quail feeding in brushy woods.*

ABOVE: *Wildlife habitat next to field.*
BELOW: *Ears of corn were tied to corn stalks to demonstrate how wildlife feeding can be accomplished by leaving a little corn unhusked near good cover. Note the fox squirrel and male, ring-neck pheasant.*

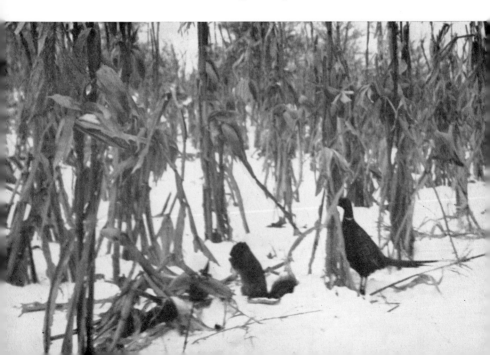

imported into this country to help keep the green bug in check. Birds can help to control the damage-dealing army worm and similar pests. Snakes prey on rodents. The earthworm is the best soil builder known, and other tiny life forms add to the productivity of the soil.

Overuse of the land tends to destroy the valuable forms of wildlife, but oddly enough does not eliminate the pests. Poison sprays may hold the insect pests in check for a time, but because sprays also destroy the natural predators of the pests, they offer no lasting benefit. To wage war on all insects is both ineffective and harmful to the farmer's best interests.

The farmer does not destroy his pasture because weeds grow there. Instead, he uses selected practices to discourage undesirable plants and to encourage desirable ones. When the grass is weakened, he finds that the weed plants invade and grow rampant; on the other hand, a strong stand of good grass will dominate the weeds. The only effective control for poisonous plants which invade a rangeland is the improvement of the grass cover to the extent that it drives out the livestock killers or reduces their numbers and vigor so much that they offer little threat to grazing animals. This situation is analogous to the control of insect pests.

There are controls for wildlife pests, but they should be used carefully to avoid destroying beneficial forms. There are also positive measures for the encouragement of desirable forms of wildlife.

1. PROVIDING FOR BIRDS, BEES, AND SMALL ANIMALS

On most farms there are areas which could be dedicated to wildlife without loss to any other farm enterprise. On other farms the use of better soils as wildlife habitats can be justified by the benefits received. The best management of woodland, pastures, and cropland will encourage wildlife.

Nature's Acres

Nature's acres may comprise the entire woodland area if it is protected from fire and intensive grazing. They may be composed of pastures of native grasses or introduced plants, for when these are managed for best grazing there will remain good cover for birds and smaller animals. They may be cropland acres where border strips, cover crops, and rotations are used, and where crop residues are managed for good soil and water conservation. All of these may encourage wildlife, although their primary use is for the production of woodland products, grazing animals, field crops, or fruits. They can produce food, cover, and nesting places for birds, small animals, and insects, and water may be available in pastures and woodlands for fish.

However, in areas where pastures are heavily used and cropland is left bare for considerable periods of time, other areas must be provided as the principal wildlife habitat and dedicated almost exclusively to wildlife. Their location, development, and management are worth careful study. Some of these sites are chosen because of soil type or erosion conditions, because they would provide better farm arrangement, or because they are areas which cannot be effectively adapted to other uses. Examples of areas commonly used as wildlife habitat are the following.

Class VIII *land.* In the discussion of land classification early in this book,[1] it was pointed out that there is a type of land which cannot safely be used for the harvest of timber products, grass, or field crops. This land, wherever it exists, is suitable only for wildlife and should be protected from other uses. Large areas of this class exist in the mountain states, for example. Colorado has given such land a colorful name and charges people to look at it, as well as to hunt and fish on it. Smaller areas

[1] See pages 31–32.

also exist on many farms throughout the nation. Regardless of how small such an acreage is, it should be fenced to exclude livestock, and all vegetative growth should be encouraged to protect any soil that remains. Wildlife suited to the area will find it and make it their home.

Erosible soils. Large gullies, areas of smaller gullies, rocky spots, very shallow soils, bluffs, creek banks and escarpments, and similar sites may be subjected to continued severe erosion in their present use despite any practical conservation measures that might be applied. Many of these may be protected and dedicated to nature.

Of course, some areas in this category are Class IV or VII land which may be planted to grass and used for pasture, but often the cost of realigning the pasture fences to include the spot will be more than the value to be received from grazing. Other such areas, already in pasture, may continue to erode and would require fences for the exclusion of livestock if adequate protection is to be given. Suggestions for the treatment of such areas are given later in this section.

Miscellaneous sites. Fence rows, windbreaks, post lots, permanent markers for contour strip cropping, field borders for turn rows, odd corners, inaccessible areas, wet spots, and similar sites may be on good land quite suitable for other uses, but for field-arrangement purposes would be better used as homes for birds, small animals, or insects.

Wildlife Habitat Improvement

Treatment should be based on the needs of the area for erosion control, the types of wildlife desirable and practical, and economic limitations. Because each site presents a different problem, because the requirements of each type of wildlife vary widely throughout the states, and because adapted plants and methods of treatment also vary, the farmer should consult local specialists for specific recommendations.

Game birds and animals require feed, cover where they may hide from their natural enemies, water in arid areas, and nesting places. Cover is less important for insects, except in their nesting places, but they, too, require food.

If possible, food plants should be planted in the wildlife habitat. Trees that bear small fruits or berries, grains, grasses, weeds, and smaller edible plants are used in the protected area to provide food, cover, and the necessary nesting places. The plants should be perennial or reseeding annuals. Grain may be left in the fields for additional food, or a separate small enclosure may be provided adjacent to the refuge and planted annually for supplemental wildlife feeding. Most of the beneficial pollinating insects, like bees, depend on nectar from blooming plants and store it for the maintenance of their colony. Their presence is encouraged to benefit legumes, fruits, cotton, and similar plants, and these crops generally provide sufficient food.

If the food plants do not provide adequate cover, other plantings should be made for this purpose unless natural wild growth affords ample cover. Such birds as quail and most small animals also require travel lanes as part of their cover. They must leave their habitat to get a large part of their food, and a well-protected habitat surrounded by barren land would be a poor home for them. But windbreaks, hedgerows, field border strips, fence rows, good waterways, gullies, or draws or pastures with good cover enable them to move about with comparative safety and provide sources of additional food.

Near-by and dependable sources of water are desirable for game animals, but, except in arid areas, are not so important for birds, who get most of their moisture supply from the insects on which they feed, from dew, and from precipitation. A good running stream or well-protected farm pond near the habitat is helpful for all types of wildlife.

Supplemental feeding is often needed during times of extreme drought, heavy snowfall, or icy conditions. Nature warns her wild creatures of the approach of such unfavorable conditions, and they eat as much as they can of the available food. But when their supply is nonexistent or is covered by ice or snow, birds and animals should be fed. This is a small chore if protected feed bunkers are wisely located and a sufficient supply of feed is placed in them to last out the unfavorable weather.

Protection

The protection of wildlife includes the measures taken to develop the habitat, to exclude livestock, to prevent and control fires, to keep out predatory animals, to control hunting, and to mitigate the unfortunate results of harmful spraying and other efforts of the farmer to fight damaging insects and other pests.

Fencing. Fencing is primarily for the exclusion of livestock. A gullied area in a cultivated field that is not grazed heavily may not need additional fences. Heavy growths of brush or trees may effectively exclude grazing animals, and a row of multiflora rose or other hedge plants may provide a living fence as well as food and shelter for wildlife. If the site that is to be developed into a wildlife habitat is in a pasture, but is adjacent to a field which is not grazed heavily, the pasture fence may be moved to include the area in the field and thus reduce or eliminate the need for additional fencing materials.

Fire control. Although farmers have learned that fires are damaging to woodland, grassland, cropland, and the farm improvements, there is still need for caution in intentional burning. Fireguards may be needed for the control of accidental

191

fires. Any burning may completely destroy feed and cover and render the refuge worthless. The farmer will realize the need for the protection of any wildlife habitat that he intentionally develops, but he may overlook the value of fence rows, weedy corners, creek and gully banks, and brushy spots that may be as valuable to his wildlife as the developed site. Even when there has been no conscious effort to encourage wildlife, such sites may furnish the needed cover and nesting places, especially for insects that are valuable in the farming enterprise. These sites are sometimes burned to destroy the nesting places of harmful insects, but as has been pointed out, nature keeps a better balance if beneficial insects and birds are encouraged. If the farmer knew of the beneficial insects that live there and how valuable they are to his crops, he would be less likely to burn over such spots.

Insecticides. Indiscriminate use of insect sprays, like careless burning, is one of the greatest enemies of beneficial insects, birds, reptiles, and other animals, even fish in farm ponds. Spraying cotton to eliminate harmful insects or worms may destroy both their natural predators and the other insects needed to pollinate the cotton. Poison washing from the fields may kill fish in near-by farm ponds and poison the feed and water used by other forms of wildlife.

The need for spraying field and fruit crops is acknowledged, but the resulting damage to honey bees and other pollinating insects is alarming to bee keepers and to the growers of many seed or fruit crops which depend upon these beneficial insects. Some states have passed laws defining the types of insecticides which may be used and the time and methods of application. Some counties have established boards of control on the basis that both the control of pests and the protection of beneficial forms of wildlife, including the pollinating insects, are a community problem.

Among insecticides, arsenical poisons are more damaging

than the hydrocarbons (including DDT, DDD, and chlordan), and of the hydrocarbons, chlordan is the most toxic. HETP and TEPP (phosphate poisons) are also more damaging than the hydrocarbons. The poisons from the more toxic of these chemicals may remain on the plant and cause injury for days, and even weeks, after application.

Perhaps more important to the preservation of wildlife than the types of insecticides used are the time and method of application. The spraying of plants which attract the pollinating insects while the plants are in bloom invites disaster to the insects. Early spraying, even spraying the fall before, has proved effective in the control of harmful insects in the field, while it has caused little or no damage to bees in their refuges, apiaries, or on other fields.

Airplane spraying is seldom controlled application. The drift may poison insect refuges and other fields being worked by pollinating insects for a distance of a mile or more. Even application with spray equipment on tractors or trailers may permit excessive drift unless the air is very still. In all cases care should be exercised to prevent the drift from reaching habitats where desirable insects find shelter. The same precautions used in the application of weed sprays when other crops that may be damaged are near by are applicable for insect habitats.

Predators. Many predators are damaging to wildlife. Some, such as wolves and coyotes, beat the hunter to the game. Others prey on the young or the eggs in the nests. Among the latter are terrapins, rodents, and snakes. In a natural environment the desirable game survives in plentiful numbers, but in most agricultural areas the environment is weighted against them, and control of predators may be necessary. Sportsmen in each community are usually aware of the predators that are creating local problems and are willing to assist the farmer in developing methods of control. Rod and gun clubs often feature this activity as part of the co-operation they offer farmers in improving wildlife habitats for their mutual benefit. Other towns-people are also learning not to dump unwanted kittens in rural areas to grow up into predators.

2. DEVELOPMENT AND MANAGEMENT OF FISHING WATERS

In recent years fishing has become the most popular outdoor sport in America. Streams once furnished most of the fishing water, but many have become clogged with silt or debris or polluted with salt water, chemicals, or sewage, and the angler has moved to man-made lakes and farm ponds.

Within the last few years new services have been developed by state and federal agencies to assist farmers in building ponds and stocking and managing them for fish production. One purpose is to help provide healthful recreation for both farmers and townspeople; another is to provide new sources of an excellent food and thus raise the standard of living in areas where this kind of food is needed. A well-managed acre of water can produce all the fish an average family can use.

Present programs have been developed largely to provide sport and recreation, and controls for harvesting the fish are largely the same for the grower and the sportsman. This equal treatment is justified on the ground that state funds for this work have been derived largely from the sale of fishing licenses to sportsmen. However, further improvement is needed to make this valuable food source more accessible to the average farm family. Thus it seems logical that the farmer who builds and stocks a small farm pond primarily for his own use should be able to harvest the crop as it matures, for the waters of the pond can support only so many pounds of fish. For most practical purposes the fish should be taken as they are ready, so that there is room for the development of a new crop. In some sections the farmer can buy young fish from a private source and harvest them as he sees fit, but the "take" from a lake stocked with fish furnished from a state or federal hatchery must be in compliance with laws applying to sportsmen. Furthermore, fish cannot be placed on the market except in accordance with state or local laws. If changes were made in the regulations to allow the farmer certain privileges in harvesting and marketing his fish, a new source of healthful food and a profitable new enterprise for the farmer would result.

These suggested changes apply only to the harvesting and use of the fish where regulations now restrict such activity. The principles of developing, stocking, and managing the fishing water would be the same.

The best fishing water, whether in stream or impoundment, is found where erosion is controlled on the watershed. Muddy water is not conducive to fish development; therefore, the drainage area should be in good grass or trees or cropland which is well protected from erosion. This factor is important in selecting a site for a farm pond, whether or not it is to be used for fish production.

A pipe should be placed through the dam with a filter housing over the inlet end to prevent clogging and with a valve placed within the fill below the frost line. The pipe should be one and one-half inches in diameter or larger so that it may be cleaned more effectively when necessary. This pipe could be used to drain the pond or supply water to a stock tank below the dam. This "controlled" water is also much better for livestock to drink than the muddy and contaminated water in which animals are allowed to wade.

The entire pond, dam, and spillway should be fenced to exclude livestock and encourage vegetation which can control erosion along the shore line. If livestock water is needed from the pond and a pipe is not provided to fill a stock tank as described above, a wide lane should be built to the edge of the water at a deep part of the pond. With the rest of the pond fenced, the spawning grounds for the fish would not be disturbed, and the muddiness caused by the cattle would be kept to a minimum.

Local recommendations should be followed for the kind and numbers of fish to be stocked in a new pond. The Soil Conservation District office, the state game and fish departments, or the Fish and Wildlife Service will help the farmer in ordering the fish.

Local recommendations should also be sought if the pond is to be fertilized. Commercial fertilizers and limited amounts of poultry or sheep manure may be used during the months when the water is warm enough to permit the growth of microscopic plants which serve as fish food and which are also beneficial in other ways. The water in the pond will be no more fertile than the land on which it is located and will have the same mineral deficiencies. Nitrogen and phosphorus are usually needed, and sometimes potash is required. Mixtures vary from a 10-20-0 formula to 8-8-8. Usually applications average one hundred pounds per surface acre per month from spring until fall, although the greater portion is used during the rainy period when large amounts of fresh water are entering the lake. The fertilizer and manure are broadcast around the shallower edges.

Stocking rates vary according to whether or not the owner plans to fertilize. If a heavy stocking rate is used, or if the fish population becomes large, the pond should be fertilized regularly. Of course, a well-fertilized pond will produce more pounds of fish than unfertilized waters. One method that biologists use to determine the fertility of the water is called the elbow test. In water that is not muddy a white object held twelve to eighteen inches below the surface should be very dim, or invisible. This indicates a heavy growth of tiny water plants. Such water is fertile and will encourage fish propagation much better than clear or muddy water.

Fishing should begin after the fish have spawned the first time, which, in southern waters, is usually a year after the pond was stocked. Heavy fishing will maintain better-balanced stock for a longer period, contrary to the belief of some that fishing should be restricted to keep people from "catching all the fish." Experts believe that it is impossible to deplete the warm-water fish population of a pond with a hook and line, and they recommend that all fish caught, including the little ones, be kept or thrown away to hold the population down as long as possible.

All of the common varieties of fish multiply very rapidly when conditions are favorable. The numbers grow to such proportions that there is not enough food and the fish become stunted. Poor fishing often results. When this condition exists, the pond should be drained or the fish killed and the water restocked. Assistance is available from trained biologists at fisheries to determine the condition of the fish in an old pond or lake and to direct measures for renovation. In many states it is against the law to kill out the fish in an old pond without the approval of the state agency or department charged with the protection and development of wildlife resources.

Carp and other rough fish are not desirable in a farm pond. Since minnows used for bait often are the young of undesirable species, the angler should never empty his bait bucket into the pond when he is through fishing.

3. THE FARMER AND THE SPORTSMAN

Many studies show that neither the fish in the pond nor the game in the field are seriously depleted by sportsmen. Very rarely will hunting or fishing, under existing laws and regulations, reduce any game or fish species by more than the annual increase. Poor hunting and fishing conditions are primarily the result of poor environment and the lack of adequate food, shelter, and nesting places. The elements, accidents, disease, and predators take a much larger toll of game than do the hunters.

The thinly veiled feud frequently existing between farmers and sportsmen who would hunt or fish on the farmers' lands has little relation to the protection or encouragement of game, birds, animals, or fish, although many farmers sincerely believe they are aiding their wildlife by posting their lands against hunting.

Certainly the sportsman should conduct himself like a sportsman. He should get permission before entering private land, and in some manner he should repay the owner for the privilege. His hunting and fishing licenses and fees do maintain state departments that assist in the propagation of wildlife. Rod and gun clubs help in many ways, and generally they stand ready to co-operate in any program that will improve wildlife conditions.

Game, with the possible exceptions of fish in a pond or other wildlife raised in pens, is not private property. Game is for the benefit of the sportsmen, whether they be farmers or city dwellers. The way to better hunting and improved wildlife conditions will be found in a program of co-operation between sportsmen and farmers. Each has a job to do for their common good, and a better understanding should be developed between them.

VII: Special Programs in Conservation

1. WATERSHED PROTECTION AND FLOOD PREVENTION

THE NATION's river systems are sick, and some are dying. The trouble stems from man's use of the land. Virgin forests and verdant native grasslands that once protected mountains and plains are gone or are badly depleted. The protective forest canopy, with the leaf mold beneath, and the tall, luxuriant grass protected the soil from the devastating power of the falling raindrops and held runoff water back until most of it soaked into the ground, protecting the soil while the surplus water moved slowly off to clear streams. That was the situation before the white man had dominion over the soils of this continent.

Today, fifty to three hundred years after man began to conquer the land with axes, plows, sheep, and cattle, there is little natural protection for the soil, and there is even less planned protection established by the most successful group of woodsmen, farmers, and ranchers the world has ever known. The Midas touch of the conquerors of the land turned natural resources of grass and trees into money.

But the land is bare.

Many of the nation's forests have been ravished, and most

of the rest have been impoverished. The forest land produced crops for a while, and then gullies, where torrents of muddy water, unhindered, carried the remaining soil to creeks and rivers. The grasslands were either plowed or overgrazed, often with the same erosive effects. But even where erosion did not develop, the grass lost its ability to hold back the rainfall and to let it soak into the ground.

Cropland too often is tilled, planted, and harvested with never a thought of protection or of the damage being done to the structure of the soil. The rain packs the unprotected soil instead of enriching it, thus permitting less and less of the rain to go into the soil and more and more to run off, carrying with it huge quantities of topsoil to be deposited on the bottom lands and in the channels of creeks and rivers.

As man's dominion of the land became more complete, floods and flood damage increased in frequency and intensity. Of course, there were floods before the white man occupied the land, but these floods generally improved the soils of the bottom lands. They are generally credited with bringing such lands to a high state of productivity. Most of the soil they deposited was good and fertile or contained valuable minerals. Certainly the grass or forest cover that protected these bottom lands permitted little scouring.

Of course, there were bare areas on the hillsides that eroded and sent sterile sand, stones, and other material onto the bottom lands. But these areas were relatively few, and on the bottom lands nature won the fight to build a fertile soil.

There may have been some benefit to the bottom lands when floods first brought topsoil from the hillsides after the protective cover had been destroyed by the plow or axe, for this soil was at first fertile, even though generally not as fertile as that already on the bottom lands. But soon gullies had cut through the fertile topsoil on the hillsides, and sterile subsoil and sand was being deposited on the bottom lands. The upper reaches of the creeks became clogged with debris and silt as the rushing waters from the hillsides reached a flatter grade, where they slowed down and spread and deposited their loads —unable to carry down the flatter gradient of the stream the material they had been able to tear loose and carry down from the steep hillsides.

This condition fed on itself. The soil became less able to hold the water, so more ran off. It also became less able to resist erosion, so more poor soil material was carried from the hillsides and deposited in the lowlands. All the while more timber was being cut, more grassland was deteriorating, and more land was being plowed to erode and add its load of water and silt to the overburdened stream channels.

Then the upper stream channels began to disappear because of siltation. This situation also fed on itself. Silt fans progressed downstream to destroy more channels and cover more bottom land with less fertile and even sterile soils. And more runoff water and more soil materials came from the uplands and slopes to add to the burden.

This situation continues and is becoming progressively worse each year. Great avalanches of mud move into and down all of the nation's river systems, carried by more and more water as the soils, the ranges, and the forests deteriorate.

Rivers and creeks which once carried a steady flow of water throughout the year become raging torrents during heavy rains and then dwindle to trickles during the dry months, because the rainfall runs off instead of soaking in to renew the underground watercourses which used to feed the streams during the dry season. The Missouri River had its worst flood in history a few years ago, and more recently the Río Grande dried up for the first time.

The loss of lives in floods is recorded as news. Damage to property, especially in cities, makes the headlines when a great river goes on a rampage. Losses of crops are sometimes re-

Soil Conservation

counted, but the damage to the land by scour and silt deposition is seldom mentioned. In newspapers, floods are generally attributed to big rains upstream, but the contributory factors of range, forest, and cropland deterioration are not recognized.

"The worst flood in history" on this creek or that river is often reported in the press. "The river reached the highest crest on record." But frequently the rain that caused it was not the heaviest or the most intensive on record. The worst rain may have occurred years ago, when the soil with its protective cover of trees or grass was able to stand the shock and absorb the water or hold it back—when torrents of mud did not add to the volume of the flow.

The reader is probably familiar with the history of public efforts to control flooding. A big dam that was not big enough caused the Johnstown flood. The Mississippi levees were built to keep flood waters out of New Orleans. Then the levees had to be built higher and higher, until the river bed now approaches the level of the streets of the city. Later large dams were built on the great tributaries of the Mississippi and other rivers, with flood pools to store surplus runoff waters. And all the while the amount of surplus waters was increasing because the rate of runoff from the watershed was increasing. The successes and the failures of this type of control are common knowledge.

Then came a new type of flood control. It started with the treatment of the watershed, acre by acre and field by field. When this was done, gully and land stabilization measures were used to control erosion on critical areas of the uplands. Between the uplands and the bottom lands, detention reservoirs were built to catch the runoff which land-treatment measures had not caused to be stored in the soil.

The world's first completely treated watershed under this program was dedicated on Cloud Creek, Washita County, Okla., July 8, 1948, by H. H. Bennett, former chief of the U. S. Soil Conservation Service and originator of the idea of water-

Good farm pond management. ABOVE: Pond is fenced to prevent livestock damage to dam and spillway and to encourage fish spawning and development. Pipe through dam and stock tank below insures clean drinking water for cattle at all times. BELOW: Fertilizing farm pond for increased fish production.

ABOVE: *A creek showing deposition and damage from floods.*
BELOW: *A detention reservoir for flood control. Note the water being discharged by the drawdown structure (lower right).*

shed protection and flood prevention as the first step in flood control. So effective was the land treatment on this watershed that the reservoirs had not filled eight years later. On this small watershed, crops had been lost every year on six hundred acres of bottom land, and siltation was progressing at an alarming rate before land treatment and flood-prevention measures were installed. Since then no flooding or siltation has occurred. Soil Conservation Service economists estimate that within fifty years this bottom land, as a result of its protection from siltation and scour and its increased yields from crops, will return $2.50 for every $1.00 that the project cost—and this does not include benefits from land-treatment programs to farmers on the uplands.

The new program, rapidly gaining popularity with the people and with Congress, starts treatment where the water falls, causing as much as possible to soak into the ground, guiding the surplus off slowly to reduce its erosive power, stopping its gullying and silt-producing action, and finally detaining excessive runoff above the bottom lands. The surplus will drain slowly through the detention reservoirs and reach the main water channels after the runoff from the rain which falls below the reservoirs has passed on downstream.

The program has proved effective on all watersheds where it has been installed. How effective it would be on an entire river watershed after all of its tributaries have been treated is still a matter of debate. Elmer T. Peterson, staff writer for the Oklahoma City *Daily Oklahoman,* believes that since the total is the sum of all its parts, the treatment of each tributary of a major stream will result in effective flood prevention on the river itself. Certainly such treatment will result in greatly increased protection for the river bottoms.

For a closer look at the Soil Conservation Service's flood-prevention program, a study of the Washita River project in Oklahoma and Texas, one of the first approved by Congress, will be helpful.

The Washita River Project

There are 367,000 acres of rich bottom land subject to flooding on this watershed. Seventy-two per cent, or 265,000 acres, is on the creeks, and only 102,000 acres are on the river. None of the bottom land on the river can be flooded unless a heavy rain has fallen first on one or more of the tributaries and flooded the bottom land of these creeks. On the other hand, many normal floods originate in one or two creek basins, flooding the bottom lands there and the bottom lands on the river for ten to thirty miles below the mouths of the creeks. By that time the swifter water in the river channel usually has reduced the crest so that flooding proceeds no farther downstream. In such cases, the land flooded on the tributaries is far greater than that flooded on the river. A general rain of high intensity over a large portion of the upper watershed may produce enough flood water to cover all of the river bottom, but, again, more land has been flooded on the tributaries than on the river.

The old type of flood control would call for two or more large dams on the upper portion of the river and dams on its principal tributaries. Such dams have been planned on the Washita. In many cases they would be placed below the greater part of the bottom land on each tributary, where they could not protect it, but where they would inundate large areas. Protection would be given to but a small percentage of the total bottom land area of the river watershed.

Of extreme importance is the protection of the drainage area above a water impoundment of any type. When erosion on the uplands is severe, as it is on most of the river systems in the Plains states, any plans for lake development should be coupled with a watershed-protection program, such as the one that comes in a package deal with the S. C. S. flood-prevention projects. To neglect this phase of the problem is to invite abject failure for the large reservoirs.

Like many similar rivers, the Washita carries a large load of silt at flood stage. Its flood waters have been measured one-eighth silt by volume. Lake Texoma, at the mouth of the Washita on Red River, is rapidly filling up at its headwaters. For the protection of this large lake and any others proposed on such streams, the upland flood-prevention program should be established as soon as possible.

Obviously this problem does not exist on streams where the watershed is well protected by trees or grass, but in intensively cultivated areas the upland flood-prevention program could be the salvation of the large dam projects of the Army Engineers and the Bureau of Reclamation.

Paradoxically, the watershed-protection program of the S. C. S. meets stiff opposition from the agencies mentioned. Friends of the program are asking for a greater share of the money appropriated by Congress in the name of flood control and for less red tape and restrictions in the development of watershed-protection projects. Friends of the large-dam builders fear that the emphasis on watershed treatment will cause delays for their program. Proponents of both sides agree that there will be a large measure of flood prevention where the watershed-protection program is being installed; and to that extent the program may reduce the justification for some of the larger downstream impounds. In addition, there will be less justification for building the larger structures to impound water for municipal supplies and irrigation.

The dwindling flow of rivers during dry seasons has caused restrictions to be placed on the use of this water for irrigation and has forced small cities which have depended on it for municipal supplies to look to the larger impounds for their future needs. Flood waters swirling down the rivers after heavy rains benefit neither the irrigator nor the cities mentioned. But when these crests are reduced and the flow during dry seasons is increased, both types of users are better supplied.

This has happened on a small segment of the Washita watershed in western Oklahoma.

On the 100-square-mile Sandstone Creek sub-watershed, the S. C. S. built twenty-two floodwater detention reservoirs and thirteen drop-inlet dams in 1951 and 1952. Prior to this time heavy rains had produced damaging overflows on the main creek channel; then the flow completely stopped for most of the year. Since 1952, the annual rainfall has been less than the twenty-five inches normally recorded. However, heavy rains have occurred which would have caused severe flooding on the bottom lands. Damage was reduced 90 per cent. But during the excessively long dry periods between rains, stream flow increased in duration and volume. As the reservoirs held floodwaters back on the uplands to recharge the underground water supplies, the water table was raised and springs came to life again. These significant increases in volume and duration of flow were recorded by one of the stream gauges on the lower part of the main creek.

1952: After a long period when there was no stream flow, water began to run on February 7. The flow lasted 99 days and produced 600 acre-feet of water.

1952–53: Flow began again December 8 and lasted 162 days, to June 11, 1953. It produced 1,027 acre-feet of water.

1953–54: Flow began still earlier and lasted nearly two months longer; it began November 19, 1953 and ended June 10, 1954. There were 8,686 acre-feet of water produced, including some flood water from a high-intensity rain of 2.2 inches on April 29.

1954–56: Flow started eighteen days earlier in the fall of 1954, beginning on November 1. It did not stop at all in 1955, in spite of the fact that no rain of any consequence occurred between May of 1954 and May of 1955. In the first ten months of the period, the stream gauge recorded a flow of 3,600 acre-feet even though ten irrigation systems had been installed above the gauge to take water from the stream.

If the entire Washita River watershed were given the same treatment, there would be less need for impoundments for flood control or for municipal water supplies or for irrigation. All of the bottom land would have a good measure of protection from flooding, while not more than 50 per cent can be protected by large dams. All of it could remain in production, and most of it would have access to a flowing stream to provide irrigation. With judicious water management, municipalities could also get adequate low-cost water supplies from the river rather than high-cost water from the large impoundments.

Fast-growing cities and cities wanting to attract new industry may need still larger water supplies and may seek larger impoundments to supply the need. Before they are built, however, engineers must investigate the ability of the reservoir to provide a dependable water supply and calculate the silt load carried by the water source, for the silt load determines the length of time the reservoir can be expected to last. The history of water rationing in cities depending on such a water supply attests to the fact that the movement of more people and industry into them is not wise. Investors who make a more careful study of these factors than wishful civic leaders point out that high tax rates or high water costs are the result of such expensive projects, while silt-filled reservoirs show the result of improper planning.

When these factors are reconciled satisfactorily, the cities must still consider the value of the displaced section of their agricultural industry in relation to the value of other industry which might, or might not, be attracted.

The conditions of river systems vary according to the intensity of agricultural use and the amount of erosion which occurs on the watershed. Many observers believe that the agricultural watershed-protection program and the large down-

stream reservoirs can be justified on most streams, with watershed protection preceding the large dams where needed. This view is likely to prevail since both the Congress and the public are becoming increasingly aware of the vulnerability of the large reservoirs which are located below watersheds that produce large volumes of silt. Furthermore, more people are becoming aware of the fact that the watershed program can minimize this silt problem. It is also becoming evident that evaporation losses are no greater in the detention reservoirs used in the watershed program than they are on the large lakes, and that no evaporation occurs on water that is forced into the ground to recharge the springs which make the streams flow more steadily during dry seasons.

Development of the Watershed Program

Three Congressional acts have authorized upland flood-prevention and watershed-protection programs. Their purposes are similar, but procedures vary widely. All are administered by the Soil Conservation Service.

In 1946, work was authorized on eleven river basins, one of them being the Washita River in Oklahoma and Texas. Under this program the government takes the lead when sufficient interest is shown by the people in any creek watershed and the work is recommended by the governing body of the soil conservation district in which this sub-watershed lies. The S. C. S. makes a plan for flood-prevention measures to be co-ordinated with land-treatment measures to be initiated by farmers operating the land. These farmer-installed conservation measures and the provision of easements and rights of way are counted as the costs of local participation. The federal government pays the costs of the flood-prevention structures, except for modifications to give special benefit to local interests, such as increasing the size of a reservoir to provide additional water storage for irrigation or municipal supply.

In 1953, Congress passed the "Pilot Watershed" program, which was designed to introduce the work in areas not reached by the original program. More local participation was required, but the S. C. S. still took the lead. About sixty projects were approved. These were not on a river-basin basis, but included only a creek watershed, or that portion of the creek watershed which lent itself to watershed treatment.

The immediate popularity of the program called for an extension of the authority to reach a larger number of watersheds. Thus in 1954, Congress passed the Watershed Protection and Flood Prevention Act, Public Law 566, which called for still greater participation by local groups, the terms of which were to be outlined by U. S. D. A. officials. More than 250 small watersheds came under consideration for assistance under this program by the middle of March, 1955, when Secretary of Agriculture Ezra Taft Benson outlined the policy under which the program would operate.

Under this law, a local sponsoring agency is expected to take the lead in the program and provide assurance that local interests will pay their proportionate share of the costs of construction, and, as in the other programs, install farm conservation measures, provide easements and rights of way, and assume responsibility for maintenance after the project is completed.

Costs to the local group can be estimated from the Secretary's words: "It is the policy that local organizations will be expected to assume that part of the cost of installing works of improvement . . . which is equal to the ratio of local benefits to total benefits . . . ." One exception is made: "The Federal Government may share a portion of the costs otherwise accruing to the local organization when justified in the work plan and the reasons for so doing are set forth in detail."

Under previous programs most of the benefits considered in

justifying a project were local, with only minor downstream benefits noted. More nonlocal benefits are considered under the new law. One of the first projects approved by U. S. D. A. under this law was on Long Branch Creek in the Black Bear Conservancy District near Perry, Oklahoma. Local interests were originally asked to pay more than 50 per cent of the estimated $235,000 cost. District directors offered to pay 10 per cent in a counterproposal which was accepted by the Department. A vote was planned to determine whether landowners would accept the project on these terms.

The second National Watershed Congress meeting in Washington in December, 1955, reported that "Farmers are disillusioned, discouraged, and disgusted with 'red tape' and what they consider favoritism on the part of Congress toward big dams." Oliver Hyatt, of the Little Hoosick Watershed Association of Cherry Plains, New York, headed a study committee which reported that "Criticism of the handling of the watershed program is mounting. Paper work has shown some progress, but even here, out of 402 applications received in Washington, only 110 have been approved and only 25 are expected to be put before Congress at the next session.

"The program requires almost unanimous local approval before even submitting an application. After this obstacle is hurdled there are more stumbling blocks at the state and federal levels. Other federal agencies interested in water control must approve the plan. These requirements cause delay and discouragement.

"The cost-sharing provisions of the program, as compared to other federal water control programs, are inequitable."

Hyatt said that the Watershed Congress was not asking for a government handout, but for treatment comparable to that received by the Army Engineers and the Reclamation Bureau, which build dams for which the local communities do not have to pay one cent.

Special Programs in Conservation

Initiation of the Program

Under any circumstances, a watershed program is sponsored by local groups such as soil conservation districts, conservancy districts, or flood-prevention associations, who assure the government that local people want the program and are ready to do their part in conservation, by providing sites for the flood-control works and by paying their share of the costs. Since the government does not buy the land on which the works are to be located or pay landowners for possible damage, the individual farmer or local group must assume the responsibility for making this contribution.

In most states, co-operation between the local sponsoring agency and the federal government is direct, although a state agency is required to pass on applications under the 1954 act. Generally there has been no active support of the small-watershed program by individual states.

The Oklahoma legislature, however, brought that state into the picture early in 1955, by passing a bill giving soil conservation districts the right of eminent domain when needed to secure rights of way for structures planned in the flood-prevention program. It backed up this measure with an appropriation to be used by districts in purchasing sites from landowners not willing to co-operate.

In effect, the local sponsoring agency says to the Soil Conservation Service: "We will see that the sites for construction are available when needed and that local interests will meet other obligations which might arise. We further assure you that our farmers are willing to proceed with the plans and practices of the land-treatment program on the watershed above the structures. Therefore, we request that you send in your engineers and other specialists to prepare a flood-prevention program for the local creek basin."

After assuring himself that local interests are informed and willing to assume this responsibility, the state conservationist will schedule his flood-prevention specialists to make preliminary examinations and, finally, a complete plan for the watershed unit.

He feels assured that the project will be a success if the people in the watershed area have voted a conservancy district into being. A conservancy district is a legal subdivision of state government voted into being for the purpose of sponsoring this work. It has the power to levy taxes on the land benefited by the flood-control project and to condemn and buy lands needed for the improvements if farmers do not offer them voluntarily. Such an organization provides the greatest assurance that local obligations will be met.

In other cases the record of accomplishments of landowners within a soil conservation district and the character of the land above the bottom land in a watershed may indicate that individual owners will co-operate in providing construction sites and will do needed conservation work without condemnation processes or other forceful measures, and the district will assume the responsibility for promoting the project. They may, or may not, be assisted by an unofficial agency such as a flood-prevention association or conservation association. The district usually does not have any power to force co-operation on any landowner who feels that the project will not benefit him. They do not generally have the money to pay damages or purchase land, unless it is raised by subscription, and normally they do not have condemnation rights. The district therefore runs the risk of being unable to deliver on its promise, and it may see the project fail after a great deal of public money is spent in planning and a great deal of effort expended in attempting to secure voluntary co-operation.

Although the planning technicians co-operate in locating structures as close as possible to sites desired by the individual landowners, it is necessary to have control of all segments of the watershed unit if the objectives of the program are to be attained.

A brief comparison of the merits of a conservancy district and a less effective organization is revealing. Although any property owner will immediately question a proposition that may increase his taxes, he regularly votes taxes on himself for schools, roads, and other public improvements. He will learn that he is voting taxes on himself only if his land is being damaged by overflow and if it will be protected by the flood-prevention measures, for the taxes are to be levied only if they are needed, only on lands benefited, and only to the extent that the lands are benefited. Most owners of bottom lands which are damaged by floods do not object to paying taxes for protection once they understand the program.

If a conservancy district is organized with the power to issue bonds, levy taxes for their repayment, and condemn land for the structures, there is still a likelihood that little money will be needed for this purpose.

The farmer who has a reservoir planned for his land generally realizes its value to his property and prefers to retain the benefits to be derived from it. If he signs a voluntary easement, the land and the water remain his. He may use the water for irrigation or stock water. He may charge for fishing or other public use. He may continue to use the parts of the basin not covered by water for grazing or cropping. He has a free lake, with the provision that the structure will be permitted to act as a flood-prevention measure.

But if condemnation is necessary, the land and the water will not belong to him, and he will receive no benefits from it. He receives a price set by appraisers or by the courts. His holding is not improved by the reservoir, but is decreased in size and value. Therefore, most owners give the needed easements. Actual expenditures by the conservancy district should generally be small and the resulting taxes insignificant.

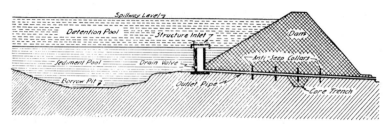

FIGURE 12. *Section of a typical floodwater retarding structure.*

The next step is the actual planning and evaluation of the watershed unit. Surveying parties will make detailed surveys of sites where dams are considered to be most effective. The elevation of the draw-down tube, which determines the permanent water level, is figured accurately with reference to sealevel elevation. Accurate calculations are also made for the flood pool. These determinations are arrived at by relating the capacity of the proposed basin at the various elevations to the storage needed to hold a certain number of inches of runoff from the watershed of the individual structure.

Sedimentation specialists determine the amount of sediment from this area that will be trapped in the proposed detention reservoirs and relate it to the size of the reservoir basin. In particularly critical silt source areas, these specialists recommend special treatment to reduce silting. For a gully or ravine where bank cutting or overfall progression is active, a gully plug may be recommended. Diversion terraces may be used to remove water from this or other types of eroding lands. The farmer also enters the picture here, since such areas may need to be established to permanent grass to further reduce erosion and siltation in the reservoir.

Expert hydrologists calculate the effectiveness of the proposed flood-prevention works on the basis of information furnished by field engineers and sedimentation and other specialists.

Economists consult farmers on the bottom lands to get actual case histories of flood damage—the amount and value of crops lost, the extent and frequency of flooding, the possibility of putting idle land into cultivation when flooding is controlled, or the possibility of using better-paying crops. From this and related information, they determine the average annual cost of flood damage in terms of land, crops, pastures, livestock, farm property, public property, and even human lives. When hydrologists have completed their part of the planning and have determined just how much reduction in flooding will be obtained by the proposed works, the economists relate this information to the farmers' reports and compute the average annual benefit, farm by farm, to the bottom lands of the watershed. The estimated costs, both to the government and to local interests, are divided by fifty (to determine the average annual cost for fifty years). The result is compared with the average annual benefit to obtain the cost-benefit ratio.

Of course, the benefits are expected to last more than fifty years, but the government expects the costs to be amortized in fifty years. Therefore, the total costs divided by fifty must at least equal the average annual benefit. If it is the same, the cost-benefit ratio is one to one, or an average annual benefit of one dollar for an average annual cost of one dollar over a fifty-year period. On this basis the completed plan is approved.

After approval comes the implementation of the plan. This means the inauguration of land-treatment measures above the proposed structures and the securing of easements or the purchasing of land, depending on the methods chosen by the local sponsoring agency. When the way is cleared for the execution of the completed plan, the state conservationist of the Soil Conservation Service may order work to start when funds are available.

It goes without saying that priorities are established on watersheds when construction funds are limited. A watershed which has a cost-benefit ratio of one to one would have a lower priority than one where the benefits are greater in proportion to the costs. A watershed where most of the conservation land-treatment measures are established would have priority over one where less work has been done by the farmers, because erosion and siltation would be greater on the watershed which has undergone less land treatment in the form of terraces, waterways, retirement of poor lands to permanent cover, regular use of crop rotations, stubble mulching, contour farming, and other needed practices. In clarifying the importance of land-treatment measures in setting up priorities for flood-prevention work, this quotation from the Washita County (Oklahoma) Soil Conservation District's Program and Work Plan may be helpful:

Since flood prevention means the control of run-off waters, such control should start on upland fields and pastures, and in that sense is the same as erosion control because run-off water is not only the cause of floods, it is one of the major causes of erosion.

When run-off water becomes excessive, it causes erosion and begins what is known as flood damage. As this water concentrates in gullies or streams, or spreads on cropland, the damage increases. By the time it gets into the larger streams and rivers, much of the true flood damage has already been done, although these larger concentrations are what are commonly recognized as "floods."

So the first step in flood prevention is land treatment—the use of crops, grasses and tillage methods to cause water to go into the ground, rather than to permit it to flow off of the land. To supplement this, terraces and good waterways will slow the excess water down, reduce its erosive powers, and prevent it from concentrating quickly in the larger watercourses. This also reduces its silt load, and consequently its volume. If this silt is kept back on the uplands, flood crests are reduced. And in tying this soil down, much of the balance of the flood crest would be forced into the ground where it fell. The remainder would be slowed down in its race to the sea.

So flood prevention comes in many parts: The proper use of the land, the maintenance of good cover on grasslands and woodlands, adequate use of erosion control measures on cropland, the control of erosion on roads, farm ponds and gully control structures, the protection of streams and watercourses, and the measures planned in the USDA–SCS flood-prevention program administered through districts. None of them is complete in itself, but all are important for complete watershed treatment.

To tie this argument down, the document quotes figures from a flood-prevention plan made for Cavalry Creek, a 70-000-acre watershed in the same district.

These are the benefits which a staff of technicians tell us may be expected from complete treatment of Cavalry Creek:

Benefits from land treatment	$226,882
Benefits from measures taken by farmers primarily to control flooding on their own lands (dams, dykes, etc.)	13,228
From channel improvement and floodways	5,338
From detention reservoirs	45,868
Total benefits from a complete program	$291,316

From this it can be seen that most credit is given to the farmer's conservation program. Even more convincing is the dollar value of benefits received (for flood prevention alone) against a dollar of cost:

For land treatment	$4.55
For channel and floodway improvement	2.93
For storage of water in detention reservoirs	1.68

The damage being done on Cavalry Creek at the time the flood-prevention plan was made was estimated to be $32,969 annually. The specialists believed that good land treatment alone would reduce the damage to $22,373 annually, or more than $10,000. When the flood-prevention storage structures were added to the protection, the annual damage would drop nearly $20,000, to $2,790. Then, if damaged creek channels below the reservoirs were opened and made effective again, the annual damage figure would drop to $958. The planners realized that it would be all but impossible to eliminate all flood damage completely, but the whole project would reduce the annual damage more than 95 per cent. They said: "The combined program of land treatment and flood prevention measures would reduce the 10 major floods to minor floods, and prevent damage from 40 of the 80 minor floods such as occurred from 1923 to 1942, inclusive."

Reduction of overbank deposition and indirect damages brought the benefits from reduced flooding to $38,761 annually. To this sum was added the more positive benefits from a more intensive use of the flood plan, which amounted to $25,-673. Total average annual benefit, $64,434.

Cavalry Creek watershed is intensively used agriculturally. More than 64 per cent of the land is cropped, more than 25 per cent is heavily used pasture, nearly 8 per cent is abandoned cropland, and the remainder is composed of urban areas, roads, and other miscellaneous land. The production of wheat, cotton, and beef cattle constitutes the major farming enterprises.

The 70,000-acre watershed includes 6,205 acres of bottom land. The largest flood in the twenty-year period used as a basis for planning covered 3,454 acres. Nine major floods covered more than 3,100 acres, and there were 91 smaller floods. The average was five floods per year, occurring mostly in the spring months. Rainfall averages 25 inches a year, but has exceeded 40 inches. Frequently the storms are of high intensity. Steep slopes and shale and clay soils on the uplands combine to cause a high rate of runoff. Erosion tends to be severe, and the planners estimated that 249 acre-feet of soil were lost from cultivated lands annually. Two miles of large U-shaped gullies from 15 to 40 feet deep and 50 miles of V-shaped gullies are found

Irrigation. ABOVE: *A leveled field receiving a heavy preplanting irrigation. Note the even distribution of water from end to end; this affords complete control of water, none of which is lost from runoff.* BELOW: *This sprinkler system irrigates 60 acres of ladino clover–orchard grass pasture.*

Proper drainage. ABOVE: This field is well drained only 12 hours after a 4½ inch rain. Note excellent field drainage; row direction and lateral ditches carry away excess water. BELOW: The main ditch and laterals afford drainage for large area.

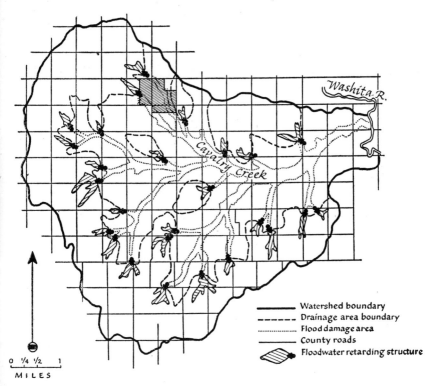

FIGURE 13. *Cavalry Creek Watershed.*

in the watershed, adding materially to the silt being carried onto the bottom lands.

The ring of thirty detention reservoirs are located so that 51.3 per cent of the entire watershed lies above the reservoirs and is thus controlled by them. This results in extensive protection for the basin's bottom lands.

The flood-prevention program of the Soil Conservation Service is a combination of treatments on a watershed basis. It is something more than soil conservation, but land treatment is generally the most important phase of the program.

Special flood-prevention measures planned for a specific area may vary from the example given here, just as conservation practices vary to meet specific needs in various parts of the nation. But the goal and the approach are the same—to treat the land for maximum control of runoff water, and then add special structures as needed to secure maximum flood prevention.

The work is planned on a small-watershed basis. The watershed may be a tributary of a river or even of a large creek. Several very small watersheds may be grouped together to facilitate planning and construction. However, each watershed must be a hydrologic unit—that is, its bottom land must not be affected by overflow from another watershed, or a part of a creek watershed may not be included when other parts of the watershed will cause flooding of the principal bottom land areas of the tributary.

Work on each watershed must be justified by the value of protection given to bottom lands by the reduction of flood damages, siltation, and scour. Each structure planned for the watershed must be justified in the same manner, on the basis of protection given to that area of bottom land which it serves. These values must, over a fifty-year period, equal the total cost of the project, or, in other words, have a cost-benefit ratio of one to one. Also, values resulting from land-treatment measures applied to the uplands cannot be considered in estimating the benefits of the structures; nor can larger structures be built to compensate for the lack of treatment on the watershed. However, after the flood-prevention measures have been justified, the costs and values of conservation treatment are computed and made a part of each plan.

Since only the values derived from the protection of bottom land are computed in the justification of flood-prevention structures, especially in the Washita program, land-stabilization measures have not generally been installed to control gullies and silt source areas upstream. Benefits from more intensive use of land affected by the gullies could be used as economic justification for such measures.

Further justification for all parts of the program could be found if the planners were permitted to compute the wildlife and recreation benefits accruing to the people of the community, the benefits derived from irrigation and from rejuvenated stream flow such as has occurred on Sandstone Creek, and benefits to downstream cities which depend on river flow for municipal water supplies. All of these benefits are real and should be used in justifying the watershed-protection and flood-prevention program.

2. IRRIGATION

"Irrigation is more than crop insurance," says T. H. Quackenbush, irrigation specialist with the Soil Conservation Service, Washington, D. C. "The farmer who has invested in an irrigation system and desires maximum returns from his investment must become an *irrigation farmer*."[1]

Irrigation has generally been considered more practical in the arid West, but is more widely used and is more profitable in the humid areas than is generally recognized. However, as Mr. Quackenbush points out, farmers who install irrigation systems on a hit-and-miss basis and plan to use them only as crop insurance when their crops begin to wilt will find that they have an expensive system and get inadequate returns.

Irrigation, whether used to supplement rainfall or as the principal source of crop moisture, is a system of farming which should be adequately planned and installed, and then properly used. Irrigation is a system designed to control the moisture in the soil before crops reach the wilting point. This is one of the

[1] T. H. Quackenbush, "It's More than 'Crop Insurance,' " *Soil Conservation*, Vol. XIX, No. 6 (January, 1954), 124–25.

secrets of successful irrigation. Others include the use of crops which will be profitable under irrigation, the control of soil fertility, and the prevention of damage to the soil. They are so important that the farmer who contemplates irrigation should make adequate and complete plans for the installation and operation of the system, or leave it alone. He should become an irrigation farmer, or continue with his old method of farming. It is not an experimental process.

The sustained high yields which attract many farmers to irrigation are the result of the application of a number of scientific principles rather than the application of water. The man who is not ready to accept a new system of farming, or who does not have the water or the land to permit him to irrigate with profit, should be discouraged *before*, rather than after, he has invested time and money in irrigation facilities.

Basic Principles

At some time in his farming experience almost every farmer is confronted with the necessity of deciding whether to irrigate or not to irrigate. In some cases, irrigation may be feasible, and the farmer's preference for farming method is the deciding factor. In other cases, irrigation is mandatory if the farm operation is to survive. In still other cases, irrigation is impossible or uneconomical. How can the average farmer discover what his position and his prospects are? A simple study of the basic principles underlying irrigation as they would apply to any farmer in the country may help to clear up confusion and misunderstanding.

First of all, the three essential factors in the decision to become an irrigation farmer are availability of water, suitability of land, and prospect of profits. These factors are discussed below in the form of answers to three basic questions the farmer should ask himself about irrigation.

Special Programs in Conservation

Is water available? Since water is the prime requisite for installing an irrigation system, each farmer must determine if there is a source of water and if he has a right to use it. He must determine if the water is suitable for irrigation. If he lives in an irrigation district where the water comes from a common source, such as a lake, he may quickly get the answers to all his questions from a local authority, such as the officers of his irrigation association, the county agent, or the Soil Conservation Service.

If he contemplates using water from streams or wells, he should immediately enlist the services of an agricultural agency to help him make the necessary investigations. Their services are free, and the information acquired will be needed in later planning.

If the stream is small, the farmer must ascertain the amount of water available during the dry periods when it is needed—in other words, the flow must be measured. If the stream is large, he must find out whether there is a limit to the amount of water he is permitted to use. This brings up the subject of water rights and definitions of these rights.

Riparian rights, generally in effect in the Eastern states, restrict the use of the waters of a stream to property owners whose lands border that stream. Also, in theory at least, the use of the water must not reduce the quality or quantity of the flow.

Priority rights, generally observed in Western states, mean that rights belong to the first person to put the water to beneficial use. But rights for community use, human consumption, or fish propagation may prevent a farmer from appropriating the water for irrigation.

Correlative rights, in California, make up a complicated system requiring local interpretation.

In addition, the right to use water from wells must also be established in many states.

When the farmer has learned that water is available and that he has a right to it, he must find out whether it is suitable for irrigation by sending a sample to a laboratory for analysis. Samples from flowing streams should be taken when the flow is low, as it would be when irrigation water is needed most, for the water at this stage may be poor in quality because of salts leached from the soil of the drainage area.

Of course, the only way to determine the quantity and quality of water from a well is to drill the well and make tests. Even in areas where wells generally furnish sufficient quantities of suitable water, the farmer should drill a test hole and test production with a pump. If there is a question of availability of water, he should put down a smaller hole, say six inches in diameter, and test it with a pump. If the test is good and the water analysis satisfactory, the technicians assisting the farmer can continue with their plans before the hole is enlarged and permanent well equipment installed.

Does the farmer have suitable land? Topsoil should have sufficient depth and moisture-holding capacity to make irrigation practicable. Shallow or very coarse soils that can hold only a few days supply of moisture would require such frequent applications of water that the irrigation of more than a few acres might be impractical, although if the water is cheaply secured and applied, even these soils may be irrigated profitably. The extent of irrigable soils may be determined from maps available at the local soil conservation office or from technicians assisting the farmer.

Will irrigation pay? If the farmer has learned that he has the proper land and water for irrigation, then he, with the help of the technicians assisting him or experienced irrigation farmers in the general neighborhood, should carefully study the possibilities of producing and marketing crops that will yield sufficient profits to offset the added expense or irrigation. He must set up a cost-benefit ratio for his own proposed enterprise.

Costs must be carefully calculated. In addition to the initial cost of drilling the well or obtaining water from other sources, there is the cost of leveling the land and installing borders, or of buying pipe and sprinkler systems. Some new farming equipment is usually needed, as well as an expanded labor force to operate the system. If this labor is not available in the family, the cost of hiring must be calculated. The costs of seed, fertilizer, insecticides, and other items will likely be more than in the past. Maintenance and amortization of the investment must also be included in the total.

Now the returns must be totaled, also. They include calculated income, whether for the entire enterprise or on a per-acre basis. Factors to be considered are the types of cash crops that are suitable to the soil and climate and for which a market exists. High yields of beans, carrots, lettuce, or other vegetables may be expected, but labor costs are also very high, and the market is limited and subject to wide fluctuations. Local processing facilities must be available for such crops, or the farmer must process and market his own. Crops normally produced under dry-land farming conditions will produce better under irrigation, but the farmer must determine whether the increased production will offset the added costs. Permanent or semipermanent hay or grazing crops may be included in the plans. They are valuable for maintaining soil condition and fertility. The cost of their production is usually lower than that of row crops, but benefits are usually less, except where valuable seed crops can be taken.

When a farmer has undertaken this study with competent assistance, he may find that his old farming operations for one hundred to two hundred acres entailed a cost of $5,000 a year with an income varying from $5,000 to $15,000 a year. Some years he did not make any money, some years a fair amount, and some years his operations had a high cost-benefit ratio.

Under his carefully planned irrigation system of farming,

he might irrigate thirty to fifty acres, continue dry-land farming on some acres, and retire all of his poorer land to permanent grasses to cut operating costs. His total costs may be calculated at $10,000 a year, income at $15,000 to $20,000 a year.

His risks for the nonirrigated cropland are the same as they were before. They are reduced on the land retired to permanent pasture. The irrigated land makes the difference in cost and security of income. He is assured against drought, although some crop damage may be expected from hot, dry winds, insects, or plant diseases. Therefore both his costs and his income may fluctuate. He cannot say, "I am averaging $10,000 a year income now and would average $17,500 with the irrigation system, so I will make $7,500 more." Since his costs have been established to be around $5,000 more, his *average* increase would be only $2,500. He does, however, have the assurance of a more reliable annual net profit if he becomes a successful irrigation farmer, for he is eliminating the element of chance from one part of his farming operations—that of inadequate rainfall. But he is establishing a higher annual cost, regardless of rainfall.

In this connection it must be pointed out that in years when rainfall is adequate and irrigation is not needed, the amortization and maintenance costs of the irrigation system go on, even though no water is applied. In one irrigation district, supplied by a multi-purpose reservoir, there is a basic charge of $5 per acre per year, and there is an additional fee for all water over a set amount.

In this area water is delivered to certain parts of the farms in canals belonging to the irrigation district. The farmers themselves built laterals on their own farms, established and leveled borders for flood irrigation, installed cutouts and disposal systems for surplus water, and constructed other appurtenances at a cost of $35 to $75 per acre. Came a rainy year or two, and the farmers did not need irrigation water. Many paid their $5 per acre base charge and wished they hadn't obligated themselves. Some decided that they didn't need irrigation after all and tilled their land by the old system they had followed under dry-land farming, thus destroying the effectiveness of the expensive border system they had installed.

Came the dry years again. The short-sighted farmers had to re-establish their irrigation systems before they could make use of the irrigation water. This cost another $15 to $25 per acre, and their crops were late, or they had to miss a year of needed irrigation. Occasionally sufficient water was not available, and one year no water at all was available. The farmers did not again destroy the effectiveness of their systems, but maintained them annually by the approved methods. And, of course, they continued to pay their $5 per acre per year base charge.

Regardless of whether the water comes from wells, streams, or impoundments, a certain amount of money from the profits must be set aside each year to repay loans, with interest, or to amortize the investment and provide for maintenance and replacement. This is a common-sense business procedure followed by all well-established businesses.

Now, this does not rule out farmers in more humid areas, for rainfall records indicate that dry spells which reduce crop production are more frequent than is commonly recognized. Here supplemental irrigation has proved to be profitable when properly applied and the cost can be kept at a satisfactory level in relation to the calculated added income from the crops grown.

The farmer should not take irrigation casually or treat it as a minor expense. He will be a successful irrigation farmer only if he calculates the costs carefully and applies water properly to crops which will bring a better income than they would under dry-land farming conditions.

It should be clear by now that the farmer must determine

whether irrigation will pay before he starts spending money on any type of irrigation improvement. He cannot experiment with irrigation to get the right answer, for he is apt to install a wholly inadequate system or the wrong type, or he may not apply water properly or use the right crops. A failure may make him decide that irrigation will not pay, even though a properly planned system might.

The prospective irrigation farmer may start by irrigating a small acreage, expecting to expand his operations as his water supply, land resources, labor, and financial ability permit— *after* he has become used to irrigation and knows that he is willing to shoulder the extra burden that irrigation farming places on him. If he does start on a small scale, he should install and operate the smaller system adequately and completely. This type of experimentation is feasible only when the initial cost of installation is not prohibitive. Expensive installations commit the farmer to irrigation farming whether he likes it or not, and can result in bankruptcy for the average man if he has not carefully calculated the costs and benefits.

Into this study of the cost-benefit ratio must come some very personal appraisals. The farmer should study the actual irrigation farming methods practiced by others and ask himself a few questions: Am I willing to undertake the added responsibility and work? Can I depend on the help that is available? Is my health adequate? Is my temperament suited to the long hours and steady grind often required for successful irrigation farming? The answers will show whether the extra profits expected are worth the effort to the individual.

Such honest appraisals of his own temperament and interests will also help the farmer to decide on the type of irrigation enterprises he should adopt. If he does not want to farm intensively, supervise pea pickers or boll pullers, and market his produce carefully, he should not undertake this type of farming. He may prefer to establish his irrigated acres to hay and pasture crops and market dairy or other livestock products. Then his benefits would be calculated on the basis of returns from such enterprises, and his cost-benefit ratio would differ from that based on income from garden produce or other cash crops. But his plan might still be profitable and more satisfactory to him.

By consulting with the technicians assisting him and by observing irrigation systems and methods used on other farms, the farmer has learned most of the details outlined below. If he is going to irrigate, he has decided on the type of system he will install, the kind and sequence of crops he will use, and the methods he will employ to determine the need for water and the rate of application. He should have a plan for the maintenance of soil fertility, prevention of erosion, conservation of water, and use of nonirrigated lands on his farm. This plan should be made in detail, in consultation with competent advisors, and written down, so that the farmer will not lose sight of his goal. As with all other farm plans, it may be altered in details, but the basic principles of irrigation farming must be scrupulously followed if maximum returns are to be obtained.

Types of Irrigation Systems

The type of irrigation system is determined by the relative costs, the amount of land and the permeability of the soil to be irrigated, the water supply, and the maximum rate at which it should be applied. Some of these factors will also dictate the design of the layout. In one place it may be necessary to use a sprinkler system because the soil is too sandy to permit a proper spread of the water in flooding, or because leveling operations would not be practical. In other cases, flooding may be cheaper and more efficient.

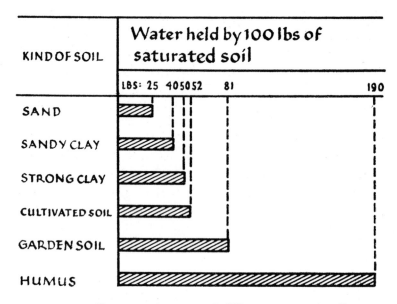

FIGURE 14. *Comparative water-holding powers of soils.*

The farmer should carefully follow the recommendations of qualified technicians who will determine which irrigation system is best for his land and how it should be installed.

The technicians will study the soil to determine depth and moisture-holding capacity. Following is an approximation of the moisture-holding capacity of one foot of different types of soil: 2.1 inches for medium to fine-textured soils; 1.2 inches for sandy loams containing more than 70 per cent sand and for loamy sands containing up to 85 per cent sand; 1.0 inch for loamy sands containing 85 to 90 per cent sand; and 0.7 inches for sandy lands which are more than 95 per cent sand. Thus, if a crop requires one inch of water per week, the sandier lands must be watered every five days when the crop gets its moisture from only one foot of soil, which may be the zone from six to eighteen inches deep. But under the same conditions, clay soils would need to be watered only once every two weeks. Evaporation losses and other factors not considered in the formula must be compensated for in the actual application of water, but this formula is the basis for determining the required capacity of the distribution system.

Infiltration tests determine the rate at which the water is absorbed by the soil. Freely permeable sands may absorb water so rapidly that if flooding is attempted, the land near the water supply may be overwatered while that farther away may not receive enough water. On tight soils the water may be spread evenly and give adequate irrigation to all of the border. On intermediate soils the length of the border must be shortened to prevent uneven irrigation, or the rate of application must be increased to speed the coverage of the entire area and provide even infiltration.

The soils men may also discover structural defects, such as a plow pan which must be eliminated to permit proper infiltration, clay pans which limit the amount of water that can be applied or which may catch salts in the water supply and finally render the land worthless, or coarse sands in the deeper layers of the soil which will drain off the soil moisture too rapidly and thus affect both the quantity and frequency of application.

When this information is correlated with the quality and quantity of water available and the types of crops to be grown, the farmer and the technician can decide on the type of irrigation system to install, and the technicians can offer plans for the design.

Wild flooding is a primitive method accomplished by merely opening a ditch to release water to find its way down the slope without direction or control. It may be employed on pastures and hay fields or on very gentle and even slopes. Otherwise severe erosion and improper use of the water is apt to result.

Controlled flooding is accomplished by a system of lateral ditches, with dams and controls to direct the water where it is wanted, and with turnouts or siphon tubes to release the water. Gated pipes on the surface or buried pipes with surface valves are sometimes used to conserve space otherwise occupied by ditches. From such water distribution systems water is released into *level borders,* which are even-width strips bounded on all sides by small dykes and leveled so that water will stand at an even depth in all parts.

Graded borders are leveled from side to side, but have a grade of from 0.05 to 0.25 feet per 100 feet from the water source to the tail-out end, where surplus water escapes into a disposal system which may lead the water off of the farm or to another area for use. There is no dyke on the lower end since that would cause an accumulation of water and over-irrigation at that place.

Contour borders are similar to the above, except that the strips are not of even width. Contour (level) lines are established around the field, the land leveled between, and small dykes established on the line and at the lower end. They are satisfactory for sown crops, but row crops are more difficult to manage on them because of the point rows.

Row or corrugation irrigation denotes the release of water into furrows, trenches, or small ditches between crop or orchard rows. Release of the water is accomplished by the use of valves in gated or buried pipes or by siphon tubes which take water from open lateral ditches. The grade of the rows must be established and the rate of discharge must be planned to assure even irrigation throughout the length of the row. The grade, length of row, and size of siphon tubes or valves are determined by the permeability of the soil and should be part of the original plan. In use, crops are planted on the bed, and water is applied in every furrow or in alternate furrows, according to the plan.

Sprinkler irrigation systems appeal to many farmers because of a mistaken belief that they can buy whatever equipment is available and "luck" their way through, providing water to supplement rainfall when crops begin to wilt, and then, if the experiment is not successful, sell their equipment without too much loss. If water is taken from streams or an impoundment with little cost other than pumping, they may actually be able to liquidate in case their experiment fails, but, as has been pointed out, irrigation is not an experiment, and such trial methods are apt to result in failure or greatly reduced benefits. Adequate technical assistance is available to most farmers without cost, and it is highly important that the sprinkler system be as carefully planned as a flooding or row irrigation system. From what has been said, it can be seen that the ability of the soil to take and hold moisture as correlated with crop requirements will determine the rates and frequency of application, regardless of the distribution system used. Since most sprinklers spread the water in a circle, the spacing of these circles to avoid too much or too little watering in the overlap and the effectiveness of the sprinkler head in throwing the water evenly must be considered.

Some combinations of these systems may be possible. For instance, borders may be built so that the land may be flooded prior to planting or when in sown crops, or the land may be irrigated in furrows when row crops are planted. But on the whole, the farmer chooses the type of irrigation he wants and sticks with it.

Soil and Water Conservation

The irrigation plan should provide for the safe disposal of excess water, just as it should provide for the application of water. A heavy rain just after irrigation should be safely drained off of the land, or it will result in a temporarily waterlogged soil. Excess water should be drained off into properly constructed and protected disposal ditches or waterways, without erosion and with damage to the irrigation system.

On the other hand, the system should make the maximum use of the rainfall that does occur. When irrigation water costs from $5 to $10 per acre-foot, the saving can be substantial.

Irrigation systems in which no water is lost, as in bordered, level basins, are the most efficient. But when it is necessary to design a system which discharges water from the lower end, measures should be taken to catch and reapply the water when possible. It may go into other bordered areas, or it may be diverted and spread on permanent grasslands which are lower and adjacent to the irrigated fields. Ponds or tanks may store the surplus for stock water or fish production. Consideration should be given to such possibilities for reuse.

Finally, unused water should be guided from the land in protected channels and disposed of in a natural drainage way where it will not damage the lands of neighbors.

Crops and Tillage

Crop sequence. Crops should be planned to make the most effective use of available water and labor. A division between cool-season and warm-season crops may enable the farmer to stretch his water supply over more acres because their water requirements fall in different seasons. The situation is the same for the labor supply. Farmers should continue to study and improve their plans, learning the crops that will pay best under irrigation.

Perhaps the most important aspect of crop sequence concerns the use of crop rotations which will best maintain soil fertility and structure. This is perhaps more important in irrigation farming than in dry-land farming since intensive use and more frequent tillage tend to exhaust soil fertility and damage soil structure.

When water was first applied to the land in one irrigation project, cotton yields jumped from a range of one-fourth to one-half bales per acre to a range of one to one and one-half bales. Then yields started dropping. Commercial fertilizers helped, but fertilizers alone failed to maintain cotton yields at a profitable level. Alfalfa was introduced into the rotation plan every fourth year for the improvement of fertility and soil structure, and yields jumped to a new high of one and one-half to two bales an acre. Although alfalfa did not pay its way as a hay crop, it generally was profitable when a seed crop could be taken. However, as part of the rotation, it paid its way in increased cotton yields in succeeding years.

Maintaining a good soil structure and a high level of fertility is perhaps even more important in irrigation farming than in dry-land farming. The principles are the same. Irrigation farmers use heavy, residue-producing crops to add large amounts of organic matter to the soil, deep-rooted crops to keep the soil opened up, and legumes, manures, or fertilizers to add plant foods as needed.

A special problem exists on fields newly leveled for irrigation. A large part of the field will have the topsoil removed to fill in low places within the borders. The exposed soil will contain less organic matter, and the soil structure may be damaged. Manure and mulches of straw and other organic matter should be spread and worked into the soil. If possible, a deep-rooted crop capable of producing a heavy growth should be raised for green manures as the first crop. This intensive treatment should be followed as frequently as practicable with other soil-improving crops until tilth and fertility reach the desired stage.

The first crop planted after a field has been leveled should be an annual crop since additional leveling may be required to fill in low places which appear after irrigation water has been applied for a season.

Tillage methods. Once a field is bordered and leveled for irrigation, it is obvious that the farmer cannot use tillage implements that will move the soil out of place. Chisels and sweeps are used for land preparation and disk furrow openers for bedding the land for row crops. Two-way plows that move the soil up and then move it down again, in two operations, should be used cautiously. One-way and moldboard plows are generally not used on leveled irrigation land.

Irrigation Water Management

After the irrigation system has been adequately planned and properly installed, the final and perhaps the most important factor in making irrigation pay is the farmer's diligence in applying the water. If he waits until the crops begin to wilt, he is too late. If he misjudges the value of a rain which has fallen, his crops will suffer. He cannot rely on a schedule of applications based on the amount of water needed for the particular crops grown during the different weeks of the growing season. These things entered into the planning of an adequate system, but the application of the water cannot be reduced to a simple formula because of variations in evaporation and transpiration losses which cannot be calculated or the rains which cannot be foretold.

There is but one way for the farmer to know when it is time for him to water his crops. That is for him to determine how much readily available moisture there is in the soil where the roots feed. For most row crops, the roots will feed in a zone from six to twelve inches deep. The readily available moisture must be determined for a greater zone for alfalfa and other deep-rooted crops.

Readily available moisture is that which the plants can obtain easily from the soil while maintaining rapid growth. It is highly important that the farmer know how much readily available moisture is in the soil between field capacity and the wilting point. *Field capacity* is the amount of moisture in the soil two days after it has been thoroughly soaked by irrigation or a heavy rain. *The wilting point* is the moisture level at which plants with mature root systems begin to show drought symptoms.

To prevent crop losses, water must be applied before the wilting point is reached—before drought symptoms can be observed in the crops. The best way to maintain rapid growth is to irrigate when the level of readily available moisture in the six- to twelve-inch zone is between one-fourth and one-half of field capacity.

To estimate the amount of readily available moisture, the *ball test* is recommended by C. H. Diebold in *What's New in Crops & Soils*. Following his recommendations, the farmer uses a spade to get a handful of soil from the six- to twelve-inch depth. Then he squeezes the ball firmly three or four times. If the soil is too dry to form a ball, it contains less than one-fourth as much readily available moisture as it would have at field capacity, and irrigation should be started immediately.

If it forms a ball, it contains at least one-fourth as much readily available moisture as it would have at field capacity. If the farmer wants to find out whether it has more than one-half of field capacity, he tosses it about one foot into the air four or five times. If it breaks with five tosses or less, the soil has less than one-half the amount. This is the ideal time to start irrigating. If the ball remains intact after five tosses, the soil contains more than one-half the available moisture it would have at field capacity, and irrigation is not needed. At three-fourths of field capacity, the soil ball will dampen the hand. When one-fiftieth of an inch or more of the soil sticks to the thumb after the soil has been squeezed firmly between the thumb and the hand, the readily available moisture is between three-fourths and full field capacity.

This method of estimating the moisture content of the soil is helpful in dry-land farming as well as irrigation farming. Tillage should not be done in either type of farming when the six- to twelve-inch layer of soil shows more than one-half of field capacity. Tillage pans or plow-soles are more easily formed when the moisture content is above this level.

3. *FARM DRAINAGE*

A drainage channel helped David O. Shirey of Reading, Pennsylvania, to produce eighty bushels of shelled hybrid corn per acre on land that a year before supported little more than a muskrat population. The sixteen-hundred-foot channel helped him establish a conservation cropping system that paid off.

Corn yields were increased from fifteen to seventy-five bushels per acre when an old and ineffective drainage system was rebuilt on one hundred acres added to the farm of James A. Cottman in the Somerset Soil Conservation District in Maryland. In addition, the modernized drainage program enabled Cottman to cut the number of his fields from twenty-nine to six and to return land to cultivation which had not been plowed for thirty years. Work on his land was made possible by a community drainage project known as the Dublin Tax Ditch Association. His farm leadership abilities earned him a position on Maryland's Production and Marketing Administration Committee (now the Agricultural Conservation and Stabilization Committee).

Good farm drainage, properly installed, is one of the conservation practices needed to bring wet and cold soils into production consistent with their inherent fertility, which is usually adequate. When air replaces the water that is drained away, the soil will warm up better and plant roots can penetrate deeper to find plant food elements and give proper anchorage for the plants. Plants which start growth on wet soils have shallow root systems which cause the crops to suffer drought damage in dry periods.

On well-drained land, work can start earlier in the spring,

seeds germinate faster and a better stand is obtained, there are no wet spots, and crops are not lost at harvest time.

Types of Drains

Two types of drainage are commonly used, and a third is sometimes used: surface drains, subdrains, and vertical drains.

Surface drainage is usually accomplished by open drains or ditches, which are used because of smaller initial costs or because the density of the soil will not permit internal drainage. Surface drains may also be needed in connection with underdrains. This type of drainage, however, is not always satisfactory and is frequently objected to on the basis that such drains occupy a considerable amount of ground, interfere with farming operations, and require more annual maintenance than other types.

Subdrains, usually of tile pipe, are laid underground, where they occupy no land surface and do not interfere with farming operations. Generally they are more effective in draining the soil to the full depth needed for good root development. Annual maintenance costs are low. Fields can be kept clean of weed plants which might get a start in open channels and spread to cropland. The principal drawbacks to this system of drainage are the high initial cost and its ineffectiveness in heavy soils which have no internal drainage or so little that the cost of an adequate system of closely spaced tile is prohibitive.

Gravel, logs, and brush have been used in the bottom of trenches and covered as a primitive method of underground drainage, but such drains are short lived. Although special equipment is required to construct "mole drains," they are used successfully in some areas. They, too, are short lived, but the initial cost and the cost of re-establishment is relatively low, too. As indicated by their descriptive title, mole drains are underground tunnels or channels, established by special equipment. No tile or other lining is used. They are effective only as long as the tunnels remain open, and for that reason are not effective on all soils and are used primarily on clay, clay loam, and organic soils.

The third type of drainage uses what are called *vertical drains* and consists of wells to allow water to penetrate impervious soils to underground cavities or strata of sand or gravel. The opportunities for such drainage are limited, and the cost is usually high. The substratum must be capable of taking large amounts of water rapidly without being sealed off by silt entering the well from the surface. It is not usually possible to determine whether this can be done prior to an actual trial on each site. Generally the wells should be cased, and the surface entrance should be protected against trash or sediment.

Drainage costs. Each drainage system should be carefully planned by a trained technician who can give an estimate of relative costs of the types of drainage which may be applicable. The farmer can then decide whether returns will offset the cost of installation and maintenance.

Drainage systems which cost over $150 per acre, based on costs and crop values of the mid 1950's, would probably be profitable only when valuable truck crops are used and in areas where the demand and market can be expected to remain high. In this category are vertical drainage systems and tile systems which require drain spacings of around 50 feet. In the same relationship, if 80-foot spacings are adequate for good drainage, costs may drop to $100 to $125 per acre and may be practical for crops with a smaller per-acre value. If spacings can exceed 100 feet for tile, most good cash crops can amortize the investment within a reasonable length of time and yield profits.

In the cost-benefit ratio, the value of the land occupied by surface drains and the costs of maintenance must be considered. Frequently the average annual cost over a reasonable length of time will be so low that the farmer will decide in favor of the more desirable tile drains.

Surface Drainage

Only by adequate planning with the surveys and assistance offered by trained technicians can effective drainage be secured and costly failures avoided. The necessary services can usually be obtained without cost from field assistance agencies such as the Soil Conservation Service, Forestry Service, the Soil and Moisture Conservation Operations of the Indian Service on Indian lands, and occasionally from technicians of the Extension Service or state agencies. The farmer is advised to consult any of these agencies and arrange to secure this assistance.

Some of the decisions that must be made are these: The type of drainage needed and the method of doing the work; the value of the land to be drained, its fertility, the probable effectiveness of the system, possible crops to be used, and their value at the market place; effect on neighboring farms and whether the system should be installed as a group project rather than on a farm-by-farm basis; and whether or not an adequate outlet is available.

In addition, the farmer will need a map showing the area to be drained; any existing drains; location and relative elevations of all swales, knolls, and watercourses; location and relative elevations of all possible outlets on the land through which the channels are to be established; and the area that will drain into each part of the system. Only by careful surveys, plotting, and planning can an effective system be established.

Planning really begins with the outlet. It must be low enough to secure adequate flow from the area to be drained, regardless of the type of drainage. It must be large enough to carry its present load, plus the water to be added, without damage to the channel or neighboring lands, and therefore its capacity and load must be calculated. Water should have free flow from the farm into the main outlet at all times without clogging and without backing up water in the system. Pumping should be resorted to only when there is no other method of disposal and when the land to be drained is very valuable.

The outlet end of the disposal ditch should be protected by an overfall structure, sod flume, or pipe outlet. The overfall structure is needed when the quantity of water to be handled is large, when the drop into the public ditch or channel is great, and when the outlet end cannot be widened and shaped to a suitable grade and protected with vegetation to form a sod flume. The pipe outlet may be used when the quantity of water to be handled is small enough to be discharged through a pipe. Maintenance is required on any type of outlet. Burrowing animals may undermine the masonry or concrete overfall structure or may create a channel through the earth-retaining dyke above the pipe outlet. The sod flume must be kept free of silt and debris, and if and when erosion occurs, the grade and shape must be re-established and the sod replaced.

The collecting ditch and field ditches may be either narrow with nearly vertical sides or V-shaped with three to one or four to one side slopes. The V-shaped ditches are easier to maintain and may produce a hay or grazing crop of value to the farmer, especially the larger ditches. Field ditches, if the sides are properly sloped, may be sown or planted to the regular crops.

Although random ditches may be established to drain small and isolated wet spots with irregular fields between, the ditches for larger areas should be laid out parallel to permit land to be plowed with the dead furrows falling at the ditches. Such lands are back furrowed to the center to maintain a crown in the center. Such field ditches are spaced 50 to 150 feet apart and are dug 12 to 24 inches deep, depending on soil conditions. The size and shape of all ditches are designed to handle the expected runoff. Structural checks may be used to keep the ditches from washing out and enlarging when the grade of any part is excessive.

In the digging of larger ditches, where the excavated material cannot be blended into the field slopes and farmed, the spoil banks should be located far enough back from the edge of the ditch to permit the operation of equipment between the ditch and the banks. Spoil banks should be flattened on top and the sides graded to permit the sowing and mowing of hay crops, if the soil is suitable for their production. Such shaping will also reduce bank erosion, which carries the soil into the field or back into the ditch.

Ditching operations begin after the job is carefully staked out by an engineering crew according to the plan developed from the plotted notes of the original survey. Stakes are set to guide construction so that the size and shape of each ditch will conform to the needs of the system. Cut stakes indicate the depth of excavation so that the flow line in each ditch will be even and regular and properly adjusted to the collection ditches that carry the water to its final disposal. Stakes are set to mark the location of the spoil banks.

Equipment used in excavating the ditches will vary according to the job to be done and the availability of machinery. Special ditching machines may excavate ditches to exact grade with specified bottom width and side slopes. Bulldozers, graders, and other earth-moving machinery may also be successfully employed. Smaller ditches are often dug by hand, and much of the maintenance is done with hand tools.

Dynamite is commonly used for ditching in wet ground where heavy machinery would bog down, but it may be used under many other conditions. Dynamite is placed in holes dug by hand or inserted to the proper depth with an Ashley core punch in wet soils. Straight or nitroglycerine dynamite is usually used. The size of the charge, depth, and other blasting conditions are determined by the type of soil and the size of ditch wanted. Properly used, dynamite will give a broad, clean-cut, U-shaped ditch. Ditching with dynamite should be done under the supervision of a qualified blaster and according to plans drawn up for the job, so that the resulting ditch will have the proper size, grade, and depth.

Tile Drainage

Underground drainage removes excess water from the soil rather than from the surface. It flows into the tile at each joint (not through the walls of the tile) and then into larger and larger drains until it reaches its outlet in a stream or channel. This type of drain may be used on all soils except those which are too dense to permit water to move through the soil profile. Proper interpretation of land capability maps of individual farms indicates which soils are not capable of underground drainage, or a soils technician may be consulted. If the soil is uniformly too wet for cultivation but is otherwise suitable for crop production, a complete system of tile drains should be installed. Wet spots may be drained by random lines.

Careful planning, under the supervision of a competent drainage engineer, is even more important in the establishment of this more expensive drainage system than in surface drainage. The correction of errors is costly. Again, the technical assistance needed for the preliminary surveys, planning, staking, and installation is usually available from the field assistance agencies of the agricultural departments of the state and federal governments. Most of these offices also have personnel who are capable of estimating the cost of the project and assisting farmers in calculating possible benefits, to determine whether the project is feasible.

Four-inch tile is the smallest size commonly used for underground drainage. Five-inch tile has nearly twice the capacity of four-inch tile. The greater the grade at which the tile can be laid, the more effective it will be, and grade, along with the acreage each line is to serve, are factors in the design. The spacing between the drains and the depth at which the tile is placed are largely determined by the permeability, or openness, of the soil. In sandy soils tile drains are spaced wider and placed deeper than in clay soils. Expert assistance is needed in determining these factors so that proper drainage is assured. Tile should be covered at least twenty-four inches deep to prevent breakage by heavy machinery, and deep enough to be free from damage by freezing.

A good grade of hard-burned clay or ground shale tile should be used. All tile should be inspected to make sure that it is free of faults, is not porous, and is strong enough to stand the pressure that will be put on it. Common or vitrified tile is best, but concrete tile is satisfactory if it is well made, smooth, and straight. If the soil or the ground water contains either acids or alkali salts, the tile should be resistant to the substance. Tests of both water and soil should be made, and special recommendations should be followed. If grades of main tile drains exceed two feet fall per hundred feet, bell-type sewer pipe with sealed joints should be used to prevent pressure from forcing water out of the pipe. Relief wells (smaller pipe extending from the drain to the ground surface) should be used under such conditions. Extreme care should be used in the selection and testing of the pipe used, since it may reduce the cost of finding and repairing breaks and pipe joints that fail.

Y-joint tile should be provided rather than T-joint or elbow junctions. The lateral should enter main tile drains at the angle provided by such junctions and slightly from above. All turns in the line should be made in wide, sweeping curves, which may be constructed by chipping and fitting regular joints together and covering spaces which are too wide with pieces of broken tile. Openings between joints should be one-eighth of an inch or less and should not be more than one-fourth of an inch without the spaces being covered.

Wheel excavators and endless-chain trenching machines are commonly used instead of hand labor in digging the trenches for the tile. When the job is properly staked for line, curve, and depth, these machines can usually dig the trenches accurately.

A supervising engineer should check the trenches before they are backfilled—either before or after the pipe is laid—to be sure that a proper grade has been attained. After the pipe has been accurately laid with junctions made properly and the larger spaces covered, the line is "blinded." This means that a workman stands astride the tile in the trench, or astride the trench itself, and shovels in four to six inches of soil around the pipe to hold it in position. The soil is worked in under the sides of the tile and under the junctions. Topsoil, straw, pine needles, or other organic material, or gravel may be worked in around the tile in this operation, especially in clay soils, to improve the movement of water to the pipe and prevent sealing of the joints. After this, the trenches are filled with a bulldozer, drag, scoop, shovel, or with whatever equipment is available.

A concrete headwall, or bulkhead, should protect the discharge end of the line, where the water spills into a creek or other channel. This structure is designed to prevent damage to the line when the channel carries a large stream of water. A fifteen- to twenty-foot length of strong metal pipe, set at a downstream angle to the channel, may be satisfactory, if firmly anchored. The pipe or structure should be recessed into the bank of the channel so that a flow in the channel will not exert pressure against the outlet. The pipe, which should be about two inches larger than the tile, should be slipped over the last tile for about six inches and cemented. Surface water should be diverted away from the outlet end of an underground drain.

A rodent guard should be placed over the end of the outlet

to prevent animals from entering the pipe and making nests which might clog the outlet. A swinging gate or screen covering the outlet should be fashioned so that it will raise when pressure is exerted against it from inside the pipe, but which cannot be pushed open from the outside.

When it is desirable to allow surface water to enter an underground drainage system, *surface inlets*, accompanied by *silt wells*, are generally used. A silt well is a concrete box or large section of sewer tile, open at the top and extending some distance below the level of the tile drain. The section below the drain traps silt, which should be cleaned out periodically. The open top should be covered with a grill to prevent debris from entering. Silt wells may be located in fence lines or on field boundaries so that they will not obstruct farming operations.

Wet spots may be drained with *blind inlets*. In this type of inlet the tile is uncovered, and the trench is filled to within one foot of the surface with cobblestones, then with soil. Water will penetrate the foot of soil and then flow readily through the rock to the tile drain.

Relief wells, run from the tile drain to the surface, permit water to escape from the drain before the pressure built up by a clogged outlet causes breakage or damage to the line. The relief well is made of pipe smaller than the line which it is designed to serve, and because it is not meant to let surface water enter the line, no silt well is provided. This pipe should also be covered with a screen, grill, or a solid covering which will open from pressure on the inside.

Surface inlets and relief wells should be located on fence lines or field boundaries, if possible, so that they will not interfere with farming and are in less danger of being damaged by farming equipment. A tile drainage system should be accurately mapped and the map kept for reference, so that any part of the system can be readily located should trouble develop. If feasible, some marking on the field is advisable.

Maintenance is seldom a problem in a properly installed system. However, some precautions are needed to keep tile drains working properly. The outlet end must be kept open, and any damage that occurs should be remedied immediately. The lines should be patrolled once or twice a year within a few days after a heavy rain. Wet spots indicate that the system is not working properly, and if they are discovered, the line should be uncovered to determine if the pipe has been broken or displaced, or if a blind drain is needed to aid the water in getting to the line. Failure to make prompt repairs to a damaged line may cause the whole line above the damaged area to become filled with silt, which will necessitate replacement of the line.

Deep-rooted legumes, such as sweetclover or alfalfa, will improve the drainage in soils whose structure has been damaged by the constant use of clean-tilled crops. This fact emphasizes the value of a conservation cropping system in the maintenance of a drainage system. Soils that have been allowed to deteriorate will not drain, just as they will not absorb rainfall properly in dry-land farming.

VIII: Public Assistance in Conservation

MANY FARMERS are not aware of the vast amount of assistance available to help them solve their problems. Often they do not understand how freely this assistance is given, and are timid about asking for it.

On the local level there is excellent educational assistance from all of the farm agencies, from vocational agriculture teachers, from experiment stations, and from private organizations such as banks, lumber companies, or foundations which conduct demonstration farms or offer advisory service to farmers in the area.

There are also local agencies which give financial assistance. The federal government gives direct financial assistance in the establishment of approved conservation practices, through loans for approved projects in irrigation, drainage, and water facilities, or for land purchase and improvement. Private banks, however, are perhaps still the greatest backers of well-planned farm improvements through their farm loan or personal loan departments.

Field assistance on technical problems of land use, soil conservation, and water use and preservation is available in most parts of the nation through soil conservation districts and, to a limited extent, through other agencies. This assistance is perhaps least understood by farmers for whose benefit it is made available. In areas where districts are not organized, many farmers are not aware of the fact that it is the policy of the federal government to establish Soil Conservation Service units where the farmers organize and ask for them. Within districts where this service is available, it is often thought that there is a charge for the service, especially when it involves a large expenditure of time in surveying, planning, designing, staking out, supervising, and checking of intricate jobs in irrigation, drainage, terracing, pond construction, or other high-cost projects. Too often there is a mistaken belief that if the farmer receives assistance on one project he will be required to accept all other plans, programs, and projects, which may be beyond his means or which he does not want.

In addition to educational, financial, and technical assistance, there are many special services available to the farmer in most localities. Price-support programs of the federal government on many commodities, marketing information and assistance from the state and federal government and locally organized groups, rural electric and telephone services, weather forecasting with storm and frost warnings, and many other services are invaluable to the alert farmer. Many special programs, such as drought and disaster relief and reclamation projects of various types, are made available in rural areas when necessary.

There are so many services offered by federal, state, and local units of government, by associations of farmers organized for their own special interests, and by private groups, that the farmer may scarcely know where to look for a helping hand or appreciate the efforts made in his behalf. This is the picture of the assistance available to him on the local level, and even better is the picture of the larger efforts designed to bring ultimate benefits. Feed, seed, and fertilizer controls, organized efforts for forecasting crop production and market trends, national programs to market agricultural surpluses to prevent them from being a drug on the market, control of freight rates and shipping costs, and, perhaps most important of all, the contributions of the many scientists who work in a multitude of fields for private and public agencies which seldom have contact with the farmer on the local level—these programs and people are largely responsible for the success of American agriculture. But how can the farmer understand or appreciate these things and people that he cannot see, cannot contact directly, and usually does not hear about?

Most of these activities are carried on without thought of public recognition. It is sufficient if they are effective in helping the farmer conserve his soil, produce more abundantly or more efficiently, market his produce more profitably, and live in health and happiness. The welfare of the individual and the public is thereby served. The co-ordination of all of these activities for the benefit of the American farmer, and for the consuming public which he serves, is a miracle of modern agriculture.

This glimpse into the intricacies of public service for farmers is made to bring out one point: Without fully understanding the many efforts being made in his behalf, the farmer can, if he tries, receive the benefits of all the scientific and industrial advances—as well as all of the public aid programs—through services available to him in his local community.

When the farmer asks his county agent to look at some bugs or worms found in a field of corn, cotton, or tobacco, he wants to know what scientists have learned about this pest, its habits, and its control. This knowledge may affect him and his financial well-being, and he wants information which will enable him to recognize the danger to his crops. He wants the latest news concerning insecticides, methods of application, and other devices that will control the pest. He is not asking for one man's opinion; he is asking for information based on the latest results of research in entomology and chemistry.

251

When the farmer asks his conservationist to visit his farm to consider an erosion problem, he wants to know that the advice he receives is based on sound soils technology, the result of adequate research in vegetative and mechanical erosion-control measures adapted to local conditions and his own individual needs.

If the problem cannot be adequately solved by his agent or conservationist, he is reassured when he finds that there are specialists who may be called in to help with the problem. He may be further reassured to know that all the work of his local agricultural office is regularly checked by these specialists, and that local personnel undergo regular training in order to have the latest information concerning scientific advances in their particular fields.

A farmer cannot master all of the skills needed in his farming operation or keep abreast of all of the information required for his enterprise. He occasionally needs special services, information, and assistance in marketing or other fields. This information and assistance are provided by the local offices and state and national agencies designed to give him the necessary help.

Each local office has many programs, and its personnel are trained to assist farmers with normal problems in each of these programs. However, problems arise from time to time which require the assistance of highly trained specialists in particular fields. These specialists, who may be called in to assist with the more difficult problems, are provided on an area, state, or regional basis.

This book is primarily concerned with soil and water conservation. Therefore, only programs and agencies through which assistance is given in these fields will be discussed. Other programs (covering such activities as marketing, crop controls and acreage allotments, and crop insurance and storage under the

Agricultural Stabilization and Conservation Service) will be omitted, except as they affect conservation.

Public assistance, whether governmental or otherwise, takes many forms. It is best explained by classifying the functions and organizations of the groups which render soil conservation assistance to the farmer. Such agencies fall within one of the following classifications: (1) farmer-controlled groups, (2) agencies whose primary function is to provide technical field assistance, (3) agencies which provide financial assistance, and (4) agencies which assist in education or research.

1. *FARMER-CONTROLLED GROUPS*

These groups are composed primarily of soil conservation districts, conservancy districts, wind-erosion districts, drainage or irrigation districts, Agricultural Stabilization and Conservation Service and Farmers' Home Administration county committees, and associations of farmers organized to promote special programs. The districts have a legal entity; that is, they are organized under state laws and are subdivisions of government. The committees are farmer organizations established by the Agricultural Stabilization and Conservation Service and Farmers' Home Administration to take certain responsibilities in administering special programs in counties and parishes and in handling funds. Associations have no definite responsibilities for the administration of programs, but are organized by the farmers themselves to promote special programs of any type and to co-operate with administrative groups or agencies sponsoring special programs.

Soil conservation districts have become outstanding examples of democracy at work. They are legal subdivisions of the state government, organized under state laws by vote of the farmers and administered by elected officials, and are free to act without interference from any agency. It is through such districts that the federal government makes available to farmers most of the facilities of the Soil Conservation Service. Soil conservation districts often serve as outlets for at least part of the services of other agencies, but none of these agencies is in a position to dictate the policies of a district or of the state and national associations of soil conservation district supervisors. It is the policy of the United States Department of Agriculture that all of its agencies assist districts to organize and promote soil conservation activities. Although the S.C.S. has been more closely associated with such districts, the Extension Service and vocational agriculture teachers have often taken the lead in assisting with their organization and the educational aspects of their programs, while Agricultural Stabilization and Conservation Service committees generally co-operate closely with districts in conservation activities.

All of the state and territories of the nation have passed laws under which districts organize and operate. They generally make annual appropriations to maintain a state soil conservation board or similar agency to administer funds and other state assistance given to individual districts.

The organization of a district (or a change in its boundaries) is usually achieved by a petition for organization, annexation, disannexation and formation of a new district, or disannexation from a district and annexation to another existing district. On receipt of such a petition, signed by the required number of farmers, the state agency holds hearings in the district to determine if public sentiment will justify calling the requested election. If the reaction is favorable, a vote is called in the area concerned. If the majority vote for the proposition, the new district is formed or the area is annexed to another district in accordance with the terms of the petition and vote.

The district governing body, called the Board of Supervisors, Commissioners, or Directors, usually consists of five members, who are chosen in various ways in the different states. In some states the governor or state board of agriculture appoints two members, the remaining ones being elected by the farmers. In other states all members of the governing body are nominated and elected by the farmers themselves. Members serve for stated terms of one, two, three, or five years.

Districts are empowered to seek and receive assistance of any kind from any source. They often receive money, equipment, property, and personnel assistance from private, state, and federal sources. Such aid is generally received in accordance with the terms of an agreement reached between the agency and the district, with the exception of state aid, which is given in accordance with terms of the legislative act which made it available.

A district may own and operate equipment on a rental or fee basis; buy and sell equipment, seeds, fertilizer, or other conservation materials; act as a contracting authority; or function in any other capacity it deems fit.

The activities of a district begin soon after organization with a study of the needs for the conservation of soil, water, and plant resources of the area, including the social, economic, and climatic conditions that might affect the district's work, the facilities and assistance that may be made available, and any other factors affecting its program and work plan. The essentials of this study and a resulting plan of action are usually mimeographed or printed and made available to farmers and co-operating agencies. On this basis a program is launched to conserve and improve the soil, water, and plant resources on individual farms of the district.

This program calls for the dissemination of information to farmers and the general public on the "why" and "hows" of conservation. This information is spread through and by the Extension Service, S.C.S., Agricultural Stabilization and Conservation Service, Farmers' Home Administration, schools, clubs, churches, and other groups and organizations in meetings, in newspapers, and by way of radio or other means available. It requires the co-ordination of all the agencies and forces available in assisting farmers and promoting the planning and application of conservation measures.

The soil conservation district, by the nature of the organization and under the terms of its agreements with the S.C.S. and other agencies, is the liaison office between the farmer and these agencies. Since the services of the S.C.S. and, to some extent, of other agencies is given to the district rather than to the individual farmer, the district must set up the terms under which this assistance is made available to the farmer. These terms are generally embodied in a written agreement between the farmer and his district. Other responsibilities of the district include the determination of priorities for assistance to farmers in the area. It may be that small groups of farmers working together will be given preference over individuals; one area may be given a priority because of the severity of the erosion problem; certain conservation practices may have priority over others because they are of greater value; and one watershed may be given preference because of the possibility of a flood-prevention project's being established there. Because there is a general lack of adequate assistance in most districts, it is the responsibility of the district governing body to direct the available assistance in channels where the most immediate good can be accomplished.

As with all farmer-controlled groups, the district should continually appraise the activities for which it shares responsibility to be sure that maximum value is being obtained for the farmers it represents. And it should continually take steps to encourage farmers to make the best use of the facilities available.

Also, districts generally recognize a responsibility to keep the public and legislators informed of the progress of conservation and the needs of the program. To do this on a broad scale, they have organized themselves into state and national associations of soil conservation district supervisors, and they support programs on these levels to publicize their broader interests and accomplishments, maintaining contact with state and national legislatures and state and national offices of the agricultural agencies and organizations.

There are 2,667 soil conservation districts, which cover more than 90 per cent of the agricultural land in the United States. In these districts there are 13,000 governing members who, in a very real sense, represent the conservation interests of the farmers of the nation. And, for the maintenance, stabilization, and development of the agriculture which supplies most of the food and fiber for this country, these members of the soil conservation districts, in an equally real sense, represent the hopes of the nation's consumers.

In the fiscal year ending June 30, 1955, there were more than 1,500,000 farmers and ranchers in the United States who had active conservation agreements with their local farmer-managed soil conservation districts, and two of every three of these agreements outlined complete plans for the use and treatment of every acre on the farms and ranches covered. With the addition of 136,000 farms and ranches containing 42,000,000 acres, a total of 454,000,000 acres were brought under conservation programs by the end of the fiscal year.

The astounding rate of application of conservation measures is indicated by the following statistics, which show practices applied in 1955, on farms and ranches of 789,264 district co-operators.

TABLE V
Conservation Practices for 1955

Practice	Extent
Contour farming	2,949,666 acres
Conservation crop rotation	7,148,130 acres
Strip cropping	806,964 acres

Stubble mulching and crop residue utilization	11,174,432 acres
Grassland brought under systems of proper use	23,166,739 acres
Planting permanent grasses	2,944,625 acres
Tree planting	287,716 acres
Field terracing	42,316 miles
Diversion terrace construction	6,493 miles
Pond construction	73,348
Waterway development	66,323 acres
Improved irrigation water application	1,655,536 acres
Drainage	1,318,972 acres
Land leveling	446,003 acres
Land clearing	605,947 acres

Although certain practices are omitted from the above table, it shows the more important conservation practices installed on farms of district co-operators through the district program and with the assistance of co-operating agencies.

Agricultural Stabilization and Conservation Service committees, which are charged with the primary responsibility of administering federal funds used for cost-sharing projects in conservation work under the Agricultural Conservation Program, are important in every county and parish in the nation. They have duties in connection with other programs of the Agricultural Conservation and Stabilization Service, but by "holding the purse strings," they may help or hinder the conservation program in a county or state.

They are not an independent subdivision of the state or federal government, but are appointed or elected under rules laid down by the secretary of agriculture and serve at his pleasure. However, they do represent the interests of farmers in the area they are named to serve—a community, a county, or a state.

State committees are appointed by the secretary of agriculture. They apportion federal funds to the counties according to need and yearly set up a conservation-assistance program for the state within the framework of the national program. This program is developed in co-operation with state offices of the Soil Conservation Service, Forestry Service, Extension Service, and the land grant colleges. Community committeemen are elected by farmers in each community who co-operate with all phases of the Agricultural Stabilization and Conservation Service program. Heads of each community committee meet to select the county committee.

Election procedures, established in the fall of 1954, call for a county election committee, of which the county farm agent is chairman and committee membership is composed of representatives of each leading farm organization (the Farmer's Union, Farm Bureau, and Grange where they are active) and the county heads of the Soil Conservation Service and Farmers' Home Administration.

This committee names three co-operating farmers within the boundaries of each county subdivision established by the Agricultural Stabilization and Conservation Service. These men are the community nominating and election committee. They nominate other co-operating farmers for community committee posts and conduct the community elections. Names may be added to the ballot by petition. Farmers vote for five candidates. The one who receives the highest number of votes becomes the chairman of the community committee and delegate to the county convention which will name the county committee. The one receiving the next highest vote is vice-chairman of the community committee and alternate delegate to the county convention. The next three, in order, are member and alternate members who would serve as community committeemen in the event of disqualification, removal, or death of one of the three regular members.

If a county is not subdivided into communities, the election

259

is conducted as for a community, and the three candidates receiving the largest number of votes, as outlined above, become the county committee. Otherwise the delegates meet in county convention to select three qualified farmers, who may or may not be elected members of community committees, to serve for the year as the Agricultural Stabilization and Conservation Service county committeemen.

The county farm agent, if not named as secretary of the committee, acts as an ex-officio member. In matters pertaining to the agricultural conservation program, the county committee consults with members of the soil conservation district governing bodies and representatives of the Soil Conservation Service and Forest Service.

Within the framework of the national and state Agricultural Conservation Programs, the county committee and its advisers select practices needed in the county to secure maximum soil and moisture conservation, set the rates and terms of cost sharing, receive applications from farmers for these practices, and make final certifications for payment.

The Agricultural Conservation Program is designed to assist farmers in the application of expensive conservation practices and to secure adequate use of other conservation practices not being employed to the extent needed. For instance, land leveling for irrigation, drainage, terraces, waterways, and farm ponds are expensive projects. Grass, legume, and small-grain crops for soil protection and improvement may not be expensive, but, when they are not a part of an accepted way of farming in a county, costs may be shared through the Agricultural Conservation Program to encourage a greater use. Limestone and fertilizers needed for the establishment of protective grass and legume cover, cultural practices for seedbed preparation and planting, and the price of seed may be included in the costs of the practice.

The program is set up to repay farmers for 50 per cent of

these costs; however, when more incentive is needed to secure adequate use of a practice, a higher rate of cost sharing may be approved by the state committee. The government's share of some expenses may be paid directly to a vendor (earth-moving contractor or seed or fertilizer dealer) to prevent the farmer from having to pay the full cost and wait until the early part of the next year for a repayment of the government's share, which is important in most of the high-cost practices.

All practices for which the government is willing to share in the costs must be bona fide conservation programs, designed to help the farmer do those things which he cannot do alone. Although most of these practices will improve a farm's productive potential, they cannot qualify for government aid if they are strictly "production" practices.

For example, legume cover crops may increase fertility enough to pay for their costs in one or two years, but their inclusion in the program is justified when they are not being used to the extent needed, for they not only protect the soil from erosion while they are on the ground, but they condition the soil to resist erosion by adding large quantities of organic matter, and their root systems tend to break up compacted layers of soil below the surface.

Farm ponds may provide needed water for stock, but if the farmer has been able to provide enough water to allow his grazing animals to use the grass near the site of the proposed pond properly, he would not be eligible for financial assistance on this practice. To qualify for financial aid, the pond project would have to provide water in an undergrazed area so that livestock could be moved there to reduce the damage around the water supply in another area of grassland, which has been overgrazed because of it.

Deep plowing, which has been approved in sandy areas as an aid in controlling wind erosion, qualifies only when an adequate amount of suitable clay material can be brought to the surface and when it is followed by a cropping program which holds this clay material and prevents wind or water erosion from reducing the land to the same state as before plowing.

Deep chiseling, or subsoiling, is designed to break up compacted layers of soil below the surface, so that conservation grass or legume crops can send down deep root systems and prevent the plow pan from forming again.

Both of the latter practices may be temporarily valuable for increasing the water intake and improving crop yields, but are not approvable for financial aid as crop-production practices.

More detailed discussions of the values and limitations of all conservation practices are found elsewhere in this book.

Soil conservation districts and Agricultural Stabilization and Conservation Service committees are generally the most important farmer-controlled groups from the standpoint of conservation. Members of the district governing bodies have very limited expense accounts and receive no pay. If they are very active in promoting the district program, they serve at considerable cost to themselves in time and money. A representative budget allows $70 a year for each member, but he earns it only if he attends the twelve regular monthly meetings, the annual area meeting, and the annual state meeting. Special meetings, tours, and other work that he may do within or outside of his district do not count and are undertaken at his own expense. National meetings are attended at his own expense. The member pays to serve, and the more he serves the more he pays. But in the opinion of many district officials, this is a source of strength to the district program, since only men with a sincere interest in conservation and a dedication to the democratic principles of the district movement are willing to make the necessary sacrifices.

This is also true of Agricultural Stabilization and Conservation Service committeemen. Their budgets, while somewhat larger, are inadequate to meet the expenses entailed by active service.

Special district organizations, such as conservancy districts, wind-erosion districts, and drainage or irrigation districts, are legal subdivisions of government organized under state laws. Since state laws vary, no general explanation of their organization is possible, but competent advice can be obtained from legal authorities in each county or parish.

These special district organizations are contracting and taxing authorities for specific projects which involve a number of farms. They are democratic, since they represent the will of a majority of the farmers concerned. They have the right to enforce the specific aims for which the district was organized, even against the will of a minority of farmers concerned, but may pay damages from money provided by bond issues and amortized as taxes on the land benefited.

A conservancy district may be organized to assure the establishment of an upland flood-prevention project on a watershed. When the organization is completed according to the enabling laws of the state, the district can condemn and purchase land for the location of detention reservoirs and other works of improvement, or they may pay damages to the owners of such lands. Taxes are levied only on the bottom lands protected, according to the acres and the effectiveness of the protection afforded. Farmers, other than those owning protected bottom land, or those on whose lands the work is to be installed, are not affected by the conservancy district. The district, when it has purchased land for a reservoir, may sell the impounded water for irrigation or for other uses, may develop the site as a recreation area, may sell or lease it, or may otherwise use it to produce revenue to help amortize the bond issue.

A drainage district may be organized among farmers concerned with a particular drainage project. The district may condemn lands for the principal drainage ditches and outlets according to a previously adopted plan. It may contract for the construction of the commonly owned ditches and appurtenances, and arrange for their maintenance. Again the bond issue required to pay for this work is repaid through taxes levied according to the benefits the individual landowners receive. Field ditches and laterals on individual farms are usually not a part of the common project, but are installed separately by each farmer.

Irrigation districts are similar. Their purpose is to provide canals and a source of irrigation water for individual farms. Repayment may be made through taxes or charges for the water made available to the individual farms.

Wind-erosion districts enforce land-use regulations to prevent unprotected land from "starting to blow" and spreading damage to other lands. The district has the authority to enter lands not being properly protected, perform the needed emergency tillage operations or plant the needed soil-protection crops, and charge the costs against this land in the form of taxes.

Land-use regulations of a similar nature may be voted by farmers within soil conservation districts, in most states, to give this district the same powers. Unless states have delegated such power, soil conservation districts have no right to levy taxes. They cannot use the powers vested in conservancy, irrigation, or drainage districts.

Associations of farmers organized to promote specific projects have no legal entity unless incorporated. They have no powers of enforcement or of taxation. Their principal purpose is to enlist the forces of public opinion by using publicity or personal work, to form a working agency through which voluntary programs may be carried on, to direct such work, and to administer funds, as needed, which may be secured through contributions.

They may function as effectively as legally constituted districts when voluntary co-operation can be secured and when it is not desirable to issue bonds for high-cost projects and repay them by taxation. Associations of farmers do sponsor many worthwhile conservation projects, but their effectiveness is by no means limited to conservation. This type of organization is flexible and informal enough that it can be molded to fit any need. Usually a president and a secretary are elected. Other officers, boards of directors, and committees may be selected as needed.

2. TECHNICAL FIELD ASSISTANCE AGENCIES

While almost all agencies give technical field assistance in some form or other, there are a number whose primary function is to give such assistance in the field of soil conservation. They are the Soil Conservation Service and the Forest Service of the U. S. Department of Agriculture, the Soil and Moisture Conservation Operations Office, Indian Service, Department of the Interior, and state departments of forestry and conservation.

The Soil Conservation Service was set up in 1935 by the unanimous vote of both houses of Congress, and succeeded the old Soil Erosion Service. In the first years, its work was primarily demonstrational and was conducted through Civilian Conservation Corps camps and demonstration projects, facilitated by work in nurseries and erosion-control experiment stations. Gradually its operations have been altered for the purpose of reaching more farmers and doing for them only those things of a technical nature which they cannot do for themselves.

The S.C.S. gives basic information on the capabilities and condition of soils, water, and plant resources and helps the farmer develop a plan for their maintenance and improvement. Direct assistance, especially in establishing proper land use and conservation treatments, is offered in the general fields of agricultural engineering, agronomy, and biology. Special programs in flood prevention, drainage, and irrigation are offered when needed. All of these programs are discussed in detail in other parts of this book.

All services are given free of charge in accordance with approved standards to farmers co-operating with soil conservation districts or the Agricultural Stabilization and Conservation Service. After the passage of state laws permitting the establishment of districts, it was the policy of the S.C.S. to channel all of its aid to farmers through these districts. Soils information, planning assistance, and many of the Service's other activities are still available to farmers only through their local districts. However, in 1952, the Service was assigned the responsibility of providing technical approval and layout for many individual practices for which the Agricultural Stabilization and Conservation Service makes payment. Thus farmers who co-operate with the Agricultural Stabilization and Conservation program may receive limited assistance from the S.C.S., whether or not they are in soil conservation districts.

Generally, each soil conservation district has a field office of the S.C.S., called work units. Large districts may be served by more than one work unit. In counties where there is no soil conservation district, a S.C.S. representative is stationed in the county seat to service Agricultural Stabilization and Conservation Service co-operators, but a full-sized work unit is not established there. These offices are contact points for individual farmers seeking S.C.S. assistance.

Specialists in the several sciences pertaining to agriculture are stationed in areas and state offices to give technical supervision to field men and direct assistance to the individual farmer, through the local work unit, on difficult problems. Administratively, the lines of authority extend from the local work units to an area conservationist, to the state conservationist, to the administrator in Washington, and to the secretary of agriculture.

Soil and Moisture Conservation Operations Office of the

Indian Service, U.S.D.I., is assigned to do those things on Indian-owned land that the Soil Conservation Service does on other agricultural land. The Soil and Moisture Conservation Operations, however, may enforce land-use regulations and require the operators to install all conservation measures necessary to "protect, maintain and augment the productivity of Indian lands, properly utilize water, reduce flood crests and overflow, and minimize reservoir sedimentation."

It is the policy of the Bureau of Indian Affairs to co-operate closely with soil conservation districts and to enter into co-operative agreements for the exchange of services and equipment. This encourages the formation of new districts and the inclusion of Indian land within districts. This policy is important, in the conservation picture, because of the large amount of Indian-owned land in the Western states.

Forest Service, U.S.D.A., was formed in 1905, when the Bureau of Forestry and the Forestry Division of the General Land Office were merged. It took over 56,000,000 acres of forest lands at that time, but in 1955 it was responsible for and managed more than 181,000,000 acres. It is in charge of conservation operations on woodlands, grazing lands, and croplands in the National Forests and other public holdings, and with the development of the forest resources of the nation. When areas of this public domain are leased to private operators for the harvesting of timber or for grazing or cropping, the Forest Service formulates plans for the maintenance of the timber and grass resources and for soil protection and water management.

The first major effort of the federal government in resource conservation was directed toward the protection of public forests. Management for the improvement of timber stands and the control of harvesting led quite naturally to the protection of soil and ranges, and, in its larger aspects, protection of watersheds at the head of many of the nation's large rivers.

The Forest Service has at times been hampered by pressure

from selfish private-interest groups who have sought to weaken the regulations on timber cutting and, particularly, grazing on public lands. Ranchers, who see the good grasses on the public lands and who honestly believe that more pasturage could be taken, seek longer grazing seasons, higher stocking rates for leased land, or want to open restricted areas to grazing.

The wise controls placed on the use of the national forests— and the efforts to reseed depleted grass areas, replant and manage damaged woodlands, control fires, and other activities —are preserving for future generations these basic natural resources, the wildlife they support, and the last vestiges of the great natural resources with which this country was blessed. But perhaps most important, even to people who are remote from the area of these activities, is the control of the watersheds which produce water for cities, irrigation, power, and recreation.

Assistance is also given to private owners in timber and range management. Woodland protection, management for natural improvement of timber stands, reforestation, and cruising and marking for timber harvests are valuable aids to the owners of private forests. Also, determinations of safe stocking rates based on range condition, other management practices, and range revegetation are aids to ranchers in areas served by the Forest Service.

3. FINANCIAL ASSISTANCE IN CONSERVATION

The government gives financial assistance in conservation by sharing the cost of practices of the Agricultural Stabilization and Conservation Service, by direct loans through the Farmers' Home Administration, and by carrying on certain programs in flood control and watershed protection through the S.C.S. and Forest Service, as outlined elsewhere. The principal financial assistance agencies are listed below.

Agricultural Conservation and Stabilization Service, at all levels, administers many programs, including acreage controls and price supports on basic crops. It also sponsors soil conservation projects through the Agricultural Conservation Program. State and county offices have no authority or responsibilities other than those assigned to its committees, as discussed above under "Farmer-Controlled Groups." Yet its operations are unique in that it is financed by federal funds, which technically lose their identity as federal funds once they have been allocated by the state Agricultural Stabilization and Conservation Service committees. At the same time, the committees are appointed by the secretary of agriculture, serve under his direction, and administer all funds within the framework of policies laid down in Washington.

Administrative expenses are deducted at the state level, and the balance is allocated to the counties or parishes on the basis of need. In the counties, part of the funds are retained for handling the work and for reimbursing the S.C.S., which is paid for assistance given to Agricultural Conservation Program co-operators. Thus the S.C.S. is reimbursed for assistance over and above that previously given to farmers in regular operations through soil conservation districts. The latter fund is worthy of special comment.

In appropriating funds for the Agricultural Conservation Program, Congress provided that county Agricultural Stabilization and Conservation Service committees shall reimburse the S.C.S. for the additional services required of that agency, since technical responsibilities for Agricultural Conservation Program work were assigned to the S.C.S. by the secretary of agriculture in 1952. This allocation is limited to 5 per cent of the country's Agricultural Conservation Program allocation. This money is transferred to the state offices of the S.C.S. and administered by them.

This money repays the S.C.S. for all work done under the

Agricultural Conservation Program on farms which are not under district agreement. This work includes the determination of need and feasibility, site selection, layout, supervision, and checking. For some practices this includes only a determination of need and feasibility, as in the case of grass and legume plantings, deep plowing, and subsoiling. Other practices, such as the construction of farm ponds, terraces, and waterways, include all of the assistance mentioned above.

On farms of district co-operators, the "5 per cent" funds are to include only those services which the S.C.S. did not previously provide as regular assistance to a district co-operator. In some cases, this may include only the measuring of terrace lengths, determining acreages of waterways, certifying for payment, and similar services. For other services, which were not included in the regular district program, it may include all assistance given on the practice.

This provision has led to friction on both county and state levels between the two agencies. On the one hand, Agricultural Stabilization and Conservation Service committees may take the position that the S.C.S. should be able to service Agricultural Conservation Program co-operators with the funds appropriated for the S.C.S. by Congress, since the S.C.S. has been given full authority for field technical work, or that it should be able to do the work for less money than requested by the S.C.S. representatives. On the other hand, S.C.S. county and state offices attempt to get adequate funds for the additional work they perform so that regular assistance to districts will not be curtailed.

When a S.C.S. work unit spends most of its time servicing Agricultural Conservation Program applicants, it becomes, in effect, an adjunct of the Agricultural Stabilization and Conservation Service office. Consequently, the district program suffers, since an adequate program includes far more than the application of the practices for which the Agricultural Conservation

Program shares the cost. The present arrangement, in effect, reduces the assistance given to districts.

Most experienced observers believe that the annual "5 per cent" funds, allotted on a county basis, constitute an unfortunate arrangement, and that Congress should make appropriations directly to the S.C.S. for all work within its scope. This would remove causes of friction and enable the S.C.S. authorities to better administer its program by giving greater assistance where the work load is greater. It would remove the tendency to pay part of the expense of the local work unit from Agricultural Conservation Program funds without giving added service to the county.

Lines of authority in the Agricultural Stabilization and Conservation Service extend from community committees to county committees to state committees, and then to the Washington administrator who is responsible to the secretary of agriculture. Employees in the county offices are under the direction of the county committee, but those in the state office, except for its head, have classified civil service protection.

Farmers' Home Administration, a nation-wide lending agency in the Department of Agriculture, has fifteen hundred offices serving all of the agricultural counties of the nation. Public Law 597, passed by the Eighty-third Congress in 1954, greatly enlarged the scope of its activities by making or insuring loans to farmers for water facilities and soil conservation; this is in addition to its regular activities of making and supervising loans for land purchase, home improvement, and farm operations.

Representative Clifford R. Hope, chairman of the House Committee on Agriculture, in speaking of the expanded Farmers' Home Administration program, said:

"I think it is difficult to overestimate the effect which this legislation [Public Law 597] may have on the future agricultural progress of this country. In addition to its great importance in advancing conservation work, the program authorized by this legislation should materially assist in facilitating long-needed land-use adjustments. It should aid substantially in bringing about desirable uses of acres diverted from the production of surplus crops, as well as relieve the impact of drought conditions and stabilize the agriculture in various areas of the Nation."[1]

The program now represents an effort to gear public and private credit to the repayment abilities of individual farmers engaged in establishing conservation programs. In the first year $11,500,000 was appropriated for direct loans, and the agency was empowered to insure $25,000,000 in private loans each year, with the Farmers' Home Administration processing and collecting all loans.

The loans, at 5 per cent interest, are available to individual farmers, to incorporated associations, soil conservation districts and similar groups for services directly related to soil conservation, water conservation and use, or drainage of farm lands.

Individuals may borrow up to $25,000. Associations and similar groups are limited to $250,000. Loans are secured by the best liens obtainable on chattels, crops, and real estate to the extent necessary to protect the government's investment adequately. Payments are scheduled according to the ability of the borrower. Individuals may have up to twenty years to repay, associations up to forty years.

The regular land purchase and operational loans of the Farmers' Home Administration are continued under similar terms. The new types of loans are made only for the soil and water conservation practices recommended by the Soil Conservation Service, the Extension Service, and other agricultural agencies, who continue to give technical field assistance in planning and application.

[1] *Soil and Water Conservation Loans.* A committee print, 2nd Session, 83rd Congress. Washington, 1954.

A farmer is eligible for a loan when he has sufficient experience or training to indicate that he has reasonable prospects of conducting successful farming operations, and is unable to obtain the necessary credit on reasonable terms and conditions from private and co-operative sources.

The local three-member committee of the Farmers' Home Administration determines the eligibility of all applicants and takes whatever steps are necessary to make sure that loans are used for authorized purposes and meet required standards. The committee and the county supervisor generally help individual borrowers prepare farm and home plans, and they work with these borrowers throughout the years, giving whatever assistance is needed to carry out the improvements in farming methods made possible by the loans. Furthermore, they enlist the aid of the Soil Conservation Service or other agencies in the detailed planning and application of conservation projects within their fields.

Loans may be made for such conservation work as the construction and repair of terraces, dykes, ponds, pasture improvement, basic applications of lime and fertilizer, and tree planting. Loans may be made for such water facilities as tanks, wells, cisterns, pumping and irrigation equipment, and similar work. Loans may also be made for drainage.

4. AGENCIES WHICH ASSIST IN EDUCATION OR RESEARCH

In a very real sense all of the agricultural agencies assist in farm research and educational work, especially on the county or local levels. However, Congress and the secretary of agriculture have assigned primary responsibility to the Agricultural Research Service to administer and direct the activities of the U. S. Department of Agriculture in all fields of research and to co-operate with all other research agencies in co-ordinating research programs and making the results available to educational and technical agencies.

The whole field of agricultural research is interrelated, and discoveries or adaptations may be widely used for many purposes. A better plant variety developed for resistance to certain diseases, for example, may be the answer to the conservationist's need for a cover crop in a certain area. A grass developed for control of eroding abandoned lands may be the salvation of stockmen.

There are three types of research. Basic research is an attempt to learn some facts from nature without any definite plan for the use of this information. Applied research is an attempt to apply this knowledge to some useful purpose. Field trials, especially in agriculture, determine the extent to which the findings of the researchers can be made applicable to the varying conditions of soils and climates in the various communities.

Basic research, little heralded at any time, was once a one-man job. A scientist worked on a theory alone. If successful, he received recognition among other scientists. Occasionally his rewards included public acclaim and financial success. Today most basic research is a mass-production job. A promising field of study may be broken down into several phases, each part of which may be "farmed out" to different public and private research centers. As information in this field comes in to the scientist directing the project, it is correlated, tested again, and progress reported to scientists in related fields. When there are discoveries which relate to the field of agriculture, the Agricultural Research Service is informed. If facilities are available, and if the field of information seems to be one which can be developed for the benefit of agriculture, efforts will be made to determine how this new information can be used.

Applied research may include determining the uses of new

fertilizer elements, new controls for crop and animal diseases, or other processes which may be passed on to the farmer when finally adapted for practical use. This field may also include experimenting with methods for studying the reaction of crops to fertilizer elements, as was the case when it was learned that such plant foods could be made radioactive and their movement into the plants traced. Such a development in the field of nuclear physics proved a boon to studies in the field of agriculture, although this research information will not be passed on to the farmer directly.

Applied research also includes many other activities. United States Department of Agriculture scientists, who are scouting the world for plants which may be used in American agriculture, send planting material to the plants division of Agricultural Research Service which will, in turn, assign the studies to experiment stations where climatic and soil conditions most nearly approximate those in which the plant was originally found. There the plants are grown and tested. If they show promise, plantings are increased to provide planting stock or seed for other stations, and eventually for field studies. In this way many valuable crops have been introduced from other lands.

Development of crop varieties also proceeds in the same manner. A single individual plant may show desirable characteristics. This particular plant will be isolated, and its seed will be planted to determine if these characteristics are constant. For example, in a field of fescue grass, a Mr. Suiter found plants which were taller and more productive than others. He called them to the attention of research workers, who took the seed and developed a new strain of fescue known as Suiter's fescue and, later, as Kentucky 31 fescue, the latter name taken from the plot number at the Kentucky experiment station.

Field trials are a part of applied research, but are considered important enough to receive individual attention. After agricultural experiment stations and nurseries, both public and private, have improved old varieties or tested new ones for adaptability, production, and use, they can say that at this station or in these nurseries the plant shows promise. But they cannot say just how it will behave in actual farming conditions or how widely adaptable it is. This is where the farmer enters the research picture.

Through field agencies the seed of these experimental plants is allocated to one or more farmers throughout the area to which the plant seems to be adapted, and they are tried out under many variations of soil and climatic conditions.

It was in this manner that African weeping lovegrass, an important pasture plant in the Southwest, was spread. U.S.D.A. scientists found the parent plants in South Africa and sent them to the S.C.S. nursery at Beltsville, Maryland, who in turn sent seed to the S.C.S. nursery at San Antonio, Texas. The plant showed promise, and small packets of seed were sent to S.C.S. field offices in Oklahoma and Texas. At first, each field office received only two pounds of seed and very sketchy information concerning the value of the plant for grazing and methods for establishment and management. Planted under various conditions, it succeeded here and failed there. As analyses were made of the soils and planting methods used in the successful plantings and of the areas where the grass was successfully established and the results obtained from pasturing, a great mass of information was gathered to guide the further use of the grass. It is now well accepted in many areas.

Blue panicum, an Australian grass, was introduced in the same manner. Field men generally drilled the grass as they did other grasses more familiar to them. Most of the first field trials were unsuccessful. Then it was learned that the grass should be planted on a well-prepared seedbed and cultivated. The grass then made a comeback in areas where it had been abandoned, and today it leads all other pasture grasses in popularity in some of these sections. Not all field trials, however, are originated through experiment stations or other organized research stations.

In East Central Texas, Belton Latimer, a supervisor of the Nacogdoches-Rusk Soil Conservation District, read that Singletarypeas, or southern winter peas, were used in Southeastern states on extremely poor and eroded soils for cover and fertility improvement. Realizing that his district program would be benefited if this legume could be used on similar soil in his district, to condition the soil for the later establishment of permanent pastures, he ordered seed and made the first planting west of the Mississippi River. The plant met the local requirements and became widely used on soils too poor to maintain a cover of any other plant. It became customary to plant Singletarypeas, with fertilizer, on the land for two to five years and then to replace it with valuable pasture and legume plants. This individual experiment was worth many thousands of dollars to a large area of eastern Texas, southeastern Oklahoma, southwestern Arkansas, and Louisiana.

Possibilities for such experimentation are unlimited. Generally the farmer should be assisted by researchers or local agricultural workers, and certainly his findings should be reported regularly to these men. There are no funds for this type of experimentation, and often the farmer will have to buy his seed and fertilizer and do all of the work himself. The experiment may fail and result in a complete loss to the farmer. If it succeeds, he may have little more than the satisfaction of knowing that he has served the interests of agriculture in his community. But sometimes he has a planting that will furnish a valuable seed crop and add to his income.

Farmers who desire to serve in this capacity have the able assistance of local agricultural workers who know of crops which might serve a useful purpose in the community, but which have not been tried. The author is now working with several farmers who are conducting such trials. Four or five received small seed supplies of Rhodesgrass, an importation from South Africa which has proved valuable in South Texas, Arizona, and California, but which to date has not been able to live through Oklahoma winters. These men plant the seed in their gardens, and each year harvest enough seed to replant a small plot again. If any plants survive the winter, they will be protected, and seed from them will be planted separately in an effort to discover a strain that can withstand Oklahoma winters. Since the grass grows rapidly and is excellent for grazing and erosion control, the success of the erperiment would be valuable to agriculture in southwestern Oklahoma. Other farmers are experimenting with creeping alfalfa, shrub alfalfa, and with other grasses, and some work is being done with the lespedezas. Most successful has been the introduction of blue panic grass, which developed from seven acres on one farm in 1952 to 2,000 acres on 250 farms in 1955 in one representative soil conservation district.

All agricultural research is dedicated to the benefit of the farmer, and in the final testing he is the key figure. Experimental results lead to agricultural improvement only when the crop or practice can successfully and profitably be adapted to actual farming conditions. A farmer who is alert to the needs of agriculture in his community may make lasting contributions in this field whether he is following the lead of organized research agencies or forging ahead on untried paths.

The Agricultural Research Service is the co-ordinating arm of the U.S.D.A. and operates stations, nurseries, laboratories, and other research facilities in the fields of crops, soils, soil conservation, hydrology, biology, forestry, and the like. It co-operates with state and private research centers, correlates findings from all sources, disseminates information to agencies and individuals, and sets up criteria for further studies according to recognized needs. Each educational and field action agency has representatives who keep Agricultural Research Service informed of research needs, and who study the research reports to get information of value to the group or agency they represent. One exception is the Soil Conservation Service, which continues research in soil classification since it is responsible for all the soil-mapping operations of the Department of Agriculture.

Educational agencies in agriculture disseminate information on all agricultural practices and developments to individual farmers and students. Theoretically, at least, any services rendered to farmers is incidental to the instruction process. Since in many localities expert services in many fields are not available, teachers and farm and home demonstration agents find it necessary to give much time to service calls. When this results in the public realization that there is a need for trained men to give these services and such specialists are provided, the effectiveness of the education program becomes apparent.

This has been true in the field of soil conservation. County agents and vocational agriculture teachers introduced many conservation practices into their communities, and for a time they were the only trained technicians available to assist farmers in this field. The farmer was generally unable to make practical use of terraces, strip cropping, farm ponds, drainage, irrigation, and other practices unless guide lines were surveyed or other assistance was given. When the demand for these services increased to the point where the agent or teacher could no longer meet it, soil conservation districts were organized so that a unit of the Soil Conservation Service could be secured to carry on the work.

Pioneer work done by these educators in the culling of poultry flocks, treatment of animal or plant diseases, cruising and marking of timber stands, and in many other fields led to the establishment of adequate local sources of assistance. Thus, the purposes of education were served and the cause of agriculture was advanced. Therefore, it is not always possible to differentiate between the educational and service aspects of the educational agencies.

The land grant colleges, in agricultural states, originally encouraged by the federal government and now operated by the states, are perhaps the best examples of federal-state co-operation in the field of agricultural education. They not only are centers of learning for youth in agriculture, but around them revolve agricultural research, both state and federal, and the best of the adult agricultural education programs, the Extension Service, which is closely integrated with the college on the state level.

In addition to the classrooms, laboratories, libraries, and other facilities found in any modern college or university, the school may include a dairy, hog and sheep barns, fields, woodlands and pastures, silos, feeding lots, slaughterhouses, and all of the other appurtenances of the farming industry in the state. Students learn from both classroom lectures and actual experience in laboratories, fields, and barns. They help to plan and carry out experiments and evaluate the results. Much of the agricultural leadership of the state is centered in these state or agricultural and mechanical (A. & M.) colleges, and all agencies work closely with their programs.

The Extension Service is a federal agency, with a central office in Washington. On the state level it is a federal-state organization closely integrated with the land grant colleges. On the county level it is a federal-state-county office operating under the joint direction of the state organization and the county governing body, each of which pays part of the costs.

On state and national levels its staffs include specialists in soil conservation and related fields, and on all levels the Extension Service has the primary responsibility of promoting educational soil-conservation activities through meetings, tours, and demonstrations in co-operation with the soil conservation districts, the Soil Conservation Service, and other groups.

On the local level it is represented by the county farm agent and the home demonstration agent, who have the responsibility of carrying the educational aspects of the agricultural and farm home arts and programs to the individual farm families. These agents work with many clubs and groups, lead tours, conduct schools and exhibits, and give individual instruction and assistance. Among the youth, they organize 4-H clubs for boys and girls and teach them, through demonstrations and projects, the arts of farming and home making.

The county agent is the handy man of agriculture in the county. If there is a new program to be developed, he is usually responsible for working with local groups to get it organized. If a cattle breeders' association, a seed-marketing group, a fair board, or any organization which promotes a special program in agriculture wants advice or assistance, they call on the county agent. He is an ex-officio member of the county Agricultural Stabilization and Conservation Service committee, heads its county election board and is usually secretary to a county soils laboratory committee, in which case he does the soil testing and makes fertilizer recommendations. He is usually expected to consult with soil conservation districts, the Soil Conservation Service office, flood-prevention, drainage, or irrigation districts, or any similar group. Generally, he is expected to handle the educational programs for all of these organizations.

These duties would seem to be a full-time job, but, in addition, the county agent is the local contact man who provides information on crop conditions, plant and animal insects and diseases, drought, flooding, wind erosion, other special conditions, and many matters pertaining to the financial health of agriculture in the county.

Specialists in many fields are on call in the state offices of the Extension Service and the agricultural college, and they are used regularly in special schools and when problems of a serious nature arise. The over-all educational programs conducted by county extension offices are remarkably good, considering the small staff available and the many fields in which they are expected to work.

In the Department of Agriculture, the Extension Service is primarily responsible for bringing all agricultural research information to the general public at the county level, when such knowledge will benefit any local phase of agriculture.

Recently a new program has been instituted by the Extension Service to help farmers in making complete farm and home plans. Additional personnel are now assigned to certain counties for this work. The services offered include planning in land use and treatment; crop planning, rotations, planting, fertilization, cultivation, and harvesting; livestock planning, management, and marketing; pasture and range use and management; marketing of all farm products, farm and farmstead improvements and machinery needs and care; home improvements and management, including the household arts and the problems of family relationships, social life, education, and health; farm and family budgeting, bookkeeping, and other matters related to financial management; and special problems.

The National Association of Soil Conservation Districts and other agencies have studied the influence that this over-all type of planning will have on the planning for special programs undertaken on many of these farms. In some instances, the soil-conservation plan, based as it is on an actual survey of the soil, water, and vegetative resources, will be the basis for land-use and land-treatment practices and will have an influence on crop rotations, range and pasture management, and the livestock program.

While details of the over-all farm-planning program of the Extension Service have not all been developed, it is evident that effective planning must be based on the capability and needs of the land and the quality of water and vegetative resources. Moreover, when the personnel is available, specialists in soil conservation, forestry, wildlife, irrigation, drainage, and financial assistance programs should assist with parts of the farm plan relating to these matters.

Vocational agriculture departments are another great educational force assisting in soil-conservation programs. Organized in most high schools in agricultural areas and frequently among veterans' groups, these departments conduct classes and projects in a wide variety of farm skills. Much of the value of these student groups lies in the education of a new generation of farm operators.

Unlike the county farm agent or his assistant, the vocational agriculture instructor is not burdened with a multitude of duties. Generally his students, who are limited in number, come from a smaller area. Thus, the instructor has more time to spend in coaching and consulting with individual students, who learn largely by doing.

While 4-H clubs are generally formed among younger boys, the Future Farmers of America (F.F.A.) groups of the vocational agriculture departments are of high school age. In the high schools, agriculture occupies a regular place in the class schedules, and, in addition, F.F.A. clubs are organized for group efforts and for individual competition. Instructors give on-the-farm supervision and training to students in the projects they have selected. In these farm visits, the instructor may also offer assistance to adult members of the family on various farm enterprises.

In veterans' classes, the instructor gives assistance to the student in all phases of his farm activities. And these farm activities take precedence over classroom instruction in this type of work.

Of course, the counterpart of the vocational agriculture departments are the home economics departments, where the arts of homemaking are taught and club work is conducted through Future Homemakers of America (F.H.A.) clubs.

Other assistance in soil-conservation education comes from many sources. Most effective are the newspapers and farm magazines which give information concerning methods and progress in conservation. On the local level, newspapers record progress and success stories of district co-operators and devote columns of space to explaining conservation practices to their readers. State papers and farm magazines have also contributed to conservation information and education.

Machinery manufacturers, meat packers, and other industrial organizations including oil companies, use advertisements urging farmers to recognize the dangers of erosion and undertake corrective measures.

Many special organizations, such as the Soil Conservation Society of America, Friends of the Land, range societies, agronomy societies, and engineering societies, carry on organized work in behalf of conservation and issue magazines with specialized information in the field.

Commercial organizations, civic clubs, and other groups have programs which sponsor conservation farming. Business firms and individuals give aid in many ways. The types of assistance and their sources are too numerous to mention individually here.

Perhaps most important, however, is the farmer working with his neighbor on a man-to-man basis. When one has tried conservation and has found it helpful, he can speak with conviction and can show the results. No other educational activity is as effective or successful.

5. CO-ORDINATION OF PUBLIC ASSISTANCE IN CONSERVATION

There is little wonder that confusion exists among the many workers in the field of soil conservation, or among those whose programs have a bearing on soil conservation. At times this has led to skepticism and occasionally to actual conflict, especially when the policies have been outlined on a national basis and one agency fears that a program is being directed in a manner that will harm its work. The same line of cleavage is found among the farmer groups sponsoring programs on a local basis.

This overlapping of policies, confusion of programs, and conflict has resulted in intensified confusion among the farmers who would take advantage of the services offered by the various groups, or who would accept information concerning conservation if the authorities were in agreement.

Much of this confusion cannot be eliminated since it is derived from varying results of different experiment stations, from varying experiences of conservation workers, and from variations of the actual problem under different conditions. Some glaring contradictions in national agricultural policies still exist, and these are recognized by the farmer. For example, acreage allotments under the Agricultural Stabilization and Conservation Service program are determined on a historical basis rather than by the capability of the land to produce. Land operators are aware that if they are to maintain a favorable acreage when controls are instituted, they must maintain high acreages in the basic crops; and when acreage controls are not in effect, many will not establish a conservation crop-rotation system or will not retire severely eroded land to grass or trees. These programs are in direct conflict and cannot be resolved until the method of calculating acreage allotments is changed.

Lack of adequate informational services at all levels of all of the agencies of the U.S.D.A. and of co-operating groups results in a poorly informed public. Recent trends indicate that the limited informational work previously conducted in the field of conservation is being transferred to the Extension Service, which is not sufficiently well staffed on the county level to assume these extra educational duties.

The best hope for the elimination of confusion among the workers whose efforts affect conservation and among the farmers who would be the beneficiaries is in the development and training of stronger local groups to control all efforts in each field of agricultural work. When the programs are under the control of county and district groups, and when each group determines that its program will be directed solely toward servicing local farmers, regardless of agency conflicts at higher levels, then most of the causes of confusion and conflict will disappear. Adequately informed farm leaders who are dedicated to securing the best service possible for their neighbors can work out effective programs in each field, within the standards required for each national program—but only if they have the freedom to act without undue influence from agency representatives. And to assist them, there should be made available trained educational leaders who have the time to conduct informational programs through tours, meetings, demonstrations, press, and radio.

Bibliography

1. DOCUMENTS AND PUBLICATIONS OF THE

UNITED STATES DEPARTMENT OF AGRICULTURE

Circulars

No. 895. *Raindrops and Erosion.* H. H. Bennett, Forrest G. Bell, and Bert D. Robinson. 1951.

No. 934. *Irrigation-Enterprise Organizations.* Wells A. Hutchins, H. E. Selby and Stanley W. Voelker. 1953.

Farmers' Bulletins

No. 1981. *Strip Cropping for Conservation and Production.* Harold E. Tower and Harry H. Gardner. 1953.

No. 1893. *Farm Fishponds for Food and Good Land Use.* Verne E. Davison. 1947.

No. 1989. *Managing the Small Forest.* By the Forest Service, Soil Conservation Service and Extension Service. 1948.

No. 1997. *Stubble-Mulch Farming to Hold Soil and Water.* F. L. Duley and J. C. Russell. 1948.

No. 2002. *For Insurance Against Drought—Soil and Water Conservation.* Tom Dale. 1950.

No. 2035. *Making Land Produce Useful Wildlife.* Wallace L. Anderson. 1951.

No. 2046. *Farm Drainage.* Lewis A. Jones. 1952.

No. 2047. *Maintaining Drainage Systems.* John G. Sutton. 1952.

No. 2080. *Grass Crops In Conservation Farming.* Tom Dale and Grover F. Brown. 1955.

Handbooks

No. 61. *A Manual on Conservation of Soil and Water.* 1954.

Soil Conservation

Information Bulletins

No. 8. *Conservation Irrigation.* Allan W. McCulloch and Wayne D. Criddle. 1950.

No. 16. *Taming Runaway Waters.* C. W. Gee. 1949.

No. 52. *Youth Can Help Conserve These Resources—Soil, Water, Woodland, Wildlife, Grass.* 1951.

No. 76. *Careers in Soil Conservation.* 1952.

No. 78. *From the Dust of the Earth.* William H. Lathrop. 1952.

No. 81. *The Great Flood.* 1952.

No. 95. *The Soil That Went to Town.* C. W. Gee. 1952.

No. 99. *Conquest of the Land Through 7,000 Years.* W. C. Lowdermilk. 1953.

No. 106. *Our Productive Land—We Can Conserve and Improve It While Using It.* 1953.

Leaflets

No. 249. *What Is a Conservation Farm Plan?* 1948.

No. 256. *Multiflora Rose—For Living Fences and Wildlife Cover.* Wallace L. Anderson and Frank C. Edminster. 1949.

No. 257. *Grass Waterways.* Harry H. Gardner and Edwin Freyburger. 1949.

No. 259. *How to Build a Farm Pond.* Walter S. Atkinson. 1949.

No. 260. *Dust Storms Come From the Poorer Lands.* H. H. Finnell. 1949.

No. 276. *Windbreaks and Shelterbelts for the Plains States.* 1950.

No. 297. *Border Irrigation.* Edwin J. Core. 1951.

No. 323. *Wood Chips for the Land.* Arthur C. McIntyre. 1952.

No. 328. *Your Soil—Crumbly or Cloddy?* A. M. O'Neal and A. A. Klingbiel. 1952.

No. 342. *Contour-Furrow Irrigation.* Karl O. Kohler, Jr. 1953.

No. 343. *Corrugation Irrigation.* William R. Stanley. 1953.

No. 344. *Furrow Irrigation.* George A. Lawrence. 1953.

Bibliography

No. 346. *Grass—The Rancher's Crop.* J. S. McCorkle. 1953.

No. 347. *Keep Your Tile Drains Working.* Paul Jacobson. 1953.

Miscellaneous Publications

No. 449. *Early American Conservationists.* Angus McDonald. 1941.

No. 543. *Some Plain Facts About the Forests.* 1949.

No. 668. *Forests and National Prosperity.* 1948.

No. 688. *A Reappraisal of the Forest Situation in the U. S.* 1948.

Program Aids

No. 69. *First Things First. Know Your Land and Have a Plan Before Starting Conservation Farming.* Albert B. Foster. 1949.

No. 71. *Use the Land and Save the Soil.* R. H. Musser. 1949.

No. 86. *Technical Skill for Soil and Water Conservation.* 1950.

No. 128. *The Measure of Our Land.* J. G. Steele. 1951.

No. 146. *Community Gains from Conservation Farming.* Vernon W. Baker. 1951.

No. 201. *An Outline for Teaching Conservation in High Schools.* 1952.

No. 204. *For Higher Production—Soil and Water Conservation.* 1952.

No. 205. *Improved Management of Irrigated Pastures Pays Dividends.* Arthur E. Miller and Carroll H. Dwyer. 1952.

Technical Papers

No. 80. *Keep Crop Residues on the Surface of the Ground.* J. H. Stallings. 1949.

Yearbooks

Grass. 1948.

Soils and Men. 1938.

Trees. 1949.

Water. 1955.

2. PAMPHLETS AND SPECIAL BULLETINS

Allen, Durward L. *The Farmer and Wildlife*. Washington, Wildlife Management Institute, 1949.

American Camping Association in Cooperation with the Soil Conservation Service, Washington. *Conservation in Camping*. Government Printing Office, 1952.

Beard, Ward P. *Teaching Conservation—A Guide in Natural Resources Education*. Washington, American Forestry Association, 1948.

Bennett, H. H., and Salter, Robert M. *Soil Erosion and Soil Conservation*. Encyclopaedia Britannica Year Books, 1943–54.

Bunch, Clarence E., and Roberts, Edd. *Circular No. 558. Know Your Native Grassland*. Oklahoma Agricultural and Mechanical College Extension Division, Stillwater, 1951.

Butler, Ovid M. (ed.). *American Conservation, In Picture and Story*. Washington, American Forestry Association, 1941.

Carter, Vernon. *Conservation or Else!* Washington, National Wildlife Federation, 1949.

Iowa Agricultural Experiment Station, Ames. *North Central Regional Publication No. 44. Economics of Some Soil Conservation Practices*. 1953.

Koroleff, A., and Fitzwater, J. A. *Managing Small Woodlands*. Washington, American Forestry Association, n.d.

Little, S., and Mohr, J. J. *Station Paper No. 67. Reproducing Pine Stands on the Eastern Shore of Maryland*. Upper Darby, Pennsylvania, Northeastern Forest Experiment Station, 1954.

Melrose, Mary, and others. *Nature's Bank—The Soil*. Washington, National Wildlife Federation, 1942.

National Association of Soil Conservation Districts, League City, Texas. *The Why, What and How of Soil Conservation Districts*. 1953.

National Education Association, Washington. *Conservation Education in American Schools*. American Association of School Administrators, 1951.

———. *Large Was Our Bounty. 1948 Yearbook*. Association for Supervision and Curriculum Development, 1948.

Bibliography

Quigley, Kenneth L. *Technical Paper No. 142. Estimating Volume from Stump Measurements.* Columbus, Ohio, Central States Forest Experiment Station, 1954.

Roberts, Edd, and Bunch, Clarence E. *Circular No. 628. Water in Oklahoma.* Stillwater, Oklahoma Agricultural and Mechanical College Extension Division, 1951.

Schaller, F. W., and Evans, D. D. *Journal Paper No. 2555. Some Effects of Mulch Tillage.* Ames, Iowa Agricultural Experiment Station, 1954.

Schwalen, H. C., Frost, K. R., and Hinz, W. W. *Bulletin No. 250. Sprinkler Irrigation.* Tucson, Arizona Agricultural Experiment Station, 1953.

Soil Conservation Society of America, Des Moines, Iowa. *Down the River.* 1950.

Texas A. & M. College System, College Station. *The Story of the Soil.* 1953.

United Nations Conference on the Conservation and Utilization of Natural Resources, Proceedings. *Vol. IV. Water Resources.* New York, International Documents Service, Columbia University Press, 1952.

———. *Vol. V. Forest Resources.* New York, International Documents Service, Columbia University Press, 1952.

———. *Vol. VI. Land Resources.* New York, International Documents Service, Columbia University Press, 1952.

———. *Vol. VII. Wildlife and Fish Resources.* New York, International Documents Service, Columbia University Press, 1952.

Wisconsin Agricultural Experiment Station, Madison. *Research Bulletin No. 183. Adoption of Improved Farm Practices as Related to Family Factors.* 1953.

3. BOOKS

Ahlgren, G. H., Klingman, G. C., and Wolf, D. E. *Principles of Weed Control.* New York, John Wiley & Sons, Inc., 1951.

Allan, Philip F. *How to Grow Minnows.* Fort Worth, The Author, 1952.

Allred, B. W. *Practical Grassland Management*. San Angelo, Texas, Sheep & Goat Raisers Magazine, 1950.

Archer, Sellers G., and Bunch, Clarence E. *The American Grass Book: A Manual of Pasture and Range Practices*. Norman, University of Oklahoma Press, 1953.

Bennett, H. H. *Elements of Soil Conservation*. New York, Mc-Graw-Hill Book Co., Inc., 1947.

———. *Soil Conservation*. New York, McGraw-Hill Book Co., Inc., 1939.

Bews, J. W. *The World's Grasses: Their Differentiation, Distribution, Economics, and Ecology*. New York, Longmans, Green & Company, Inc., 1929.

Brandwein, Paul E., Hollingworth, Leland G., Beck, Alfred D., and Burgess, Anna E. *Science for Better Living*. Chicago, Harcourt, Brace & Co., 1952.

Brasnett, N. V. *Planned Management of Forests*. London, George Allen & Unwin Ltd., 1953.

Brink, Wellington. *Big Hugh, The Father of Soil Conservation*. New York, The Macmillan Co., 1951.

Brinser, Ayers, and Shepard, Ward. *Our Use of the Land*. New York, Harper & Bros., 1939.

Bromfield, Louis. *Malabar Farm*. New York, Harper & Bros., 1948.

———. *Out of the Earth*. New York, Harper & Bros., 1950.

Canadian Nature Magazine (comp.) *Conservation and Nature Activities*. Toronto, Audubon Society of Canada, 1951.

Carter, Vernon Gill. *Man on the Landscape*. Washington, National Wildlife Federation, 1949.

Chapman, Paul W., Fitch, Frank W., Jr., and Veatch, Curry Lafayette. *Conserving Natural Resources—A Guide to Better Living*. Atlanta, Turner E. Smith & Co., 1950.

Chase, Agnes. *First Book of Grasses: The Structure of Grasses Explained for Beginners*. San Antonio, W. A. Silveus, 1937.

Chase, Stuart. *Rich Land, Poor Land*. New York, McGraw-Hill Book Co., Inc., 1936.

Cheyney, Edward G., and Schantz-Hansen, Thorvald. *This Is Our Land: The Story of Conservation in the United States*. St. Paul, Minn., Webb Book Publishing Co., 1946. Revised ed.

Bibliography

Clements, F. E. *Dynamics of Vegetation*. Compiled and edited by B. W. Allred and Edith S. Clements. New York, H. W. Wilson Co., 1949.

Cocannouer, Joseph A. *Farming with Nature*. Norman, University of Oklahoma Press, 1954.

Cope, Channing. *Front Porch Farmer*. Atlanta, Turner E. Smith & Co., 1949.

Cushman, Frances S., and MacGregor, Gordon. *Harnessing the Big Muddy*. Washington, U. S. Dept. of the Interior, Indian Service, 1948.

Dale, Tom, and Carter, Vernon G. *Topsoil and Civilization*. Norman, University of Oklahoma Press, 1955.

Deering, Ferdie. *USDA, Manager of American Agriculture*. Norman, University of Oklahoma Press, 1945.

DeGraff, Herrell, and Haystead, Ladd. *The Business of Farming*. Norman, University of Oklahoma Press, 1948.

Doane, D. Howard. *Vertical Farm Diversification*. Norman, University of Oklahoma Press, 1951.

Elliott, Chares N. *Conservation of American Resources*. Atlanta, Turner E. Smith Co., 1951.

Faulkner, Edward H. *Plowman's Folly*. Norman, University of Oklahoma Press, 1944.

———. *A Second Look*. Norman, University of Oklahoma Press, 1947.

———. *Soil Development*. Norman, University of Oklahoma Press, 1952.

Francis, M. E. *The Book of Grasses: An Illustrated Guide to the Common Grasses and the Most Common of the Rushes and Sedges*. New York, Doubleday, Page, 1912.

Frank, Bernard. *Our National Forests*. Norman, University of Oklahoma Press, 1955.

———, and Netboy, Anthony. *Water, Land, and People*. New York, Alfred A. Knopf, 1950.

Funderburk, R. S. *History of Conservation Education in the United States*. Nashville, Peabody Press, 1948.

Gabrielson, Ira N. *Wildlife Conservation*. New York, The Macmillan Co., 1941.

——. *Wildlife Management.* New York, The Macmillan Co., 1950.

Gilbert, Frank A. *Mineral Nutrition of Plants and Animals.* Norman, University of Oklahoma Press, 1949.

Graham, Edward H. *Natural Principles of Land Use.* New York, Oxford University Press, 1944.

——. *The Land and Wildlife.* New York, Oxford University Press, 1947.

Gustafson, A. F., and others. *Conservation in the United States.* Ithaca, Comstock Publishing Co., 1949.

Harding, T. Swann. *Two Blades of Grass: A History of Scientific Development in the U. S. Department of Agriculture.* Norman, University of Oklahoma Press, 1947.

Haystead, Ladd, and Fite, Gilbert C. *The Agricultural Regions of the United States.* Norman, University of Oklahoma Press, 1955.

Hitch, Earl. *Rebuilding Rural America.* New York, Harper & Bros., 1950.

Hitchcock, A. S. *Manual of the Grasses of the United States.* Revised by Agnes Chase. Washington, Government Printing Office, 1951.

Howard, Sir Albert. *The Soil and Health.* New York, Devin-Adair Co., 1947.

Hughes, H. D. (ed.). *Forages: The Science of Grassland Agriculture.* Ames, Iowa State College Press, 1951.

Jacks, G. V., and Whyte, R. O. *Vanishing Lands.* New York, Doubleday, Doran & Co., 1939.

Johnson, Vance. *Heaven's Tableland.* New York, Farrar, Straus & Co., 1947.

Joint Committee on Grassland Farming. *The New Grassland-Livestock Handbook.* Norman, University of Oklahoma Press, 1955.

Kauffman, Erle (ed.). *The Conservation Yearbook.* Washington, The Conservation Yearbook, 1953.

Kellogg, Charles E. *Our Garden Soils.* New York, The Macmillan Co., 1952.

——. *The Soils That Support Us.* New York, The Macmillan Co., 1941.

King, G. H. *Pastures for the South.* Danville, Ill., The Interstate Printers and Publishers, Inc., 1950.

King, Thompson. *Water.* New York, The Macmillan Co., 1952.

Kraenzel, Carl F. *The Great Plains in Transition.* Norman, University of Oklahoma Press, 1955.

Leopold, Luna B., and Maddock, Thomas, Jr. *The Flood Control Controversy,* New York, The Ronald Press Co., 1954.

Lord, Russell. *Behold Our Land.* Chicago, Houghton, Mifflin Co., 1938.

Lord, Russell and Kate. *Forever the Land.* New York, Harper & Bros., 1950.

McConkey, O. M. *Conservation in Canada.* Toronto and Vancouver, Canada, J. M. Dent & Sons., Ltd., 1952.

McCulloch, Allan W., and Schrunk, John F. *Sprinkler Irrigation.* Washington, Scheiry Press, 1955.

McDonald, Angus. *Old McDonald Had a Farm.* Boston, Houghton Mifflin Co., 1942.

Meyer, H. Arthur, Recknagel, Arthur B., and Stevenson, Donald D. *Forest Management.* New York, The Ronald Press Co., 1952.

Mickey, Karl B. *Man and the Soil.* Chicago, International Harvester Co., 1945.

Millar, C. E., and Turk, L. M. *Fundamentals of Soil Science.* New York, John Wiley & Sons, 1951.

Norman, A. G. *Advances in Agronomy.* Vol. 7. New York, Academic Press Inc., 1955.

Oosting, H. J. *The Study of Plant Communities.* San Francisco, W. H. Freeman and Co., 1948.

Osborn, Fairfield. *Our Plundered Planet.* Boston, Little, Brown & Co., 1948.

Parks, W. Robert. *Soil Conservation Districts In Action.* Ames, Iowa State College Press, 1952.

Peterson, Elmer T. *Big Dam Foolishness. The Problem of Modern Flood Control and Water Storage.* New York, Devin-Adair Co., 1954.

Picton, Lionel James. *Nutrition and the Soil.* New York, Devin-Adair Co., 1949.

President's Water Resources Policy Commission. *A Water Policy for the American People, Volume I.* Washington, Government Printing Office, 1950.

Rhyne, Conway L., and Lory, Ellsworth E. *Conservation of Natural Resources.* Columbus, Ohio, Berkeley, Calif., and New York, Charles E. Merrill Co., Inc., 1948.

Riedman, Sarah R. *Grass—Our Greatest Crop.* New York, Thomas Nelson & Sons, 1952.

Roberts, Edd. *Land Judging.* Norman, University of Oklahoma Press, 1955.

Sampson, A. R. *Range Management Principles and Practices.* New York, John Wiley and Sons, 1952.

Saunderson, M. H. *Western Land and Water Use.* Norman, University of Oklahoma Press, 1950.

Schneider, Herman and Nina. *Rocks, Rivers and the Changing Earth.* New York, William R. Scott, Inc., 1952.

Sears, Paul B. *Deserts on the March.* Norman, University of Oklahoma Press, 1947. 2nd ed.

———. *This Is Our World.* Norman, University of Oklahoma Press, 1937.

Shepard, Ward. *Food or Famine: The Challenge of Erosion.* New York, The Macmillan Co., 1945.

Smith, Ella Thea. *Exploring Biology.* Chicago, Harcourt, Brace and Co., 1952.

Smith, Guy-Harold (ed.). *Conservation of Natural Resources.* New York, John Wiley & Sons, Inc., 1950.

Staten, H. W. *Grasses and Grassland Farming.* New York, Devin-Adair Co., 1952.

Sykes, Firend. *Humus and the Farmer.* Emmaus, Pa., Rodale Press, 1949.

Thomas, Harold E. *The Conservation of Ground Water.* New York, McGraw-Hill Book Co., Inc., 1951.

Thompson, W. R. *The Pasture Book.* State College, Miss., The Author, 1950.

Timmons, John F., and Murray, William G. (ed.). *Land Problems and Policies.* Ames, Iowa State College Press, 1950.

Van Dersal, William R. *The American Land.* New York, Oxford University Press, 1943.

Bibliography

——— and Graham, Edward H. *The Land Renewed*. New York, Oxford University Press, 1946.

Vogt, William. *Road to Survival*. New York, William Sloane Associates, 1948.

Waksman, Selman A. *Soil Microbiology*. New York, John Wiley & Sons, 1952.

Wales, H. Basil, and Lathrop, H. O. *The Conservation of Natural Resources*. Chicago, Laurel Book Co., 1944.

Wheeler, W. A. *Forage and Pasture Crops*. New York, D. Van Nostrand Company, 1950.

Whitaker, J. Russell, and Ackerman, Edward A. *American Resources*. New York, Harcourt, Brace & Co., 1951.

Whitaker, John R. *The Life and Death of the Land*. Nashville, Peabody Press, 1946.

White, John M. *The Farmer's Handbook*. Norman, University of Oklahoma Press, 1948.

Wrench, G. T. *Reconstruction by Way of the Soil*. London, Faber & Faber, 1946.

Index

Soil Conservation

has been printed on paper designed for an effective life of three hundred years. The text has been set in Linotype eleven-point Electra on a thirteen-point body. The display type used on the title page and for chapter heads is Warren Chappell's Lydian Italic from American Type Founders.